INDIAN POLICY IN THE UNITED STATES

INDIAN POLICY
in the
UNITED STATES
Historical Essays

BY

Francis Paul Prucha

UNIVERSITY OF NEBRASKA PRESS / LINCOLN AND LONDON

Library of Congress Cataloging in Publication Data

Prucha, Francis Paul
  Indian bibliographical references and index.
    1. Indians of North America—Government relations—Addresses, essays, lectures.
I. Title.
E93.P9664   323.1'197'073   81–1667
ISBN 0–8032–3662–X   ·   AACR2

The paper in this book meets the guidelines for permanence and durability of the Committee on Production Guidelines for Book Longevity of the Council on Library Resources.

CONTENTS

PREFACE

I became interested in American Indian policy through my research on the activities of the United States Army on the frontier. The military commanders in the West played an important role as law enforcers, and much of that work had to do with Indian affairs. As I looked more deeply into the subject, I discovered that there were many aspects of United States relations with the Indians that had not been adequately covered by historians. Much had been written about the Indian wars, and the impression could easily be gained that military subjugation of the Indians had been the chief goal of the United States. But the continued government concern for regulating the intercourse between the whites and the Indians, the conviction that it was impossible for the Indians to escape extinction in their traditional state of culture, the strong thread of reform sentiment and humanitarian concern for Indian rights and Indian welfare, and the influence of Christian missionaries and Christian officials on the movement for acculturation and assimilation had been overlooked or deemphasized and in some cases seen only as hypocritical rationalization for crass avarice in seeking to acquire Indian lands.

It has been easy to look at past Indian-white relations from a late twentieth-century viewpoint, in which we are much aware of racism and hopeful of a cultural pluralism in which all races and ethnic groups can be free to maintain their heritage instead of being absorbed into a single homogeneous mass. From such a viewpoint it is understandable that there should be strong temptations to see the past in moralistic terms, to condemn the actions of nineteenth-century whites toward the Indians in the light of twentieth-century sensitivities. It has been my concern, however, to try to understand, not to judge, the past and

to investigate thoroughly the sources of the past with as few precon-
ceptions and prejudgments as possible.

My concentration has been on white action. Although it used to be
customary to call what I was doing "Indian history," I have not attempted to write the history of Indian groups and only to a limited
extent have I attempted the history of Indian response to white programs. It seems to me that the history of white policy is a legitimate
enterprise, even though, like all history, it presents only part of the
story. There can be no doubt that the actions of the United States
government toward the Indians had an important bearing on American history and affected the Indians in radical ways. I hope that by
understanding those events in all their complexity we can better appreciate the nation's history.

There are dangers, of course, in such an approach. The sources for
such a history are primarily the records of the federal government in
the National Archives and similar published records, and the historian
exposes himself to a "government view" of reality. I have tried to use
historical sources critically, but no doubt I have not always been alert
enough to the biases they contain.

Much of my research has resulted in substantial monographs published in book form, but I have also advanced my ideas and conclusions
in lectures and articles. It is these that are printed here. They have, on
one hand, allowed me to examine some questions in more detail than
would be suitable for inclusion in a broader study and, on the other,
given me an opportunity to try out ideas and to speak in general terms
about American Indian policy development. The essays, taken together,
by no means constitute a complete picture of American Indian policy,
but they touch on many topics of nineteenth-century Indian affairs,
and it seemed useful to have them available in one volume. They are
arranged in this way: The first two concern the study and writing of
the history of Indian policy, and the following two are overviews of
federal policy. The remaining essays appear in the chronological order
of their subject matter.

The essays that have been published before are reprinted here without updating or other substantial changes, but some changes in spelling,
punctuation, and capitalization have been made for the sake of conformity to a uniform style. The footnotes are those of the original,
except that they have been rewritten in a uniform style for this publication, and some references to new material have been supplied within
square brackets. In one case, footnotes omitted from the original
publication have been added. Except for the essay on the Great American Desert, which contains maps essential for an understanding of the

text, illustrations used in some of the original articles have been omitted. In brief headnotes to the essays I have indicated the circumstances under which the pieces were written, some reactions to them, and other information.

My thanks are extended to the editors and publishers who have graciously permitted the reprinting of previously published material.

FRANCIS PAUL PRUCHA, S.J.
Marquette University

1

Doing Indian History

*When the planning was done for the National Archives Conference on
Research in the History of Indian-White Relations, I was invited to give
a keynote address to open the conference. Certain Indian activists, I
am told, objected to my having that position, and the term* keynote
address *was thereupon dropped from the final program. I was allowed
the privilege, nonetheless, of giving the introductory talk at the conference, although the Archivist of the United States in introducing me
was careful not to endorse beforehand anything I might say. All the
worries, it turned out, were needless, for the talk, given on June 15,
1972, caused little stir and no trouble. The principles I discussed then,
I think, are still valid.*

The historian writing about Indian matters today is in a remarkably
enviable position. After years of comparative neglect, Indian historical
studies have come to the forefront. Experienced practitioners are in
demand and in some circles are even treated by students and other lay
people with new reverence and respect. Many historians, who turned
to an investigation of Indian-white relations in the United States long
before the subject was a popular one, may feel occasionally like minor
prophets. Demand for one's services in this advisory capacity or that—
while hardly on a par with the profitable consulting that our academic
colleagues in the sciences enjoy—brings at least the heady feeling that
comes from being wanted. And, though few fortunes have been made
from scholarly books on Indian subjects, one cannot quite restrain the

Printed source: Jane F. Smith and Robert M. Kvasnicka, eds., *Indian-White Relations: A Persistent Paradox* (Washington: Howard University Press, 1976), pp.
1–10.

hope that his or her next work will ride the wave of consumer interest to the top of the bestseller list.

This rising interest in the history of Indian affairs, nevertheless, has ambivalent qualities. On the one hand, the new probing by scholars, both Indian and white, has sharpened our awareness of subjects to be investigated, has made it possible to delineate with greater exactness the scope of our discipline, and has already produced an impressive amount of work that has broadened our horizons and deepened our understanding of this subject. Yet, on the other hand, there is danger that the popularity will lead to haste and to disregard of accepted canons of historical research, if not, indeed, to a general slovenliness and, at times, alas, to downright dishonesty.

The good features of the present situation are sufficiently recognized and universally commended. I judge, therefore, that I may be excused from commenting on them further and that I may turn at once to a consideration of some of the problems that arise in doing Indian history.[1] My comments will be both explanative and hortatory—and on occasion, no doubt, also provocative.

There are, to begin with, problems of terminology. In large part, of course, it is all the fault of Christopher Columbus. His geographical inexactitude saddles his heirs with a name for the people he found in the Western Hemisphere that was inappropriate, to say the least. But the term "Indian" was not abandoned when more sophisticated geographical knowledge showed that it was a mistake, and it has been sanctioned by long usage. It seems unwise, if not impossible, to eradicate it and replace it in general usage with an artificially contrived term—such as "Amerind" or "Amerindian," which had a brief vogue—or with the more cumbersome "native American," which is increasingly coming into use. Words are fundamentally arbitrary conventional signs to which certain meanings are attached. It is well to be reminded from time to

---

1. The choice of my title, "Doing Indian History," was influenced by J. H. Hexter's article, "Doing History," *Commentary* 51 (June 1971): 53–62, in which he argues for excellence in traditional historical writing. I have been helped, too, by the following articles in addition to those cited specifically below: Jack D. Forbes, "The Indian in the West: A Challenge for Historians," *Arizona and the West* 1 (Autumn 1959): 206–15; Stanley Pargellis, "The Problem of American Indian History," *Ethnohistory* 4 (Spring 1957): 113–24; James C. Olson, "Some Reflections on Historical Method and Indian History," ibid. 5 (Winter 1958): 48–59; William T. Hagan, "On Writing the History of the American Indian," *Journal of Interdisciplinary History* 2 (Summer 1971): 149–54.

time that some of them are not properly descriptive, but everyone knows what they mean. Intelligent discourse is not always advanced by substituting laborious circumlocutions or hyphenated nouns for simple words. I listened recently to a long disquisition on historical encounters between Native Americans and Euro-Americans, a discussion that would have moved along considerably better, and just as accurately and meaningfully, if the talk had been about Indians and whites.

But if we stick with "Indian" for our everyday discourse—and it is a point in favor of historians, I think, that they write in everyday language—what are we to do with the term "Indian history"?

Here we are on shifting ground. For too long United States history has been written exclusively by white historians. For many of them, "Indian" history has consisted of the story of events in which the Indians impinged in some way upon the course of white society. Indians, it has been noted to our shame, were often treated (along with mountains, deserts, rivers, and wild beasts) as part of the environment that had to be overcome. The commonly used textbook phrase "the Indian barrier to white settlement" is indicative of this frame of mind, as is the repeated concern during the course of American history with the "Indian problem."

Now we are coming to see that "Indian history" might properly refer to changes within the Indian communities themselves, to Indian-Indian rather than Indian-white relations, and to the interaction of the red and white races from the Indian standpoint—in which no doubt there would be considerable concern about the "white problem."

Historians today, therefore, must be more careful than many of us have been in the past to differentiate between these different meanings of the term "Indian history"—between the history of the Indian experience in America and the history of Indian-white relations. That historians are still in a transitional and confused state is illustrated in a recent issue of a historical journal that was devoted entirely to the "American Indian." Two articles dealt specifically with the writing of "Indian history"; the phrase was, in fact, used in their titles. One of the authors spoke about a "general history of the American Indian." He took a pretty dim view of the possibility of a "good," a "successful," or a "meaningful" general history (the adjectives are his), and his article became almost a litany of the different things that "Indian history" can mean, for his examples ranged all the way from books like the anthropological survey of Harold E. Driver to William T. Hagan's brief synopsis of government policy and Indian-white relations in the United States.[2]

The second author recognized the divergence in approach, and he made a clear decision. He declared categorically: "American Indian history must move from being primarily a record of white-Indian relations to become the story of Indians in the United States (or North America) over time." And he proposed a context in which his "new Indian history" might be developed.[3]

It is tempting to look upon the traditional history of Indian-white relations as passé, if not, indeed, morally unacceptable because of "racist" overtones, and to turn completely toward the new approach. Then scholars could draw upon traditional historical methodologies and social science theories and techniques alike, and anthropologists and historians could form a tight partnership. I personally think, however, that this would be a mistake—that the boat would list just as badly if we were all to rush from starboard to port.

It is an obvious fact which needs no belaboring that relations with the other group were of supreme importance both for the whites and for the Indians. To leave out these relations in the history of either group could easily lead to serious distortion. It therefore makes considerable sense for a member of the white society interested in its own history to investigate the ways in which contact with the Indians affected the course of events of the United States, just as it makes sense to study the impact of contact with foreign nations.

On the Indians' side, contact with whites was often a determining factor in their history. Great changes were wrought on Indian communities by contact with whites, and a history of strictly Indian-Indian relations would be partial to the point of inaccuracy.

So, while by no means denigrating the study of Indian history as the history of the Indian experience—a development that is long overdue—and by no means belittling cooperation between historians and anthropologists—a development that will certainly be valuable to both—I would like to assert my belief in the value of the historian's traditional tasks and in the value of the history of Indian-white relations. But I would, particularly, like to note some of the difficulties faced by practitioners of this historical inquiry.

2. Wilcomb Washburn, "The Writing of American Indian History: A Status Report," *Pacific Historical Review* 40 (August 1971): 261–81.

3. Robert F. Berkhofer, Jr., "The Political Context of a New Indian History," ibid., pp. 357–83.

Considering the significance and magnitude of the subject, there have been far too few historians who have devoted their careers to the study of Indian-white relations. Some periods and subjects in Indian policy have been almost entirely neglected by serious scholars. How many important works are there that deal with the period between the Dawes Act and the beginning of the reform movements of the 1920s? Yet that was the period of the working out of the allotment policy with its great and serious consequences. There is no satisfactory general history of government educational programs for the Indians. Too little attention has been paid so far to the administration as contrasted with the development of policies. And even the treaty system, so prominent in Indian relations, has not had adequate treatment. Largely untapped sources still exist that can help supply better answers to old questions, and new questions are continually being asked. All this is hard work—impatience is not a good virtue to promote the digging out of the necessary knowledge. It will require the work of many competent and dedicated persons.

The first requisite is accurate knowledge, which was the purpose of the conference on Indian-white relations. Historical events of the past are complex—they cannot be treated in one dimension, they cannot be pulled out of the context in which they occurred without grave danger of distortion, and they cannot be simplistically linked in a single chain of cause and effect. History, moreover, is a continuum. The beginnings and endings are often quite arbitrarily introduced by the historian for reasons of convenience, or fatigue. A history of a set period may be necessary, but if the knowledge of historians extends no farther forward or backward than their termini, some events may be considered as wonderfully unique phenomena when they are but examples of a continuing pattern. A history may properly treat a tightly limited area—a single Indian reservation, for example—but we know the fallacy of generalizing from a single example.

The facts dug out and the knowledge acquired and disseminated must be accurate and must be seen in proper perspective. But it is not an easy thing to maintain one's equilibrium when dealing with inter-racial relations. There is much to condemn in the treatment of the Indians by the United States government and its people. Injustice, callousness, and hatred, as well as ignorance, indifference, and neglect, have marked much of the whites' relations with the Indians. Many writers, some professional historians among them, have made these elements their stock in trade. Present-day activists and their sympathizers find it tempting to twist historical data to their own uses, an understandable reaction of minority groups seeking to redress an unjust balance and to gain overdue respect for rights that should have been indisputable.

But the historian's task is not activism or special pleading. History is a legitimate scholarly discipline, whose purpose is to reconstruct the past as accurately as the intelligence of the historian and the fullness of the historical sources permit. Its purpose is to supply enlightenment, understanding, and perspective and to provide sound information on which balanced judgments can be based. Its purpose is not to serve the special interests of any group or doctrine, nor to furnish ammunition for polemics and propaganda. It is a scientific study based on finely honed techniques. Its success depends upon long and careful training and on a critical evaluation of the remains of the past, seeking enlightenment for problems that plague the present.

Correction of existing historical writing comes from discovery of new sources, from application of new techniques, and from more sophisticated probing of the records with new questions. It does not come from unsubstantiated assertions about the past, nor by manipulating the evidence to suit one's preconceived positions. The goodness of a cause, moreover, is not a substitute for accurate and balanced information. Impassioned pleading for a cause and scholarly historical study both have their place, but they should not be confused as being the same thing.

Critical tools have long been at the historian's hand. Rules for the assessment of documents have been a staple of historical methods manuals and courses for more than a century, and I see no justification for throwing them out in doing Indian history. Their habitual use is what marks the "pro" from the amateur.

It is not enough, then, to write the history of the Modoc War with heavy and uncritical reliance on a story of the war told by a man who was the son of the interpreters in the conflict but who was only ten years old at the time and who never had a formal education. At least one might suspect that all the direct dialogue of which the book is composed is not really verbatim.[4]

It will not do to accept uncritically everything that is put forth as the speech of a famous Indian. Indian orations recorded in the eighteenth century all came out sounding pretty much alike and usually sounding like the men and women who recorded them.[5] Chief Joseph's

4. See Jeff C. Riddle, *The Indian History of the Modoc War and the Causes That Led to It* (n.p., 1914).

5. Alan E. Heimert, *Religion and the American Mind, from the Great Awakening to the Revolution* (Cambridge: Harvard University Press, 1966), pp. 219–21.

"surrender speech" apparently was not a speech at all but a report of his reply to the demand for surrender brought back by an intermediary.[6] Black Hawk's autobiography, while accepted as representing the chief's Indian viewpoint, was certainly not written by the Sac chieftain himself.[7] It is not necessarily a sign of authenticity when a man proclaims himself a Sioux chief, is 101 years old, and sells his memoirs to McGraw-Hill.[8]

And if one can be sure of the authenticity, the question of what weight to put on the contents of the speeches still remains. If we must interpret with great caution and critical eye the rhetoric of Andrew Jackson in his advocacy of Indian removal—as I have been repeatedly told we must—we must also cast a quizzical eye upon the rhetoric of the Indian leaders and the zealous missionaries who opposed him. If we must ask whether the statements of Andrew Jackson and Lewis Cass were self-serving, can we reasonably neglect to ask the same question in regard to the statements of John Ross or Jeremiah Evarts? Not every Indian who speaks is a chief representing his whole tribe, nor are all clergymen unbiased in regard to their own causes.

Statistics, so much discussed these days, can be used to promote causes as well as to portray accurately the past. I have been interested in accounts of the number of deaths on the tragic Cherokee "Trail of Tears," for the variety of figures is startling. Herbert Welsh, the crusading secretary of the Indian Rights Association, wrote in 1890: "The march through the wilderness caused the death of at least half the tribe."[9] Ralph Henry Gabriel declared in 1929, "A third of the people perished in the autumn and winter of 1838 when the Cherokee followed what they called the 'trail of tears.' . . ."[10] And a recent author, intent on showing the cruelty of Andrew Jackson toward the Indians, has repeated the figure of one-third.[11] Most historians speak of the

6. Mark H. Brown, "The Joseph Myth," *Montana, the Magazine of Western History* 22 (Winter 1972): 2-17.

7. See the discussion of the autobiography in Donald Jackson, ed., *Ma-Ka-Tai-Me-She-Kia-Kiak, Black Hawk: An Autobiography* (Urbana: University of Illinois Press, 1955), pp. 31–38.

8. *The Memoirs of Chief Red Fox* (New York: McGraw-Hill, 1971). For an account of the charges leveled against the book, see the *New York Times,* March 10, 1972.

9. Herbert Welsh, *The Indian Question, Past and Present* (Philadelphia, 1890), p. 7.

10. Ralph Henry Gabriel, *The Lure of the Frontier: A Story of Race Conflict* (New Haven: Yale University Press, 1929), p. 128.

11. Sidney Lens in "Book Forum," *Saturday Review,* February 26, 1972, p. 79.

death of one-fourth of the migrating Indians, although Edward Everett
Dale in the *Dictionary of American History* notes with somewhat
greater accuracy that "it is probable that nearly 10% of those who
started died on this tragic journey."[12] What is disturbing is that few
writers have made use of the records that do exist, which indicate the
number of deaths in each of the emigrating parties.[13] That even 10
percent died is a damning commentary on the whole process of forced
removal to the West, but sound historical judgment is hardly fostered
by arbitrarily blowing up the figures beyond all measure of truth.

It is interesting to note, turning to a different and less controversial
matter, that the Indian reformer of the 1870s and 1880s, Dr. Thomas
A. Bland, mistakenly appears in a substantial scholarly account of post–
Civil War Indian reform as Theodore A. Bland—a very small error, of
the kind that creeps into every history book. But a subsequent study of
the same period of Indian policy also calls him Theodore. The author
of a third work on the same subject that appeared recently also thinks
the doctor's name was Theodore. And on the tentative listing of non-
Indians for whom brief biographies will appear in the new Smithsonian
Handbook of North American Indians appears Theodore A. Bland.
Anyone who comes along now with the correct name is likely to be
ruled out of court.

These are examples—admittedly rather minor ones—of the tendency,
even among professional scholars, to accept stereotypes, to copy uncritically from previous works when a reinvestigation of the sources is
called for. The conference on Indian-white relations might serve as a
rededication to the principles of scientific thoroughness and historical
accuracy and critical use of sources that should mark such an important
endeavor as doing Indian history.

The history of Indian-white relations presents, of course, the special
problem of dealing with two diverse cultures. All historians need to understand the times and manners with which their histories deal, but
added difficulties arise for the intercultural investigator. It is necessary
to see the action on each side and to study the reaction on the other.
This means, ideally, understanding two *others,* quite diverse in themselves. It is customary to insist that we grasp something of the worldview

12. *Dictionary of American History,* s.v. "Trail of Tears."
13. See Grant Foreman, *Indian Removal: The Emigration of the Five Civilized
Tribes of Indians* (Norman: University of Oklahoma Press, 1932), pp. 310–12.
Figures on removal, with number of deaths, are given in *House Report* no. 288,
27th Cong., 3d sess., ser. 429, pp. 17–18.

of the Indian cultures (because we instinctively know they are different from our own), and we try not to judge one culture by the norms of another. What is often forgotten is that we must also understand past white societies and not assume that the 1830s can be understood and judged entirely by the norms and values of the 1970s. The brilliance of hindsight must not blind a proper understanding of, say, the Jacksonian era's views of race, of religion, or of the future prospects and rate of Western expansion. One of the goals of writing about Indian-white relations in United States history must certainly be to explain that past to white Americans. Historians must learn to understand the intellectual equipment with which nineteenth-century Americans approached the terribly difficult problems that arose in intercultural contacts and conflicts.

If our goal is not to condemn or to praise but to understand, it is necessary to be more fully conscious of the historical context in which events in Indian-white relations took place. An appreciation of the Enlightenment minds of Jefferson and his contemporaries, for example, makes one question the easy analysis of Jefferson's Indian policy as, first of all, the desire to gain the Indians' land and only secondarily, a concern for Indian welfare, when these elements seemed to have been interwoven parts of one whole. Recent careful studies of the politics involved in the Cherokee cases decided by John Marshall's court, to take another example, make it impossible any longer to see a simple conflict between justice and morality on one side and expediency and illegality on the other, which so often has been the historian's judgment.[14]

Many times it is assumed and sometimes it is explicitly argued that a person cannot legitimately investigate the history of an ethnic group or cultural community without being a member of that group. I have the uncomfortable feeling that the argument is sometimes converted into a still more questionable form—that mere membership in the group itself supplies accurate information about all aspects of the group's past. Such ethnic or racial criteria of the validity of historical research are unacceptable because they are basically anti-intellectual. "It may well be," as a recent study on the discipline of history has pointed out, "that some things are knowable only to 'insiders'; but then there are other things that are especially perceptible to 'outsiders' precisely because they are outside. That is one of the ambiguities of historical

14. See Joseph C. Burke, "The Cherokee Cases: A Study in Law, Politics, and Morality," *Stanford Law Review* 21 (February 1969): 500-531.

research: the scholar tries to get as close to his subject as possible while maintaining enough distance of space and time to afford him a sense of context and significance."[15]

But I would like to hope that historians might advance beyond a concern for "insiders" and "outsiders," so that what might prevail in the study of Indian-white relations will not be charges and countercharges but a spirit of patience and cooperation, a willingness to aid one another in a common purpose. If that common purpose is to grasp the past with sympathetic understanding, let us be slow to judge and slow to condemn.

When judgment is necessary, however, we must take care to judge all parties alike. It is true that an understanding of a culture must be governed to a large extent by the culture itself, yet it is essential to avoid adopting a double standard of judging when dealing with two cultures and their interaction. It will hardly do to see all wrong on one side and nothing but sweetness and light on the other. Breast beating over the injustices done to the Indians may have a salutary effect on public policy—although there is little evidence that Helen Hunt Jackson's *A Century of Dishonor* had any direct effect upon the members of Congress to whom she eagerly sent copies or that the book significantly changed the effective Indian reform movements of the 1880s and 1890s. What effect Dee Brown's similar book, *Bury My Heart at Wounded Knee,* will have remains to be seen. The imbalance and distortions of such books, though serving an immediate purpose of stimulating public interest in a good cause, weaken their lasting importance, and the books themselves become part of the history of Indian rights movements, not histories that can stand the test of time.

A reviewer criticized a recent book on the history of Indian-white relations by saying, "Today, most treatises on the Indian are more or less biased, and this book is no exception. White invaders are portrayed as greedy, brutal, and faithless; Indians as uniformly ingenuous and innocent. Anyone who has dealt as intimately with Indians as [the author] . . . knows that most were (and are) neither heroes nor villains but people trying (like the rest of us) to sustain their lives in a difficult environment." Those who are intent upon following professional norms would do well to heed the wise counsel with which this reviewer ends his criticism. "The historical record reveals . . . ," he notes, "that the Iroquois could be as brutal and merciless in their expansionist

15. David S. Landes and Charles Tilly, eds., *History as Social Science* (Englewood Cliffs, N.J.: Prentice-Hall, 1971), pp. 16–17.

activities as any White frontier group; and it will not do so to absolve them of critical judgment by attributing the moral responsibility for their conduct to the temptations of White traders or missionaries. If moral judgment is to be rendered upon the latter, so should it upon the former. Or, if the Indians are to be absolved of responsibility on the grounds of being naive and illiterate victims of circumstance, by what right," he asks, "can we still impose judgment upon the traders, missionaries, and frontiersmen?"[16]

John C. Ewers has expressed a similar view. "I [do not] see the role of the historian of Indian-white relations," he said, "to be that of being kind to either party in this historic confrontation. But I do think he should study this very complex theme in both breadth and depth, consulting and weighing all the sources he can find, so that he can be fair to both sides."[17]

I will be accused of offering a counsel of perfection, but the goal of historians, no matter how we all fall short of it, can be no less. A historian's inability to eliminate biases altogether does not justify the abandonment of all efforts to minimize or to surmount them in the search for truth. Perhaps the goal cannot ever be attained, but we will assuredly not get closer to it if we fail to strive for it. "Some historians do in fact come closer to it than others," it has rightly been noted. "Some history is more objective and less biased, better documented and more cogently argued. Most of us would call that better history."[18]

We must seek the truth in the story we are telling, and in the history of Indian-white relations especially we must be alert to the pitfall of having too much sympathy either for our own preconceived ideas or for one side or the other of a controversy. To be a good judge, we must not care what the truth is we are seeking. We must be concerned only with finding it. Indeed, the more we care what it is, the less likely we are to find it. We must not let our personal interests or personal pique get in the way of our judgment. We must not be too much concerned about making points for one side of a controversy or another.

Let me close with the advice offered by a sixteenth-century religious leader to his followers. "Argue in such a way," he said, "that the truth may appear, and not that you may seem to have the upper hand."

16. Murray L. Wax, review of *A History of the Indians of the United States,* by Angie Debo, in *Nebraska History* 52 (Fall 1971): 340.

17. John C. Ewers, "When Red and White Men Met," *Western Historical Quarterly* 2 (April 1971): 150.

18. Landes and Tilly, *History as Social Science,* p. 16.

Let us proceed in such a spirit as we seek the truth about the history of Indian-white relations in the United States. Then we—and the world too—can acclaim the Indian history we are doing.

2

New Approaches to the Study
of the Administration of Indian Policy

When the National Archives planned a Conference on Research in the Administration of Public Policy in 1970, it included a session on new proposals for such research, for which three historians were asked to serve as a panel. My assignment, understandably, was to discuss the administration of Indian policy. Since my own research had been confined largely to the formulation of policy rather than its administration, I was a little uncertain about how to proceed. My remarks were directed toward suggestions about areas of research regarding Indian policy administration for which there was a need and for which extensive sources were at hand in the National Archives. The talk was given at the conference on November 20, 1970. Since that time there have been some studies of Indian office bureaucracy and administration, among them Paul Stuart's Indian Office: Growth and Development of an American Institution, 1865–1900 *(Ann Arbor: UMI Research Press, 1980), which was inspired by the discussions at the conference. A good many more are needed.*

This conference, though entitled simply "Research in the Administration of Public Policy," has a strong historical orientation, and I intend to treat of strictly historical studies, which consider the course of past events, not studies of contemporary or recent situations. Too many of the latter, unfortunately, suffer because they do not rest firmly on a historical background. It seems impossible for anyone to understand a present situation without some knowledge of its past,

Printed source: Frank B. Evans and Harold T. Pinkett, eds., *Research in the Administration of Public Policy* (Washington: Howard University Press, 1975), pp. 147–52, and in *Prologue: The Journal of the National Archives* 3 (Spring 1971): 15–19.

for anyone to formulate successful administrative policy without some idea of what has been tried before and how well it worked. This presumes, of course, that historians have done their job well. But have they in fact done so?

Historical research in the administration of public policy entails two elements. There is first the formulation and determination of the policy, the definite course or method of action which guides and determines present and future decisions. Then there is the administrative execution of the policy. Neither of these can be studied effectively without the other, for a policy can be fully understood only by watching it unfold in practice; evaluation of the policy depends upon a knowledge of the problems and kinks in its administration; and changes in policy frequently come from faults or difficulties discovered in the field as the policy is applied. On the other hand, the operation, the administration, can hardly be understood unless the rationale behind the policy and its formulation is fully grasped. The intent of the formal legislation of Congress and the regulations from executive agencies needs to be known if one is to judge fairly the administration of a policy.

It may be true that the historical studies of many federal agencies have adequately covered both the formulation of policy and its execution. I do not think it is true in the case of American Indian policy and the Bureau of Indian Affairs.

What we find in historical studies is an overwhelming emphasis on investigation of policy and a serious lack of concern for the history of administration. Historians have sought to discover what the United States intended and have argued, sometimes rather heatedly, about the moral implications of the policy. Thus a good many years ago James Malin wrote a pioneering work that he called *Indian Policy and Westward Expansion,* which covered the period 1840 to 1854. In more recent years Reginald Horsman has written *Expansion and American Indian Policy, 1783–1812,* as well as a series of articles dealing with American policy in the decades before the War of 1812. Loring B. Priest's important study on the post–Civil War period has the fancy title *Uncle Sam's Stepchildren,* but the subtitle tells what the book is about: "The Reformation of United States Indian Policy." So with Henry Fritz's *The Movement for Indian Assimilation, 1860–1890,* which in dissertation form was called "The Humanitarian Background of Indian Reform." Elsie Rushmore's monograph was called *The Indian Policy during Grant's Administrations.* To say nothing of my own studies on *American Indian Policy in the Formative Years* and on the Indian policies of Lewis Cass and of Andrew Jackson.

There has been a fascination with investigating and explicating the terms of the relationships between the Europeans who invaded the continent and the Indians who were already here. Contemporary writers of the nineteenth century were intrigued by the same sort of thing— witness, to choose only one example, the rash of articles in such journals as the *Nation* and the *North American Review* in the 1870s, 1880s, and 1890s on "the Indian question," or "the Indian problem." The authors were interested in "what to do about the Indians"—that is, with the development of policy.

And what have we to match against all this on the administration of Indian affairs? Only Laurence F. Schmeckebier's now somewhat outmoded study, *The Office of Indian Affairs: Its History, Activities, and Organization,* in the Brookings Institution's series of monographs. Well, that is not quite fair. There have been some selective studies on aspects of Indian Bureau administration, of which a recent excellent example is Roy E. Meyer's *History of the Santee Sioux,* subtitled "United States Indian Policy on Trial," which shows the application of government law and regulations among a single community of Indians. There have also been a number of doctoral dissertations in recent years which have investigated in depth the working out of some aspect of Indian policy. For example, Robert Whitner's dissertation at the University of Minnesota dealt with the Methodist agencies under Grant's peace policy; and Ronald Satz at the University of Maryland is working on what promises to be a very valuable study of the administration of Indian policy during the Jackson era, 1829 to 1849. The kind of questions Satz is asking indicates the possibilities. What were the duties of the various officials engaged in Indian Affairs? How realistic was the assignment of specific duties to the various echelons in the bureaucracy? What considerations went into the selection of personnel for the Indian office and for posts in the field? What effect did the removal policy have on government agencies hitherto unconnected with Indian affairs? How adequate was the existing bureaucracy for carrying out the removal policy? How responsive was the bureaucracy to crisis situations?

All this is a beginning, but much remains to be done.

The key figure in carrying out Indian policy was the Indian agent. Herbert Welsh, the secretary of the Indian Rights Association, wrote in 1900:

> When it is considered that the Indian Agent is really the key to the proper solution of the Indian problem, the importance of securing good men for these positions and retaining them so long as they

faithfully perform their duties will be apparent. As a matter of fact, a great part of the Association's work during the past eighteen years has been to counteract the disastrous results too often caused by placing unworthy, if not dishonest, men in charge of Indian agencies. Had the Government selected the proper kind of agents and other employees, it is safe to say that the Indian problem would have been solved by this time, and the Indian Rights Association would never have been organized.

But where are the historical studies of Indian agents and their operations—not so much biographies of individual agents (although these would have great value), but analytical studies of the office of agent and the effect of the agents on Indian matters? Who has studied the kind of men appointed, their qualifications and character, their skills, their tenure of office? There are suggestive data in Whitner's dissertation on the Methodist agents from 1870 to 1882, and William Unrau in his dissertation at the University of Colorado studied the agents on the southern plains, but these are very little considering the overwhelming resources of the National Archives. Edward Hill's careful brief histories of the agencies from 1824 to 1881 give the names of all the agents. For each one there are files of correspondence in the records of the Bureau of Indian Affairs. The incoming correspondence of the Office of Indian Affairs, arranged by agency or superintendency, is largely composed of letters of agents to the commissioner about problems and activities of the agencies. For the period from 1824 to 1880 alone, these records fill more than five hundred feet of shelf space. The letters received from 1881 to 1907 fill another fifteen hundred feet. Match these statistics with those for the outgoing correspondence, the letters from the commissioner to the agents, passing down to them, as it were, the policy they had to carry out. Add to this the voluminous field office records, which take a whole volume in the preliminary inventory to describe. Can we say that we are satisfied with our knowledge of the administration of Indian affairs while these resources lie largely untouched or at least not systematically exploited?

Take another example: Indian education. Indian reformers and policy makers throughout the whole course of our history of contact between the government and the Indians have placed education of the Indians high on the list of priorities. The commissioner of Indian affairs in 1839, T. Hartley Crawford, asserted that education "is one of the most important objects, if it be not the greatest, connected with our Indian relations. Upon it depends more or less even partial success in all endeavors to make the Indian better than he is." Half a century later Thomas Jefferson Morgan, then the commissioner, declared: "Education is the medium through which the rising generation of Indians are to be brought into fraternal and harmonious relationship with their white fellow-citizens, and with them enjoy the sweets of refined homes, the delights of social intercourse, the emoluments of commerce and trade, the advantages of travel, together with the pleasures that come from literature, science, and philosophy, and the solace and stimulus afforded by a true religion."

But where are our studies of Indian schools, of how the policy was administered? The government's policy of contract schools, in which missionary groups were paid annual per capita sums for the Indian children they instructed, has received limited attention because it resulted in a critical church-state controversy, which some historians claim determined the outcome of the presidential election in 1892. But who has written a detailed scholarly history of a contract school, to say nothing of the system as a whole and its effect on the acculturation of the Indians, on church-state relations, or on educational reform? The standard bibliographies all list Alice C. Fletcher's *Indian Education and Civilization* and Evelyn C. Adams's *American Indian Education*, the first largely a compilation of statistics on Indian schools in the 1880s and the second a very small book. Is that enough?

There is no dearth of materials in the National Archives. There was off and on a special education division in the office of the commissioner of Indian affairs. Letterpress copies of outgoing correspondence on education number a healthy 352 volumes (some eight hundred pages per volume) for the period between 1885 and 1908 alone. And there are innumerable other records of the education division.

And what about the financial or—better—the "business" operations of the agencies? Just take the matter of supplies. The Board of Indian Commissioners noted in 1890 "the tedious work of receiving, inspecting, assorting, packing 27,425 packages, weighing 4,132,928 pounds and shipping the goods from the [New York] warehouse." Has the distribution of these Indian supplies been studied, and the effect they had on the life of the reservations? I have often had the feeling that the agents and superintendents were so tied up with reports and accounts that they had little time or energy left for anything else. In a famous early imprint from the northwest frontier, Lewis Cass's *Regulations for the Indian Department,* printed in Detroit in 1814, most of the items dealt with the handling of accounts. Should there not be studies on such matters? The records are here. The account books of the agencies, the auditor's vouchers, the contract books, all contain data of immense value in setting the historical balance right. The agents' work was a good deal more than making speeches at Indian councils. And who has investigated in detail the business frauds that made agents rich and infuriated the Indians?

Then there is the history of allotment of land in severalty. This has too often stopped at the policy level. The events and arguments leading up to the eventual passage of the Dawes General Allotment Act in 1887 have been exhaustively studied. The process of allotting the land has been pretty largely neglected. Yet land is the overarching element in many past as well as current Indian matters. Has anyone investigated and evaluated the work of the remarkable ethnologist Alice Fletcher, who directed the allotment of the lands for the Omahas, the Winnebagos, and the Nez Percés? The Land Division of the Office of the Commissioner of Indian Affairs has records no less voluminous than those for education.

What is the problem? Why are there such gaps in our history of the administration of Indian policy?

In the first place, I suggest, it is the very bulk of the documents. Bureaucracy, after the Civil War especially, really got out of hand. Who has the persistence to dig through such a mass of routine correspondence? Robert Kvasnicka and his staff in the Indian records section of the National Archives will testify that I have been none too courageous myself. I have had several guided tours into the stacks, "surveying" the extent of the Indian office records. I keep hoping that I might get some special inspiration as to how to tackle them—or in my more discouraged moments, that some of them would simply go away. It will take many researchers, each one digging in some special section of the files, before these riches are properly exploited. Yet books and articles of a purportedly scholarly nature keep appearing on Indian history matters, written by men who have seldom if ever set foot in the National Archives.

Secondly, a mere descriptive or narrative account of the administrative activities these records represent is not enough. Who has the creative skill to write up such a business? Rather, analysis and interpretation are necessary if this sort of administrative investigation is to be fruitful, to say nothing of being interesting. Here is where the social scientists can be of great help to the historians. There is a strong movement among historians to make use of social science concepts and theoretical structures as the framework for the investigation of historical problems. Might not these give the inspiration one needs to gather the data and at the same time supply a framework around which to fashion the study?

One might, for example, consider the theories of bureaucracy advanced by the sociologist Max Weber in order to enhance understanding of the Indian service in its wide connotation, by considering the effect of the groups of expert functionaries on the course of events. At the 1970 meeting of the Organization of American Historians in Los Angeles there was a session devoted to "Bureaucracy and the West." One paper dealt with Indian agents and investigated the reasons for administrative failures. The other treated federal bureaucrats in the West as creative agents of reform. Both authors at least bowed in the direction of Weber. The insights of the sociologist were not fully developed, but the papers pointed in a direction that might prove very fruitful in writing new histories of Indian affairs. They were a significant step beyond the mere recitation of administrative organization and activity with which so much administrative history has been concerned.

I feel a little guilty in asking others to do the work that I myself have shied away from. But it is work that will require many hands and many years. When it is done at last, we will have a sound base on which to build in the present and for the future.

3

Federal Indian Policy in United States History

I was invited to speak at the first annual Symposium on the American Indians, held at Tahlequah, Oklahoma (the old Cherokee capital), in 1973, and I used the opportunity to explore broad themes in American policy. This is a more difficult task than writing an exhaustive monograph on a small topic, but it has advantages in forcing the historian to expand his horizons. Looking at American Indian policy in the light of the social and intellectual context in which it was developed, as I attempted to do, helps to place it in proper perspective. This brief essay is only a start, but it signals the directions my thought is taking in regard to the origins of Indian policy. The essay draws to some extent upon material previously used in essays on reform in the 1840s and in the 1880s (reprinted in the present volume as numbers 11 and 15).

The policy of the federal government toward the American Indians cannot be understood as something isolated from the main course of United States history. It will not do—as many of our textbook writers assume—to treat the relations between the whites and the Indians as events that can be inserted into traditional accounts of the nation's development like foreign bits stuck in here and there to satisfy current demands for attention to ethnic minorities. Nor can we turn, at the other extreme, to the monograph writers, the specialists on Indian policy, who are likely to place their subject quite outside the general context of the cultural patterns of the times about which they write.[1]

---

1. A notable exception is the recent book by Bernard W. Sheehan, *Seeds of Extinction: Jeffersonian Philanthropy and the American Indian* (Chapel Hill: University of North Carolina Press, 1973), which explains Jeffersonian Indian policy in terms of the intellectual history of the period.

I have been disturbed for some time by both of these positions, and I keep wondering if it might not be possible to look at American Indian policy in the light of the principal social and intellectual characteristics that marked American history as it progressed period by period from the Revolution down to our own day. I do not have the temerity, of course, to tackle so immense a topic in a single short lecture. But I would like to outline the direction my thinking is taking and to propose the thesis that the Indian policy formulated from time to time by the federal government reflected—or was part of—the fundamental intellectual patterns of American life and can be understood only within that context.

We will have time, I think, to consider briefly three examples: (1) humanitarian or benevolent elements of Indian removal in pre–Civil War America, (2) the drive to Americanize the Indians at the end of the nineteenth century and the beginning of the twentieth, and (3) the Indian New Deal of John Collier in the 1930s.

The first example illustrates a pervasive factor of tremendous importance in American history. I speak of the religious and moral character of the American people—and also of the American government. The United States was an openly admitted Christian nation. It is true that the establishment of a particular church ended with the Revolution and that the Constitution prohibited any further establishment. But this principle should not obscure the fact that the American people and their government were dominated by a religious sentiment that affected all aspects of national life—including Indian policy.

It is difficult, of course, to encapsulate this religious spirit. Fortunately, recent historians of American intellectual life and of American religious history are beginning to turn to a consideration of these basic attitudes and can offer us assistance, albeit somewhat halting. Perry Miller, for example, finds the fundamental intellectual spirit of pre–Civil War America in religious revivalism. It was, he says, "the dominant theme in America from 1800 to 1860."[2] Ralph Gabriel, in an older but still significant study, sees moral concern as a distinguishing mark of America in the 1830s, 1840s, and 1850s, which included not only a demand for adherence to a strict religious code but also a deep-seated belief in a fundamental moral order in the universe which led to the spirit of optimism and progress that colored so markedly the

2. Perry Miller, *The Life of the Mind in America from the Revolution to the Civil War* (New York: Harcourt, Brace and World, 1965), p. 7.

whole Jacksonian era.[3] "The story of American Evangelicalism," says another recent scholar, "is the story of America itself in the years 1800 to 1900, for it was Evangelical religion which made Americans the most religious people in the world, molded them into a unified, pietistic-perfectionist nation, and spurred them on to those heights of social reform, missionary endeavor, and imperialistic expansionism which constitute the moving forces of our history in that century."[4]

A strong element of the revivalism and moral interest was a spirit of benevolence, which blossomed into an active reform crusade in the decades before the Civil War. The great revivalist preacher Charles G. Finney declared that the spirit of every true Christian "is necessarily that of the reformer. To the universal reformation of the world they stand committed."[5] A care for the less fortunate became a major concern of the leaders of American social thought. "Nothing in America," to use Sydney Ahlstrom's phrase, "was safe from the reformer's burning gaze during the first half of the nineteenth century."[6] It is not without significance that major changes in Indian policy have always been proposed under the rubric of "reform," and advanced with a moral fervor of frightening intensity.

We have so long been accustomed to think of Indian policy in the early national period in terms of ruthless aggression and limitless avarice for Indian lands that it will stretch our mental forms to see that Indian policy did not stand by itself outside these general trends of American thought and sentiment—but was indeed strongly affected by them and in some ways an integral part of them.

There was a strong humanitarian element in pre–Civil War Indian policy, which was in tune with the moral sentiment of the day. Thomas L. McKenney, Superintendent of Indian Trade and then first head of the Bureau of Indian Affairs, worked persistently for what he considered the best interests of the Indians. Thus he encouraged both private and public efforts to educate the Indians and to teach them the white man's social and economic patterns. And when the transformation he and other humanitarians envisaged did not quickly occur, he

3. Ralph Henry Gabriel, *The Course of American Democratic Thought: An Intellectual History since 1815* (New York: Ronald Press, 1940), pp. 26–38.

4. William G. McLoughlin, ed., *The American Evangelicals, 1800–1900: An Anthology* (New York: Harper and Row, 1968), p. 1.

5. Quoted ibid., p. 12.

6. Sydney E. Ahlstrom, *A Religious History of the American People* (New Haven: Yale University Press, 1972), p. 637. See all of chap. 39, "The High Tide of Humanitarian Reform," pp. 637–47.

earnestly endeavored to persuade the eastern Indians to migrate to the West, where they might escape the pressures and the vices of the white society surrounding them. In a typically "benevolent" frame of mind, he wrote: "Seeing as I do the condition of these people, and that they are bordering on destruction, I would, were I empowered, take them *firmly* but *kindly* by the hand, and tell them they must go; and I would do this, on the same principle that I would take my own children by the hand, firmly, but kindly and lead them from a district of Country in which the plague was raging."[7]

The Jackson administration, a very black period in many present-day accounts of Indian relations, reflected some of the same spirit. In the West, President Jackson asserted in his first annual message, the Indians "may be secured in the enjoyment of governments of their own choice, subject to no other control from the United States than such as may be necessary to preserve peace on the frontier and between the several tribes. There the benevolent may endeavor to teach them the arts of civilization, and, by promoting union and harmony among them, to raise up an interesting commonwealth, destined to perpetuate the race and to attest the humanity and justice of this Government."[8] Similarly, Lewis Cass, in his first annual report as Jackson's Secretary of War, spoke of Indian removal as presenting "the only hope of permanent establishment and improvement." He recommended instruction in the "truths of religion, together with a knowledge of the simpler mechanic arts and the rudiments of science." He encouraged severalty of property, assistance in opening farms, and employment of persons to instruct the Indians.[9] The government clearly intended to promote the civilization of the Indians in their new homes, to sweep them up into the "progress" of the times.

There is a question, of course, about the sincerity of such intentions. It has been customary with many modern historians to look at these utterances as "mere rhetoric" and to assume and often to charge specifically that the *real* intent of policy was ruthless land grabbing, that the rhetoric was no more than a cover up or rationalization for sordid motives. This dichotomy will not hold up under sharp historical

---

7. McKenney to Eli Baldwin, October 28, 1829, Records of the Office of Indian Affairs, Letters Sent, vol. 6, p. 140, National Archives, Record Group 75.

8. James D. Richardson, comp., *A Compilation of the Messages and Papers of the Presidents, 1789–1897,* 10 vols. (Washington: Government Printing Office, 1896–99), 2:458.

9. Report of the Secretary of War, November 21, 1831, *House Executive Document* no. 2, 22d Cong., 1st sess., ser. 216, pp. 30–34.

investigation. The policy stated, the motivation adduced, has to be seen, to some extent at least, as a reflection of the moral spirit of the times. There was enough plausibility in these benevolent views to catch the sympathetic vibrations of large sections of the American public and to make unlikely if not impossible the success of those who—arguing on moral grounds themselves—tried to prevent and then to reverse the removal policy. Both sides of the removal controversy, you see, spoke the same pietistic and perfectionist language—although they had radically different ideas about how the goal was to be attained.[10]

When removal of the eastern Indians had been accomplished, revivalism and benevolence came into full play in federal Indian policy. The 1840s were a tranquil interval between the upheaval of removal and the eventual cracking of the "permanent Indian frontier" that had been established in the West. It was a time when the officials of the Indian Office shared in the vital optimism of their age, an age in which the betterment of all mankind seemed within easy reach, and concern for society's unfortunates (the delinquent, the insane, the indigent poor, the deaf, the blind) appeared everywhere. Crusades for peace, for women's rights, for temperance, for education, and for abolition of slavery marched with reforming zeal and a strange naiveté through the land. Words like *benevolence, philanthropy,* and *perfectability* slipped easily from men's tongues. The plans for civilizing and Christianizing the Indians who had been removed from the main arena of American life reflected this evangelizing spirit. The Indian policy of the 1840s, indeed, can be considered part of "the first great upsurge of social reform in United States history."[11]

In 1840 the Commissioner of Indian Affairs, T. Hartley Crawford, foresaw for the Indians in their new western homes a great flowering of

10. For further argument on the removal policy, see Francis Paul Prucha, *American Indian Policy in the Formative Years: The Indian Trade and Intercourse Acts, 1790–1834* (Cambridge: Harvard University Press, 1962), chap. 9, "Civilization and Removal," pp. 213–49; Francis Paul Prucha, "Andrew Jackson's Indian Policy: A Reassessment," *Journal of American History* 56 (December 1969): 527–39.

11. The statement is from Arthur M. Schlesinger, *The American as Reformer* (Cambridge: Harvard University Press, 1950), p. 3. Other surveys of the reform of the period are Alice Felt Tyler, *Freedom's Ferment: Phases of American Social History to 1860* (Minneapolis: University of Minnesota Press, 1944), and Clifford S. Griffin, *Their Brothers' Keepers: Moral Stewardship in the United States, 1800–1865* (New Brunswick: Rutgers University Press, 1960). I am following here my discussion of Indian reform in "American Indian Policy in the 1840s: Visions of Reform," in John G. Clark, ed., *The Frontier Challenge: Responses to the Trans-Mississippi West* (Lawrence: University Press of Kansas, 1971), pp. 81–110.

the solid Puritan virtues—"temperance and industry, and education and religion."[12] Education was to be the powerful instrument in bringing about the reform. That the Indians could be educated was a basic tenet of the reformers. They admitted, of course, that the present state of the Indians was inferior. But the unfortunate condition of the red men was not irremediable. The government officials did not believe in a fundamental racial inferiority. "It is proved, I think, conclusively," Crawford remarked of the Indian race, "that it is in no respect inferior to our own race, except in being less fortunately circumstanced. As great an aptitude for learning the letters, the pursuits, and arts of civilized life, is evident; if their progress is slow, so had it been with us and with masses of men in all nations and ages."[13] Circumstances and education alone made the difference between them and the whites. So schools for Indians were advocated with great enthusiasm, befitting an age in which education was considered the "universal utopia."[14] The federal government and the missionaries joined forces to bring to the Indians fringing the western settlements the schools—largely manual labor schools—which were to bring about the transformation.

By the end of the 1840s there were enthusiastic appraisals of success. "The dark clouds of ignorance and superstition in which these people have so long been enveloped," the Commissioner of Indian Affairs wrote of the Indians in 1849, "seem at length in the case of many of them to be breaking away, and the light of Christianity and general knowledge to be dawning upon their moral and intellectual darkness." He gave credit for the change to the government's policy of directing the Indians toward an agricultural existence, the introduction of the manual labor schools, and instruction by the missionaries in "the best of all knowledge, religious truth—their duty towards God and their fellow beings." The result was "a great moral and social revolution" among some of the tribes, which he predicted would be spread to others by adoption of the same measures. Within a few years he believed that "in intelligence and resources, they would compare favorably with many portions of our white population, and instead of drooping and declining, as heretofore, they would be fully able to

12. Report of T. Hartley Crawford, November 28, 1840, *Senate Document* no. 1, 26th Cong., 2d sess., ser. 375, pp. 232–34.

13. Report of T. Hartley Crawford, November 25, 1844, *Senate Document* no. 1, 28th Cong., 2d sess., ser. 449, p. 315.

14. The phrase is from a chapter heading in Arthur A. Ekirch, Jr., *The Idea of Progress in America, 1815–1860* (New York: Columbia University Press, 1944), p. 195.

maintain themselves in prosperity and happiness under any circumstance of contact or connexion with our people." In the end he expected a large measure of success to "crown the philanthropic efforts of the government and of individuals to civilize and to christianize the Indian tribes."[15]

This was considerably overdone, for the Indians did not find utopia. But it was quite in tune with the age, when zealous reformers saw no limit to the possibilities for ameliorating and perfecting human conditions, when the insane were to be cured, the slaves freed, the prisons cleansed, women's rights recognized, and Sunday schools flourish. Can we not believe that they had comparable hopes for the American Indians, even though the fulfillment fell far short of the vision?

The end of the nineteenth and the start of the twentieth century—our second period for consideration—offers another fruitful example for my thesis. Indian policy reform in those years was initiated by a small group of Christian men and women, who were certain that they had discovered at last a solution to "the Indian problem." By persistent propaganda, they sought to awaken and to inform the conscience of the nation and thereby to force legislation through Congress and to win the support of federal officials. They gave a new orientation to Indian-white relations in the United States as they came to dominate government policy.[16]

These reformers acted through organizations that sprang up in response to spectacular revelations of Indian wrongs—such groups as the Boston Indian Citizenship Committee, the Women's National Indian Association, and the Indian Rights Association—and their work was brought into sharp focus in an annual conference held at a resort hotel on Lake Mohonk, New York. There these self-denominated "Friends of the Indian" discussed Indian reform and formulated the program they intended to promote.

The meetings took place in an atmosphere of deep religious sentiment, for the group was bound together by a common humanitarian

15. Report of Orlando Brown, November 30, 1849, *House Executive Document* no. 5, 31st Cong., 1st sess., ser. 570, pp. 956–57.

16. The discussion of these reformers here follows my account of their principles and actions in "Indian Policy Reform and American Protestantism, 1880–1900," in Ray Allen Billington, ed., *People of the Plains and Mountains: Essays in the History of the West Dedicated to Everett Dick* (Westport, Conn.: Greenwood Press, 1973), pp. 120–45. See also the introduction in Francis Paul Prucha, ed., *Americanizing the American Indians: Writings by the "Friends of the Indian" 1880–1900* (Cambridge: Harvard University Press, 1973).

outlook and by a common Christian tradition. The president of the Lake Mohonk Conference in 1891 declared: "This is essentially a philanthropic and Christian reform."[17] The goal was to guide the Indian "from the night of barbarism into the fair dawn of Christian civilization," as the secretary of the Indian Rights Association expressed it.[18] The only hope for the Indians, the reformers believed, was to bring them "under the sway of Christian thought and Christian life, and into touch with the people of this Christian nation."[19]

The term *Christian,* as these men and women used it, was defined in terms of American evangelical Protestantism, which continued throughout the nineteenth century to be a great moving force. The evangelicals, in fact, had long hoped to create a "righteous empire" in America; at the end of the century there was an intensified desire for unity, a new energization in this "quest for a Christian America."[20] And it was precisely at this time that the "Indian problem" demanded a long overdue solution. The coincidence of an ultimate crisis in Indian affairs, brought about by the overwhelming pressure of aggressively expanding white civilization upon the Indians and the intensified religious drive for a unified American society, led to a new program of Indian policy reform.

The distinguishing mark of this American evangelicalism was its insistence on individual salvation. Conversion and reformation of individuals was to be the means for correcting evils in society. The Indian reformers at Lake Mohonk came to realize the fundamental conflict between this principle and the communal life of the Indians. And they demanded the individualization of the Indians and their acculturation as individuals freed from bondage to the tribe. "The Indian as a savage member of a tribal organization cannot survive, ought not to survive, the aggressions of civilization," the Indian Rights Association declared in a typical statement in 1884, "but his individual redemption from heathenism and ignorance, his transformation from the condition of a savage nomad to that of an industrious American

---

17. *Lake Mohonk Conference Proceedings,* 1891, p. 11.
18. Ibid., 1886, p. 13.
19. Remarks of Merrill Gates, ibid., 1900, p. 13.
20. The phrases are from Martin E. Marty, *Righteous Empire: The Protestant Experience in America* (New York: Dial Press, 1970), and Robert T. Handy, "The Protestant Quest for a Christian America," *Church History* 22 (March 1953): 8–20. See also Robert T. Handy, *A Christian America: Protestant Hopes and Historical Realities* (New York: Oxford University Press, 1970).

citizen, is abundantly possible."[21] The president of the Lake Mohonk Conference declared in 1900:

> We have learned that education and example, and pre-eminently, the force of Christian life and Christian faith in the heart, can do in one generation most of that which evolution takes centuries to do.
>
> But if civilization, education and Christianity are to do their work, they must get at the individual. They must lay hold of men and women and children, one by one. The deadening sway of tribal custom must be interfered with. The sad uniformity of savage tribal life must be broken up! Individuality must be cultivated. . . . At last, as a nation, we are coming to recognize the great truth that if we would do justice to the Indians, we must get at them, one by one, with American ideals, American schools, American laws, the privileges and the pressure of American rights and duties.[22]

The evangelical reformers fought for individualization on many fronts. Most important was the drive to break up tribal ownership of land and to substitute the allotment of reservation lands to individual Indians. Communal land holding was considered the substructure upon which the tribal power rested. If it could be destroyed, the Indian could be treated as an individual and absorbed as an individual into American society.

By concerted effort the reformers got what they wanted. On February 8, 1887, the Dawes Act became law—authorizing the President to allot portions of the reservations to individual Indians and granting United States citizenship to those who received the allotments. The humanitarians rejoiced at the passage of the act; they hailed it as the "Indian Emancipation Act" and spoke of the beginning of a new epoch in Indian affairs. "The supreme significance of the law in marking a new era in dealing with the Indian problem," one reformer noted, "lies in the fact that this law is a mighty pulverizing engine for breaking up the tribal mass. It has nothing to say to the tribe, nothing to do with the tribe. It breaks up that vast 'bulk of things' which the tribal life sought to keep unchanged. It finds its way straight to the family and to the individual."[23]

The individualism of the evangelical Protestants was intimately related to the Puritan work ethic. The virtues of hard work and thrift

21. *Report of the Indian Rights Association,* 1884, p. 5.

22. *Lake Mohonk Conference Proceedings,* 1900, p. 14.

23. Remarks of Merrill Gates, *Lake Mohonk Conference Proceedings,* 1900, p. 16.

were the very basis of individual salvation. The reformers, indeed, could conceive no transformation of the Indians that did not include self-support. Allotment of land in severalty was demanded because the reformers believed that without the personal labor needed to maintain the private homestead the virtue of hard work could never be inculcated.

But what especially marked the final decades of the century in the development of evangelical Protestantism and gave it its peculiar flavor was an almost complete identification of Protestantism and Americanism—culminating a movement extending throughout the century. Two tendencies intensified this identification. One of them was the weakening of traditional theological interest to such an extent that the principles of Americanism became in large part the religious creed. The other was the growing threat to Protestant hegemony by new forces in the United States, principally the immigration of millions of new Europeans who did not fit the Anglo-Saxon Protestant pattern of America, and the growing industrialization and urbanization of the nation, which upset the rural Protestant outlook.

Under these threats to the unity of America the churches promoted new measures to strengthen conformity. The most important of these was a universal public school system, which while reflecting and continuing evangelical Protestant virtues (under a cloak of "nonsectarianism") instilled the Americanism that had become a basic religious goal. "Nothing, perhaps, is so distinctly a product of the soil as is the American [public] school system," asserted the former Baptist minister, Thomas J. Morgan, who was to become Indian Commissioner in 1889. "In these schools all speak a common language; race distinctions give way to national characteristics."[24]

The Indians were engulfed in this flood of Americanism. Their Americanization, indeed, became the all-embracing goal of the reformers in the last two decades of the century. "The logic of events," Commissioner Morgan declared in his first annual report, "demands the absorption of the Indians into our national life, not as Indians, but as American citizens."[25]

This means for Americanizing the Indians seemed to be at hand. Building on the foundation of individualism supplied by the land-in-severalty legislation and the provisions for granting American citizenship,

24. Thomas J. Morgan, *Studies in Pedagogy* (Boston: Silver, Burdett and Company, 1889), pp. 327–28.

25. Report of Thomas J. Morgan, October 1, 1889, *House Executive Document* no. 1, 51st Cong., 1st sess., ser. 2725, p. 3.

the reformers promoted a universal national school system, which would do for the Indians what the public school system of the states was doing for other alien groups in the republic. The government and the humanitarian reformers joined hands to educate the Indians as individual Christian patriotic American citizens.

Under the direction of Thomas J. Morgan the United States embarked on an aggressive program of government schools for the Indians that would promote the goals that the Lake Mohonk reformers had in mind. "The chief thing in all education," Morgan asserted, "is the development of character, the formation of manhood and womanhood. To this end the whole course of training should be fairly saturated with moral ideas, fear of God, and respect for the rights of others; love of truth and fidelity to duty; personal purity, philanthropy, and patriotism. Self-respect and independence are cardinal virtues, and are indispensable for the enjoyment of the privileges of freedom and the discharge of the duties of American citizenship." The Protestant emphasis on the virtues of hard work and regularity was evident. "Labor should cease to be repulsive, and come to be regarded as honorable and attractive," Morgan insisted. And the students were to learn the virtue of economy and to understand that waste was wicked. The schools were to be organized and conducted so that they would accustom the pupils to systematic habits. "The periods of rising and retiring, the hours for meals, times for study, recitation, work and play," he directed, "should all be fixed and adhered to with great punctiliousness." His goal was to replace what he called the "irregularities of camp life" with "the methodical regularity of daily routine." Such routine would develop "habits of self-directed toil," and teach the students "the marvelous secret of diligence." "When the Indian children shall have acquired a taste for study and a love for work," he proclaimed in significant terminology, "the day of their redemption will be at hand."[26]

To these goals of Indian education was to be added the inculcation of American patriotism. The Indian children were to be "instructed in the rights, duties, and privileges of American citizens, taught to love the American flag, . . . imbued with a genuine patriotism, and made to feel that the United States and not some paltry reservation, is their home." They were to be educated, not as Indians, but as Americans. "In short," Morgan noted in his plan, "the public school should do for

26. Thomas J. Morgan, "Supplemental Report on Indian Education," *House Executive Document* no. 1, 51st Cong., 1st sess., ser. 2725, pp. 98–101.

them what it is so successfully doing for all the other races in this country,—assimilate them."[27]

The government schools were to assimilate the Indians into the Christian nation which was the great evangelical goal. The schools, therefore, were to reflect Protestant traditions through their teachers and their programs. For the reformers were convinced of the position enunciated by the presiding officer at Lake Mohonk in 1893: "Only as men and women who are full of the light of education and of the life of Christ go in and out among these savage brothers and sisters of ours, only as the living thought and the feeling heart touch their hearts one by one, can the Indian be lifted from savagery and made into useful citizens. . . . As we get at them one by one, as we break up these iniquitous masses of savagery, as we draw them out from their old associations and immerse them in the strong currents of Christian life and Christian citizenship, as we send the sanctifying stream of Christian life and Christian work among them, they feel the pulsing life-tide of Christ's life."[28]

The reformers represented at Lake Mohonk have sometimes been dismissed as a peripheral group of sentimental men and women, who by clever machinations and unjustified propaganda foisted a program of reform upon Congress and the Indian service. Neither the men nor their impact can be understood in this narrow perspective. Rather, the reformers represented a powerful segment of Protestant church membership, and thereby of late nineteenth- and early twentieth-century American society. When they spoke, they spoke for a large majority of the nation, expressing views that were widely held. They were but the channel through which this evangelical Protestant Americanism, this vision of a Christian America, came to bear upon the Indians.

This does not mean, of course, that their program can be commended. Though sincere and humane in their outlook, the reformers were entrapped in a mold of patriotic Americanism that was too narrow to allow them to appreciate the Indian cultures. Their program broke down the Indians' heritage and cultural pride without substituting anything in its place, until the Indians became a demoralized people, lost between their historic identity and the white American culture they could not totally accept.

Let us move, finally, to the third example: Indian reform in the second and third decades of the twentieth century.

27. Ibid., p. 96.
28. *Lake Mohonk Conference Proceedings,* 1893, p. 12.

The fundamental fact to be noted here is that the concept of a "Christian America"—the context in which the evangelical reformers worked—had faded by the 1920s. That postwar period was one of strong reaction against idealism and reform, a condition growing out of disillusionment with American participation in World War I. But there was more to it than that. The very life of the nation had changed from what it had been in prewar days. Evangelical Protestantism, in short, was being displaced as the "primary definer of cultural values and behavior patterns in the nation." The belief that the United States as a nation was basically Protestant and that it was progressing toward the kingdom of God had supported evangelical crusading, and the crusade for Americanizing the Indians in this mold was no exception. But in the 1920s the old supports were crumbling.[29]

A new secularization of society occurred, and it was uncongenial to religion. Abrasive new doctrines of social freedom eroded the old mores, and the bitter controversy between fundamentalists and modernists further lessened the prestige of Protestantism. But more basic than anything else were new advances in science and technology, breeding a devotion to scientific method that led to disillusionment with religion. There was a growing optimism that science could solve all human problems, and the belief that progress depended upon religion was irreparably weakened.

There was no firm foundation, then, for the Christian reform principles that had held sway at the turn of the century. Gone were the dreams of inevitable progress toward a unified society based on the old religious values, which had been at the root of Indian reform movements at the end of the nineteenth century. Concern for the Indians underwent a marked shift in keeping with the changes in American society. The old philanthropic, benevolent approach, which saw as the highest good for the Indians the absolute imitation of their white Christian advisers, was replaced by a social science approach that aimed at cultural understanding and at a secular solution to Indian problems. The anthropologist replaced the missionary at the cutting edge of Indian policy "reform."[30]

29. Handy, *A Christian America,* chap. 7, "The Second Disestablishment," pp. 184–225, treats of this change. See also a similar account in Ahlstrom, *A Religious History of the American People,* chap. 53, "The Twenties: From the Armistice to the Crash," pp. 895–917.

30. See Kenneth R. Philp, "John Collier and the American Indian, 1920–1945" (Ph.D. diss., Michigan State University, 1968), pp. 143–44. [Published as *John Collier's Crusade for Indian Reform, 1920-1954* (Tucson: University of Arizona Press, 1977).]

The early 1920s brought a new surge in concern for Indian rights when the federal government, through the so-called Bursum Bill, wanted to permit white encroachment upon the lands of the Pueblos. From the public outcry against this administration measure developed a new crusade for Indian reform that reflected the new mood of American life and which ultimately resulted in a revolutionary change in federal Indian policy.[31]

Representative of the new direction was the American Indian Defense Association and its spokesman, John Collier, who came to the fore in a successful defense of the threatened Indian rights. Collier was a symbol of the dramatic change in viewpoint that was taking place. A social reformer in New York City and in California in the early years of the century, he had become interested in the Indians of the Southwest. But his concern for their rights was only a part of his newly found interest. He saw in the communal existence of the native Americans a model for reforming society at large. Beginning as an outspoken critic of existing Indian policy and Indian service administration, Collier soon became the architect of a new program. When Franklin D. Roosevelt took office in 1933, inaugurating a New Deal that was to reshape American society, he appointed John Collier Commissioner of Indian Affairs, and an "Indian New Deal" became part of the administration's program.

John Collier spoke about seven basic principles that guided his administration of Indian affairs. They can serve to depict his philosophy of reform.

1. "Indian societies must and can be discovered in their continuing existence, or regenerated, or set into being *de novo* and made use of."
2. "The Indian societies, whether ancient, regenerated or created anew, must be given status, responsibility and power."
3. "The land, held, used and cherished in the way the particular Indian group desires, is fundamental in any lifesaving program."
4. "Each and all of the freedoms should be extended to Indians, and in the most convincing and dramatic manner possible." Collier asked for "proclamation and enforcement of cultural liberty, religious liberty, and unimpeded relationships of the generations."
5. Positive means must be used to ensure freedom—credit, education (of a broad and technical sort), and grants of responsibility.
6. "The experience of responsible democracy, is, of all experience, the

31. This movement is discussed fully in Philp, "John Collier and the American Indian."

most therapeutic, the most disciplinary, the most dynamogenic and the most productive of efficiency. In this one affirmation we, the workers who knew so well the diversity of the Indian situation and its recalcitrancy toward monistic programs, were prepared to be unreserved, absolute, even at the risk of blunders and of turmoil. We tried to extend to the tribes a self-governing self-determination without any limit beyond the need to advance by stages to the goal."

7. "The seventh principle I would call the first and the last: That research and then more research is essential to the program, that in the ethnic field research can be made a tool of action essential to all the other tools, indeed, that it ought to be the master tool."[32]

What a vastly different world this was from the world of the Lake Mohonk Friends of the Indian with their Christian individualism! Indian corporate life was to be regenerated and individualism rejected as the highest good. Cultural and religious freedom—no matter how it might go against the established American cultural grain—was to be ensured. A secularized democracy replaced American Christianity as the essential *end* to be sought. Scientific research—the Indian administration was to be "a laboratory of ethnic relations" in Collier's view— replaced the "strong currents of Christian life" as the indispensable *means* of reform.

John Collier got his legislative program. The Wheeler-Howard Act (or Indian Reorganization Act) of 1934 incorporated his basic views. The new legislation explicitly rejected the Dawes Act and its principles, and further allotment of Indian lands was forbidden. Money was provided for the purchase of additional communal lands; authority was granted for a revolving credit fund from which loans could be made to tribes. And the act allowed the adoption by the Indian tribes of written forms of government.[33]

It might be impossible to prove that the new Indian policy was *caused* by the secularistic, scientific climate of opinion that obtained after 1920, for direct causal connections are very difficult to establish in historical study. But John Collier and his program would have been inconceivable in the 1890s.

32. These principles are set forth in John Collier, "United States Indian Administration as a Laboratory of Ethnic Relations," *Social Research* 12 (September 1945): 274–75. This article is repeated substantially in Collier, *Indians of the Americas: The Long Hope* (New York: W. W. Norton and Company, 1947), chap. 14, "The Indian New Deal." I have quoted them from this later version.

33. *United States Statutes at Large*, 48:984–88.

Was Collier's democratic vision for the Indians any more successful than Thomas J. Morgan's goal of Christian patriotism? At one time it was thought so. The Wheeler-Howard Act was received by Collier and his friends with jubilation that rivaled that of Senator Dawes and his associates when the general allotment law was passed in 1887. Historians were quick to accept Collier's own version of his principles and of their success. Yet the current and persisting difficulties among Indian communities suggest that Collier did not usher in the millennium.[34]

The tragedy is that white Americans—whether their philanthropic impulse came from Christian sentiment or from social science commitments—have never really been willing to accept a pluralistic society. For nearly two centuries of United States history the dream of the reformers has been to bring the Indians into conformity with the prevailing moods—religious and intellectual—of white society. The dominant sentiments of an age could not make room for alternative or divergent patterns of life. The formulators of Indian policy, in all the periods we have looked at today, with typical reformers' zeal swept criticism and opposition aside, for they believed that they and the nation they represented were supremely right. The Indian has been asked to march to all kinds of drummers—except his own.

34. See, for example, Alvin M. Josephy, Jr., "What the Indians Want," *New York Times Magazine,* March 18, 1973, p. 67.

4

The Dawning of a New Era:
The Spirit of Reform and American Indian Policy

In studying Indian policy I have been impressed with the "reform" aspects of its development. Each new proposal was put forward as a reform of past errors and many times as a panacea, with the aggressive zeal that seems to be characteristic of true reformers. What struck me eventually was the repetition of the rhetoric as one reform after another appeared—the old order was always changing and a new era was dawning for the Indians. I have no doubt that the spokesmen were sincere, whatever their triteness of expression, but the repeated failure of the "new day" to materialize says much about the shortcomings of American optimism and the difficulties of finding a sound and lasting set of relationships for Indian and white societies. I used this essay first as a talk at the meeting of the Oklahoma Association of College History Professors in March 1974. Since then I have adapted it for other more general audiences. One version appeared in Centennial Addresses *(Bulletin of the University of Wisconsin–River Falls, vol. 57, series 2, no. 3, September 1975), pp. 9–16. The essay has always been in a state of flux, however, for I am continually finding more examples of a "new era" descried for the Indians.*

Americans are a reforming breed. Through most of United States history they have faced national and individual difficulties with an almost illimitable optimism. Problems were there to be solved; evils in public or private life, it was believed, could be eradicated with a little good will and the application of some special remedy, and simplistic approaches abounded. Graham bread, it was argued, would end the ills of a sickened world; communal utopias would reshape society; free silver—or the single tax—would correct the economic maladies that crushed the poor and exalted the rich; the initiative and the referendum—or if not they, perhaps woman suffrage—would prevent political malfunctions; prohibition would create a new and wholesome America. We might almost say that Americans have been panacea-prone.

It should come as no surprise, then, that American Indian affairs have repeatedly fallen into the same pattern. The "problem" that resulted from the contact of Western European settlers and the Native Americans is well known. The conflicts over land, the misunderstandings that arose from agreements between two groups with radically different cultures and world outlooks, the hostility perpetuated by military encounters, the fraud and deception and injustice of men toward other men, the complexities of intercultural exchange—all this resulted in an "Indian problem" that no one could ignore. Here was fertile ground for seeds of reform, which have sprouted again and again. The withering blasts of hard practicality were considered no more than temporary discomforts, and when the winds had passed they were soon forgotten. New reforms appeared or older ones resprouted.

I would like to look briefly at some of these recurrent solutions to the "Indian problem" and to do so under a particular rubric. I have selected a number of statements that show the remarkable similarity of rhetoric used by reformers through the decades in their enthusiastic, optimistic, panacean approaches to Indian policy. I want to point out, in short, the repeated pronouncements that the evils of the past have been wiped away and that now, at last, a new era in American Indian affairs has dawned. My examples run from the 1840s to the present day.

The 1840s were the first great age of reform in American history. Women's rights, care of the insane, peace crusades, and public education received an impetus then that carried through the century. This reform sentiment touched the Indians as well, in the period of relative tranquillity following the turmoil of Indian removal. And it was education that was to be the means of change.

The Commissioner of Indian Affairs, William Medill, declared in 1846: "The cause of education has received that attention which its great importance would appear to demand. Its advantages and meliorating influences are beginning to be seen and felt in the forests and among the savages, as well as among the more cultivated regions and enlightened circles of our country. The direction which has recently been given to the system, by combining with letters a knowledge of agriculture and the mechanic arts," he continued, "has opened a new era in the progress of Indian civilization." Medill noticed the increased interest of the Indians themselves in the schools, whereas formerly there had been opposition, and he saw everywhere evidences of "increased happiness and prosperity."[1] The manual labor schools of which the Commissioner spoke in 1846 were the first of a long succession of panaceas that were to erase the past and create a bright new future for the Indians.

Just as Commissioner Medill was writing, the isolation of the Indians west of the Mississippi was being destroyed by American expansionism. Emigrants to Oregon and California cut through Indian lands, and the Indians struck back. In 1851, a council with the Indians was held at Fort Laramie and a treaty was signed, by which the tribes agreed to permit an open passageway for the whites. In attendance at that council was the famous Jesuit missionary Father Pierre-Jean DeSmet, who strongly supported what took place. He wrote:

> The happy results of this council are, no doubt, owing to the prudent measures of the commissioners of the Government, and more especially to their conciliatory manners in all their intercourse and transactions with the Indians. The council will doubtless produce the good effects they have a right to expect. It will be the commencement of a new era for the Indians—an era of peace. In future, peaceable citizens may cross the desert unmolested, and the Indian will have little to dread from the bad white man, for justice will be rendered to him.[2]

The missionary's vision, unfortunately, was clouded, for the pressure of white expansion created new Indian conflicts. By the end of the Civil War the plains were aflame with Indian wars, and a new method in Indian affairs was obviously needed. It was supplied by the "peace policy" of President Grant, which incorporated the advice of humanitarians and the religious sentiment of missionary societies into a policy that sought to conquer the Indians by kindness rather than by war. With a somewhat restrained enthusiasm, Grant's Commissioner of Indian Affairs, the Seneca Ely S. Parker, described the situation:

> Of late years a change of policy was seen to be required, as the cause of failure, the difficulties to be encountered, and the best means of overcoming them, became better understood. The measures

1. Report of William Medill, November 30, 1846, *Senate Document* no. 1, 29th Cong., 2d sess., ser. 493, pp. 225–26.

2. H. M. Chittenden and A. T. Richardson, eds., *Life, Letters, and Travels of Father Pierre-Jean De Smet, S.J., 1801–1873,* 4 vols. (New York: Francis P. Harper, 1905), 2:684.

to which we are indebted for an improved condition of affairs are, the concentration of the Indians upon suitable reservations, and the supplying them the means for engaging in agricultural and mechanical pursuits, and for their education and moral training. As a result, the clouds of ignorance and superstition in which many of this people were so long enveloped have disappeared, and the light of a Christian civilization seems to have dawned upon their moral darkness, and opened a brighter future.[3]

But the years of the "peace policy," ironically, were filled with Indian wars—an inhospitable seedbed for reform. Not until the Indians had been militarily subjugated could substantial reformation of policy take place.

Then, in the 1880s and 1890s, well-intentioned though seriously misguided humanitarians in the East mounted an aggressive campaign to revolutionize the relations of the Indians to American society. In an age of rampant individualism these reformers were aghast at the communal life of the Indians. Determined at all costs to end tribal relations and the reservations on which the tribes were based, new reform organizations devoted their money and their energy to individualizing and thus Americanizing the native Americans. The first of their goals was to allot the reservation lands in severalty to individual Indian families. They wanted a general allotment law and were no longer willing to rely on piecemeal efforts that did not affect all Indians.

They got their way in the Dawes Act of 1887, which authorized the President to allot the reservations to individual Indians and which granted United States citizenship to the allottees. The reformers were jubilant!

The Indian Rights Association declared after the passage of the act: "There can be but little doubt that this is one of the most vital and important steps ever taken by Congress in its dealings with the Indians. It may be said to make an era; to be the beginning of a new order of things." The legislation, the report continued, marked a "new departure on the part of Congress"—it established a policy "which would help the Indians to become independent farmers and stock men by making them individual land holders; which looks to the gradual breaking up of the reservations on which the Indians are shut from all wholesome contact with our civilization; which loosens the fatal tribal bonds by bringing

3. Report of Ely S. Parker, December 23, 1869, *House Executive Document* no. 1, 41st Cong., 2d sess., ser. 1414, p. 445.

the Indians under our laws, and making the way broad for their entrance into citizenship."[4]

Nor did the praise quickly die away. In 1892, more than five years after the passage of the Dawes Act, the religious weekly *Independent,* in an editorial entitled "The Red Man's Charter of Liberty," felt obliged to remind its readers of the great changes. It wrote: "The significance and far-reaching consequence of what is known as the Dawes Act, adopted in 1887, providing for alloting to Indians lands in severalty, do not seem to be fully appreciated. It marks an epoch in the history of our dealings with Indians. It is to the Red man what Lincoln's Proclamation of Emancipation was to the Black man; it overturns at one stroke the entire past, and inaugurates for the Indian a new era." The editors did not want the import of the law to be missed: "It goes without saying that this act of emancipation from the condition of wardship carries with it, of necessity, the destruction of the old Indian life and the substitution of the methods and policies of the white man. It breaks the power of the chief and utterly destroys the tribal relation. As a citizen, each Indian is his own chief, and belongs not to a tribe but to the nation."[5]

No man was more important as a discerner of the new day than Thomas Jefferson Morgan, a Baptist minister turned public educator, who served as Commissioner of Indian Affairs from 1889 to 1893. He, of course, enthusiastically supported the Dawes Act. "This radical measure," he said in 1891, "may be said to mark the beginning of a new era in the status of the Indians."[6] And he repeated his pronouncement in 1894 when he had left office to become editor of the *Baptist Home Mission Monthly*: "By the passage of the Dawes' bill . . . ," he wrote, "a new policy has been established in our dealings with the Indians, and a new era has dawned upon these unfortunate children of the forest. Gradually . . . the reservations are being broken up, the tribal relation is melting away, the community of goods is being displaced by individual holdings, 20,000 Indian children are gathered into schools maintained for them by the general government, and are being fitted socially, industrially, intellectually, and, to a degree, morally, for the grave duties and responsibilities of American citizenship. The Indians are not only becoming Americanized, but they are by this

4. *Report of the Indian Rights Association,* 1886, p. 9.

5. *Independent* 44 (April 28, 1892): 586–87.

6. Thomas J. Morgan, *The Present Phase of the Indian Question* (Boston: Boston Indian Citizenship Committee, 1891), p. 7.

process of education gradually being absorbed, losing their identity as Indians, and becoming an indistinguishable part of the great body politic."[7]

Education, for Morgan, was the key, for by its means, primarily, would the changes be wrought that he envisaged. In an elaborate fantasy that he presented in a speech at Albany, New York, while he was Commissioner, a talk he called "A Plea for the Papoose," Morgan spoke for Indian children and their hopes for a better future. He contrasted the present status of the Indians with the hopeless conditions of twenty-five years earlier. "Notwithstanding all that may be said by pessimistic observers," he asserted, "the fact remains that the Indians have entered upon a new era, and that there is for them an outlook and a future. The old order of things is passing away, and a new one is dawning. The rising generation of Indians, the children that are coming upon the scene to-day, look forward and not backward. Their faces are illumined by the rising sun, their hearts are big with hopes, their minds are expanded with expectation, their little hands are outstretched, eager to grasp that which the future seems about to bestow upon them."[8]

The momentum of the reform that was embodied in the Dawes Act and in the educational programs of Commissioner Morgan carried well into the twentieth century. So too did the rhetoric.

Samuel M. Brosius, long-time Washington agent of the Indian Rights Association, in 1903 recalled the various appeals filed and prosecuted during the past year in the courts by the Indians. "These indicate," he said, "that the Red Man realizes that he cannot longer hope to follow the beaten paths of his forefathers by seeking redress for injury through donning war-paint and wreaking physical vengeance upon his enemies. Not only this, but it demonstrates that he is alert to the need of fighting these battles for the protection of his property rights, in the manner open to him through the courts." All this, Brosius concluded, indicates that "a new era has dawned for the Indians."[9]

Robert Valentine, who became Commissioner of Indian Affairs in 1909, had a sharp eye for new dawnings. In his first annual report he reviewed the developments in new employment opportunities for the Indians, as the Indian Service encouraged industrial training and jobs on

7. Thomas J. Morgan, "Our Red Neighbors," *Baptist Home Mission Monthly* 16 (June 1894): 190.

8. Thomas J. Morgan, *A Plea for the Papoose* (n.p., n.d.), p. 18.

9. *Report of the Indian Rights Association*, 1903, p. 35.

the railroads and other off-reservation employment. "I consider these developments to be of great significance," he declared. "The systematic connecting of the industrial education of the schools with the real work of the world will mean the dawning of a new day in Indian education."[10]

In 1911 Valentine was invited to give the opening address at the first conference of the Society of American Indians, a pan-Indian organization of educated Indians who advocated assimilation of Indians into white society without forfeiting their cultural heritage. "When I first heard of this proposed meeting," he told the assembled delegates, "I felt that a new day had come in Indian affairs." "This meeting," he said, "is epochal."[11]

The high point of the assimilationists—or perhaps it would be better to call it the final gasp of the enthusiasm that began with the Dawes Act—came in the administration of Cato Sells, a small town Texas banker who served as Woodrow Wilson's Commissioner of Indian Affairs. Sells promoted with new energy the policy of eliminating government supervision over Indians. In April 1917, he issued a "Declaration of Policy in the Administration of Indian Affairs," in which he proclaimed "a policy of great liberalism . . . to the end that every Indian, as soon as he has been determined to be as competent to transact his own business as the average white man, shall be given full control of his property and have all his lands and moneys turned over to him, after which he will no longer be a ward of the Government." New rules were established for issuing patents in fee, for the sale of inherited Indian lands, for granting certificates of competency, for pro-rating trust funds, and for eliminating Indian pupils from government Indian schools.

"This is a new and far-reaching declaration of policy," Sells concluded. "It means the dawn of a new era in Indian administration. It means that the competent Indian will no longer be treated as half ward and half citizen. It means reduced appropriations by the Government and more self-respect and independence for the Indians. It means the ultimate absorption of the Indian race into the body politic of the Nation. It means, in short, the beginning of the end of the Indian problem."[12]

10. Report of Robert G. Valentine, November 1, 1910, *Report of the Commissioner of Indian Affairs*, 1910, p. 8.

11. Quoted from *First Proceedings*, pp. 27–28, in Hazel W. Hertzberg, *The Search for an American Indian Identity: Modern Pan-Indian Movements* (Syracuse: Syracuse University Press, 1971), p. 60.

12. Report of Cato Sells, October 15, 1917, *Report of the Commissioner of Indian Affairs*, 1917, p. 4.

We know now that all this enthusiasm, all these bright visions, all the new eras a-dawning led to darkness, to disillusionment, and often to disaster. The allotment of land in severalty under the Dawes Act and the subsequent loss of many of these lands by the Indians eliminated the economic base upon which viable Indian societies depended. The educational and Americanization programs destroyed the Indians' pride and their cultural heritage without completely substituting anything in their place, until the Indians became, in large part, a demoralized people with economic, educational, and health problems that seemed to grow steadily worse instead of better.

Then, in the 1920s, the pendulum of Indian policy began to swing in the opposite direction, as articulate critics and a newly aroused public demanded new reform. The movement inaugurated by the Dawes Act, it was finally seen, needed to be reversed. The religious spirit, which had dominated Indian policy in the last decades of the nineteenth and early decades of the twentieth century, was giving way to a new secular, scientific spirit. But enthusiasm for panaceas was by no means dampened, and the melioristic rhetoric which seems to be so much a part of the American way was resuscitated.

The muckraking campaigns sparked by John Collier in the early 1920s led to positive results at the end of the decade. The famous investigation of Indian affairs undertaken by the Brookings Institution, under the direction of Lewis Meriam, published its findings and recommendations in 1928. This so-called Meriam Report was unsparing in its criticism of the condition of the Indians and of the policies (allotment in severalty, for example) that had brought it about. It urged a new and extensive program of health, education, and economic welfare to correct the patent evils of the past and present, to reverse the trend toward degradation and despair. "The people of the United States have the opportunity, if they will," the Report insisted, "to write the closing chapters of the history of the relationship of the national government and the Indians."[13]

President Hoover, heeding the call for reform, appointed the Quaker philanthropist Charles Rhoads to head the Indian Bureau, and Rhoads took as his platform the Meriam Report. The movement was hailed just as we might expect. "A new day has dawned in the life of the North American Indian," wrote one observer in 1929. "The American public has finally awakened to the fact that neither are all the Indians dead

13. *The Problem of Indian Administration* (Baltimore: Johns Hopkins Press, 1928), p. 51.

nor is their problem a matter of past history." By the Meriam Report, the writer asserted, "the stage has been most auspiciously set for Mr. Rhoads and for a new order in the Indian world."[14]

The culmination of *this* "new order," of course, was the Wheeler-Howard or Indian Reorganization Act of 1934, the special project of John Collier, whom Franklin Delano Roosevelt appointed Commissioner of Indian Affairs in 1933. In the halcyon atmosphere that marked the early years of the New Deal, Indian affairs were swept up into an "Indian New Deal." The visions of John Collier, the long-time critic of Indian administration, now had their fulfillment in legislation. The Wheeler-Howard Act ended allotment and authorized the rebuilding of a communal land base, and it provided for the organization of Indian governments as a restoration of tribal authority.

We can let Collier himself describe the momentous changes. In an article in the *Atlantic Monthly* he wrote:

> In 1933, when President Franklin D. Roosevelt took office, Indian policy was changed in fashions radical and exhaustive. The change, in principle, was from maximal to minimal authority; from denial of Indian cultural values to their emphasis; from expectation of Indian doom to expectation of Indian triumph; from one-pattern policy to a policy of multiple options; but first and last from denial to intense encouragement of group self-determination and self-government. Self-determination under the impact of difficulties and challenges crowding fast. Self-determination even where failure might be very damaging. Above all, self-determination oriented toward regenerating the land and toward using it beneficially. In a word, restoration to the Indian of his two inseparable heritages wherein he had been great—democracy and land, one and indivisible."[15]

It is no wonder that one admirer of Collier predicted in the summer of 1934 that the Wheeler-Howard Act would, in his words, "open up a new era for Indians."[16]

But the bright light of this new era, like those of the past, was soon darkened by clouds of discontent and opposition. Deeply ingrained sentiments that the Indians should not occupy a special position in

14. Helen M. Brickman, "A New Day for the American Indian," *Missionary Review of the World* 52 (July 1929): 551–52.

15. John Collier, "Indians Come Alive," *Atlantic Monthly* 170 (September 1942): 78.

16. William Hughes, "Indians on a New Trail," *Catholic World* 139 (July 1934): 461.

their tribal relations with the federal government soon surfaced, and a movement to terminate government supervision of the Indians began which outdid even Cato Sells. House Concurrent Resolution no. 108 in 1953 declared it to be the sense of Congress that Indian tribes and individuals "should be freed from Federal supervision and control and from all disabilities and limitations specially applicable to Indians." Termination laws soon provided for the end of federal reservation status for the Menominee Indians of Wisconsin, the Klamath Indians of Oregon, and others.

The visions of a new order did not die. It just depended upon which side of the issue the dreaming was done. When President Eisenhower, on June 17, 1954, signed the Menominee Termination Bill, he recognized specifically that it was an outgrowth of the congressional resolution of the previous year, and he said: "The Menominees have already demonstrated that they are able to manage their assets without supervision and take their place on an equal footing with other citizens of Wisconsin and the Nation. I extend my warmest commendations to the members of the Tribe for the impressive progress they have achieved and for the cooperation they have given the Congress in the development of this legislation. In a real sense, they have opened up a new era in Indian affairs—an era of growing self reliance which is the logical culmination and fulfillment of more than a hundred years of activity by the Federal Government among the Indian people."[17]

The loss of special status and of federal funds that resulted from termination soon brought a vehement outcry from the Indians and their friends. *Termination* became a hated word, arousing fierce opposition from Indian advocates, especially as the results among the Menominees and Klamaths were more clearly seen.

Termination as a policy was shelved by the Kennedy and Johnson administrations, and Indian voices were again listened to. An Oneida Indian from Wisconsin, Robert Bennett, was appointed Commissioner of Indian Affairs, and he set about optimistically to incorporate Indian wishes into his policies. Bennett wrote in February 1967: "It is my sincere hope, bolstered by meetings with tribal groups during the past few months, that a new era in federal-Indian relations has commenced— an era in which the expressed wishes and hopes of all Indians will be fulfilled through their own active participation in the making of policy and law." He pointed to a reorganization of the Bureau of Indian

17. *Public Papers of the Presidents of the United States: Dwight D. Eisenhower,* 1954 (Washington: Government Printing Office, 1960), p. 582.

Affairs, designed "to give proper recognition to the importance of educational opportunity; to provide for close and continual liaison between federal, state, and local agencies, and with lay groups interested in Indian affairs; to hasten economic development of Indian resources; and to prepare Indian people for the day when they will want to function as communities within the framework of our American system." With the Department of the Interior, the Congress, and the Indian people joining their voices in condemning the deplorable existing conditions, Bennett concluded that "a new era is indeed dawning for America's 'first citizens.'"[18]

Bennett's administration was not notably successful, and President Nixon had to face, as his predecessors had done, the specter of termination. He finally and firmly rejected the policy. In a special message to Congress on Indian affairs in July 1970, Nixon argued that the policy of forced termination was wrong—that it was "morally and legally unacceptable," that it produced "bad practical results," and that the mere threat of termination tended "to discourage greater self-sufficiency among Indian groups." "The time has come," the President said, "to break decisively with the past and to create the conditions of a new era in which the Indian future is determined by Indian acts and Indian decisions."[19]

In August 1973, Vine Deloria, Jr., the articulate Indian-rights advocate, was the main speaker at a convention of Menominee Indians at Keshena, Wisconsin. Referring to the then pending legislation to reverse the termination of the Menominee tribe and restore the Indians to federal status, Deloria declared that the bill would begin "a whole new era of Indian affairs. It means," he said, "the federal government is finally recognizing its responsibilities and obligations to Indians."[20]

As you know, President Nixon signed the Menominee Restoration Bill on December 22, 1973. We have entered then, we may conclude, into the latest of the long series of "new eras." I say "latest" and not "last," for when the next one will appear we can only speculate.

The recurring announcements or predictions of a "new day dawning" for the American Indians—with the subsequent realization that the new era never really materialized and that the condition and status of the

18. Robert L. Bennett, "New Era for the American Indian," *Natural History* 76 (February 1967): 6–11.

19. Message of President Richard M. Nixon, July 8, 1970, *Public Papers of the Presidents of the United States: Richard Nixon,* 1970 (Washington: Government Printing Office, 1971), pp. 565–66.

20. Quoted in *Milwaukee Journal,* August 19, 1973.

Indians remained a critical problem both for them and for white society—could easily lead to cynicism. My students, I admit, sometimes do accuse me of cynicism, but I answer with a definition by Ambrose Bierce: "A cynic is a blackguard whose faulty vision sees things as they are, not as they ought to be."

But cynicism is not the proper response to the historical examples I have set before you. What we need, in order to build the better futures that all these men and movements had in mind, is a realistic understanding of the past. Reformers often wear blinders; they see only the goal ahead, cutting off from view the instructive past. Mixed with a bigger dose of history, their remedies would have had a better chance of working.

We must realize, as I suggested at the beginning, that a reforming spirit is an essential trait of the American character, which cannot be suddenly erased. The idea that the past with its evils and its contradictions can be changed with one dramatic stroke and a new age ushered in seems to be imbedded in the very marrow of the nation. It goes back, I guess, to our colonial foundations. Witness John Eliot, the Puritan "Apostle to the Indians," who with his fellow workers in 1647 issued a report of their activities and of their vision of the future in a pamphlet entitled "The Day-Breaking, if not the Sun-Rising of the Gospell with the Indians in New England." Or recall the sentiments of the Founding Fathers, who believed that they were instituting a new model of government for all the world to behold, and who boldly adopted as the motto for the Great Seal of the United States an epigram from Virgil, *Novus Ordo Saeclorum*—a new order of ages, or if you will, the beginning of a new era. "A great part of both the strength and weakness of our national existence," Richard Hofstadter noted in his study of reform, "lies in the fact that Americans do not abide very quietly the evils of life. We are forever restlessly pitting ourselves against them, demanding changes, improvements, remedies, but not often with sufficient sense of the limits that the human condition will in the end insistently impose upon us."[21]

The failure to attain the new eras for the Indians that were so confidently announced should above all convince us of the complexity of the problems involved. We need to understand why the situation is as it is before we move aggressively to change it. And explanation in history is no simple process. It means discovering, grasping, and analyzing

21. Richard Hofstadter, *The Age of Reform: From Bryan to F.D.R.* (New York: Vintage Books, 1955), p. 16.

a thousand ties which unite the many faces of reality with each other—often in nearly inextricable fashion. Events are bound to neighboring events, present conditions are tied to previous ones, immediate or remote, and to future ones as well. Simplistic solutions and panacean pronouncements are not sufficient to change deeply rooted cultural patterns—if indeed they should be changed at all—or to stamp out long-held prejudices and misconceptions.

Let me conclude by insisting that we need to know a great deal more about Indian-white relations and the advocacy of Indian reform in American history before we can offer any secure conclusions about errors of the past or hope for the future. It is my expectation, therefore, that what I have said will be taken as a preface and perhaps a stimulus to further studies in American Indian policy and not as an attempt to offer final judgments. With new scholarly reflections on this old and disturbing theme in our national history we may yet be able to speak accurately of "the day-breaking, if not the sun-rising" on our understanding of the Indians and their place in American history and in today's society. Then, indeed, we will have truly entered a "new era."

5

The Image of the Indian in Pre–Civil War America

It is truism that white Americans dealt with the Indians as they perceived them, and it has been a popular activity of intellectual historians to investigate the "images" of the Indians held by the whites as a means of more fully understanding Indian-white relations. A notable example of such study is Robert F. Berkhofer, Jr., The White Man's Indian: Images of the American Indian from Columbus to the Present *(New York: Alfred A. Knopf, 1978). My own essay in this genre is a modest one. Unconvinced by a common assumption that whites in the nineteenth century generally considered Indians inherently or innately inferior to whites, I picked out five significant figures in pre–Civil War America to test the assumption and to see what effect images of the Indian had in American Indian policy. The essay was given as a lecture at the closing session of the Northern Indiana History Conference, Fort Wayne, September 19, 1970.*

The American Indians have been a persistent and perennial problem for the United States. They thinly inhabited the vast continent at the time the first Europeans arrived and presented theoretical as well as practical problems to the new arrivals, who hoped to settle and exploit the wilderness they had discovered. Who were these red men—erroneously called "Indians" by Columbus? What was their origin and how did they fit into God's creation? Were they only a variety of the human race, or were they some new species, different from and perhaps inferior to Europeans?

The practical problems of coexistence of the two races were closely

Printed source: *American Indian Policy: Indiana Historical Society Lectures, 1970–1971* (Indianapolis: Indiana Historical Society, 1971), pp. 2–19.

related to the answers given to such speculative questions. For how the white man, who was advanced in technology and material civilization, treated the red man, who lived in a preliterate society without the blessings of Western culture or Christian religion, depended upon the image the former had of the latter, his views of the Indian's nature, rights, and ultimate potentialities.[1]

Americans answered the questions in different ways, and their views, the images they drew of the Indian, were by no means all alike. The opinions varied from the extreme disdain of the aggressive frontiersman, who equated the Indians with wild beasts of the forest, fit to be hunted down at will, to the romantic ideas of novelists like James Fenimore Cooper and poets like Henry Wadsworth Longfellow, who exalted the superhuman qualities of the "noble savage." But in between, among the responsible and respected public figures of pre–Civil War America, there was a reasonable consensus, out of which grew official government policy toward the Indians.

Let us look at a number of these Americans to see what they thought about the Indians. I have picked Thomas Jefferson, whose scientific interests matched his political acumen and his literary facility; Lewis Cass, a formulator of Indian policy as long-time governor of Michigan Territory and later secretary of war; Andrew Jackson, first American President from the new West and remembered as an "Indian fighter"; Horace Greeley, the ablest and best-known newspaper editor of the age, whose journey across the continent in 1859 gave him an opportunity to record some candid observations on the Indians; and finally, as a kind of counterpoise, Francis Parkman, one of America's greatest historians, whose interest in the forest brought him into direct as well as vicarious contact with the red man.

---

1. Theoretical considerations of race in America, including speculations about Indians, are discussed in William Stanton, *The Leopard's Spots: Scientific Attitudes toward Race in America, 1815–59* (Chicago: University of Chicago Press, 1960), and Thomas F. Gossett, *Race: The History of an Idea in America* (Dallas: Southern Methodist University Press, 1963). On images of the Indian, see Roy Harvey Pearce, *The Savages of America: A Study of the Indian and the Idea of Civilization* (Baltimore: Johns Hopkins Press, 1953), and a critique of the book in David Bidney, "The Idea of the Savage in North American Ethnohistory," *Journal of the History of Ideas* 15 (April 1954): 322–27. There are valuable insights in Winthrop D. Jordan, *White over Black: American Attitudes toward the Negro, 1550–1812* (Chapel Hill: University of North Carolina Press, 1968), though the book touches on Indians only incidentally. [See also Robert F. Berkhofer, Jr., *The White Man's Indian: Images of the American Indian from Columbus to the Present* (New York: Alfred A. Knopf, 1978).]

Jefferson was surely the most important of these as theorizer about the aborigines.[2] He was a man of tremendous speculative interests, a scientist (according to the definition of his age) as well as a political philosopher, and one who so influenced his generation that we, quite correctly, speak of his age in American history as "Jeffersonian."

Jefferson, setting the pattern that was not to be successfully challenged, considered the Indian to be by nature equal to the white. Although he strongly suspected that the Negro was an inferior creature, he never for a moment relegated the Indian to such status. Thus he wrote unequivocally in 1785: "I believe the Indian then to be in body and mind equal to the whiteman."[3] His arguments rested on two anterior principles. In the first place, he believed in an essential, fixed human nature, unchangeable by time or place, and he applied this principle of the unity of mankind to the Indian. In the second place, as an ardent American, Jefferson could not accept a position which would have made the native Americans a basically ignoble breed. In fact, his most detailed and most eloquent defense of the qualities of the Indians came in his *Notes on the State of Virginia*, in which he refuted the criticism of things American that appeared in the celebrated work of the French naturalist Buffon, who described the Indian as deficient in stature, strength, energy, mental ability, and family attachments. These aspersions Jefferson fully answered, and he entered a point by point refutation of the slanders. He insisted that the Indian's "vivacity and activity" of mind was equal to that of the white in similar situations. And he quoted from the famous speech of Chief Logan, declaring that the whole orations of Demosthenes and Cicero could not produce a single passage superior to the chief's oratory. Physically, too, the Indians were a match for the whites. They were brave, active, and affectionate.[4]

2. The views of Jefferson and the Jeffersonians about the Indians are examined in Bernard W. Sheehan, "Civilization and the American Indian in the Thought of the Jeffersonian Era" (Ph.D. diss., University of Virginia, 1965) [*Seeds of Extinction: Jeffersonian Philanthropy and the American Indian* (Chapel Hill: University of North Carolina Press, 1973)]; Daniel J. Boorstin, *The Lost World of Thomas Jefferson* (New York: H. Holt Company, 1948), pp. 81–88; Frederick M. Binder, *The Color Problem in Early National America as Viewed by John Adams, Jefferson and Jackson* (The Hague: Mouton, 1968), pp. 82–119; and Jordan, *White over Black*, pp. 475–81.

3. Jefferson to Chastellux, June 7, 1785, *The Papers of Thomas Jefferson*, ed. Julian Boyd, 19 vols. to date (Princeton: Princeton University Press, 1950–), 8:186.

4. For Jefferson's refutation of Buffon, see his *Notes on the State of Virginia* (Richmond: J. W. Randolph, 1853), pp. 62–69, 215–18.

Unable to ignore obvious weaknesses in Indian life and customs as they existed before his eyes, Jefferson (like most of his contemporaries) explained the differences by environment. If the circumstances of their life were appropriately changed, the Indians would be transformed. In that happy event, Jefferson asserted, "we shall probably find that they are formed in mind as well as in body, on the same module with the 'Homo sapiens Europaeus.'"[5]

So convinced was he of the racial equality or uniformity that he urged physical as well as cultural amalgamation of the Indians with the whites. "In truth," he wrote to the Indian agent Benjamin Hawkins, "the ultimate point of rest & happiness for them is to let our settlements and theirs meet and blend together, to intermix, and become one people." In his disappointment that during the War of 1812 the British had again stirred up Indian animosity toward the Americans, Jefferson lamented: "They would have mixed their blood with ours, and been amalgamated and identified with us within no distant period of time . . . but the unprincipled policy of England has defeated all our labors for the salvation of these unfortunate people."[6]

Since the Indian by nature possessed the capacity for civilization, Jefferson admitted the responsibility of the whites to aid the natives to that great goal. He knew, of course, that the Indians could not be transformed at a single stroke, but the movement toward civilization he held to be inexorable, and unless the Indians moved with the tide, they would surely be destroyed. That they would indeed move and eagerly accept white aid was judged to be but a corollary of their rational nature. If there was a sense of urgency in Jefferson's hope for Indian melioration, it came from his conviction that haste was necessary because of the extraordinary pressures of white civilization.

Jefferson had a linear view of civilization, an inevitable movement from the savagery of the Indians toward the European culture of his own coastal region. This he expressed in a striking comparison of geographical states with temporal ones. "Let a philosophic observer commence a journey from the savages of the Rocky Mountains, eastwardly towards our seacoast," he wrote. "These [the savages] he would observe in the earliest stage of association living under no law but that of nature, subsisting and covering themselves with the flesh and skins of wild beasts. He would next find those on our frontiers in

5. Ibid., p. 67.
6. Jefferson to Hawkins, February 18, 1803, *The Works of Thomas Jefferson,* ed. Paul Leicester Ford, 12 vols. (New York: G. P. Putnam's Sons, 1904–1905), 9: 447, and Jefferson to Baron von Humboldt, ibid., 11:353.

the pastoral state, raising domestic animals to supply the defects of hunting. Then succeed our own semi-barbarous citizens, the pioneers of the advance of civilization, and so in his progress he would meet the gradual shades of improving man until he would reach his, as yet, most improved state in our seaport towns. This, in fact, is equivalent to a survey, in time, of the progress of man from the infancy of creation to the present day."[7]

It is no wonder, then, that Jefferson urged the Indians to accept the white man's ways. And for this he had a single formula. The hunter state must be exchanged for an agricultural state; the haphazard life dependent upon the chase must give way to a secure and comfortable existence marked by industry and thrift; private property must replace communal ownership. By example and by education these changes could be wrought. Experience had shown, he asserted, that the following steps had been successful: "1st, to raise cattle, etc., and thereby acquire a knowledge of the value of property; 2d, arithmetic, to calculate that value; 3d, writing, to keep accounts, and here they begin to enclose farms, and the men to labor, the women to spin and weave; 4th, to read 'Æsop's Fables' and 'Robinson Crusoe' are their first delight."[8] The central point was conversion to farming, which was proper enough in the light of Jefferson's agrarian propensities. It was easy for Jefferson to make farming the indispensable step in the Indians' progress from savagery to civilization. Christianization came afterward; for Jefferson reversed the process of the missionaries, who considered acceptance of Christianity as a great first step toward civilization. "To begin with [moral and religious instruction] . . . ," he wrote, "has ever ended either in effecting nothing, or ingrafting bigotry on ignorance."[9]

In Jefferson's mind there was no real contradiction or equivocation in working for Indian advancement and at the same time gradually reducing the land held by the red men. It was not an opposition of policies, one working for the education and civilization of the Indians, the other seeking to relieve him of his land for the benefit of the whites. These were two sides of the one coin. He wrote in 1803: "While they are learning to do better on less land, our increasing numbers will be calling for more land, and thus a coincidence of interests will be

---

7. Jefferson to William Ludlow, September 6, 1824, *The Writings of Thomas Jefferson*, ed. Andrew A. Lipscomb, 20 vols. (Washington: Thomas Jefferson Memorial Association, 1903–1904), 16:74–75.

8. Jefferson to James Jay, April 7, 1809, ibid., 12:270–71.

9. Jefferson to James Pemberton, November 16, 1807, ibid., 11:395.

produced between those who have lands to spare, and want other necessaries, and those who have such necessaries to spare, and want lands." Nor was Jefferson unmindful of benevolence toward the Indians. "In leading them thus to agriculture, to manufactures, and civilization," he told Congress on January 18, 1803, "in bringing together their and our sentiments, and in preparing them ultimately to participate in the benefits of our Government, I trust and believe we are acting for their greatest good."[10]

Thomas Jefferson thought deeply about the nature of the Indian, and what he and his fellow scientists concluded—that the Indian was naturally the equal of the white—could not be refuted on purely practical grounds. Jefferson, however, did not live in close contact with Indians, and those who did developed a less theoretical view. One of these men was Lewis Cass, for eighteen years in intimate association with the Indians on the northwest frontier during his tenure as governor of Michigan Territory from 1813 to 1831. Cass had a scientific interest in the Indians, too, and one of his enthusiastic biographers claimed that "there has perhaps never been another man in the country so well acquainted with Indian habits and customs."[11] But his concern was less to place the Indian in his proper place in the great "chain of being" in God's creation than to investigate the prosaic elements of the red man's daily life. Cass was assiduous in collecting data, sending out in 1823 a questionnaire to Indian agents entitled *Inquiries, Respecting the History, Traditions, Languages, Manners, Customs, Religion, &c. of the Indians, Living within the United States.* From the answers he received as well as from his own personal experience, Cass formulated his views—his image—of the Indian.[12]

It was somewhat less favorable than Jefferson's. There was no hint that Cass did not accept Jefferson's conclusion that the red man was of the same species as the white, but he was chiefly concerned to delineate the Indian in his present circumstances and conditions. And here he

10. Jefferson to Hawkins, February 18, 1803, *Works,* 9:447, and James D. Richardson, comp., *A Compilation of the Messages and Papers of the Presidents,* 10 vols. (Washington: Government Printing Office, 1896–99), 1:352.

11. Andrew C. McLaughlin, "The Influence of Governor Cass on the Development of the Northwest," *Papers of the American Historical Association* 3 (1889): 323. For Cass's views, see Francis Paul Prucha, *Lewis Cass and American Indian Policy* (Detroit: Wayne State University Press, 1967); and Frank B. Woodford, *Lewis Cass, the Last Jeffersonian* (New Brunswick: Rutgers University Press, 1950), pp. 122–47.

12. Cass's questionnaire is discussed in Elizabeth Gaspar Brown, "Lewis Cass and the American Indian," *Michigan History* 37 (September 1953): 286–98.

painted a rather uncomplimentary picture. The Indians, as Cass portrayed them, were primitive and savage; they were governed by their passions, self-interest, or fear, not by any higher rational motives. They lacked enterprise, industry, and thrift, those great Puritan virtues that were part of Cass's Yankee heritage. In a burst of self-righteousness Cass asserted, in an article which was published in the *North American Review* in 1827, that a "principle of progressive improvement seems almost inherent in human nature." But he found little of this, alas, in "the constitution of our savages." He concluded: "Like the bear, and deer, and buffalo of his own forests, an Indian lives as his father lived, and dies as his father died. He never attempts to imitate the arts of his civilized neighbors. His life passes away in a succession of listless indolence, and of vigorous exertion to provide for his animal wants, or to gratify his baleful passions. He never looks around him, with a spirit of emulation, to compare his situation with that of others, and to resolve on improving it."[13]

If he would not improve his condition, and thereby become better circumstanced and ultimately like his white brothers, the Indian would be forced to give way to progress. What folly it would be, Cass said, to argue that "a few naked wandering barbarians should stay the march of cultivation and improvement, and hold in a state of perpetual unproductiveness, immense regions formed by Providence to support millions of human beings."[14]

Yet Cass's hopes for the Indians and his proposals for their betterment, though less sanguine and more hardheaded than Jefferson's, were at bottom much the same. While leaving untouched as much as possible the peculiar institutions and customs of the Indians, he would encourage them to adopt individual ownership of property, assist them in opening farms and procuring domestic animals and agricultural implements, and employ honest and zealous men to instruct them as far and as fast as their capabilities permitted.[15]

Education was essential. Cass pretty openly despaired of doing very much to change the habits or opinions of adult Indians. "Our hopes," he asserted, "must rest upon the rising generation. And, certainly, many of our missionary schools exhibit striking examples of the docility and

---

13. "Policy and Practice of the United States and Great Britain in Their Treatment of Indians," *North American Review* 24 (April 1827): 391.

14. Ibid., pp. 391–92.

15. Report of the Secretary of War, November 21, 1831, *House Executive Document* no. 2, 22d Cong., 1st sess., ser. 216, pp. 27–34, and "Indians of North America," *North American Review* 22 (January 1826): 118–19.

capacity of their Indian pupils, and offer cheering prospects for the philanthropist."[16] His aid to the missionary teacher Isaac McCoy indicated a willingness to promote in practice what he preached in principle.

Andrew Jackson, under whom Cass served as secretary of war, had his own strong views about the Indians, their nature, and their destiny.[17] Although Jackson has been severely condemned, to some extent unjustly, for ruthless dispossession of the Indians as they were removed from the southeastern states in the 1830s, he did not hold, any more than Jefferson had, that the Indians were inherently evil or inferior. Jackson had had much contact with Indians on the frontier, but his relations, unlike Cass's in Michigan Territory, had been chiefly military rather than administrative, and Jackson had no scientific bent that led him to speculate about the Indians and their origins. Jackson's dealings with the Indians had been severely practical and his policy simple: reward and protect friendly Indians, crush or chastise hostile ones, but in all exhibit a spirit of justice to red and white alike. He eagerly used Indian allies in his campaigns and respected and warmly liked individual chiefs.

Jackson viewed the present state of the Indians as barbaric, and he was convinced that it had to change. But he also believed that change was possible and would have to come if the red men were to survive. His public and private statements show a consistent belief that the Indians were capable of becoming civilized and the firm hope that they would do so. His vision appears in a proclamation to his troops after the victory at Horseshoe Bend on the Tallapoosa River in April 1814: "The fiends of the Tallapoosa will no longer murder our Women and Children, or disturb the quiet of our borders. Their midnight flambeaux will no more illumine their Council house, or shine upon the victim of their infernal orgies. They have disappeared from the face of the Earth. In their places a new generation will arise who will know their duties better. The weapons of warefare will be exchanged for the utensils of husbandry; and the wilderness which now withers in sterility and seems to mourn the disolation which overspreads it, will blossom as the rose, and become the nursery of the arts."[18]

16. Ibid., p. 115.

17. For opposing views of Jackson's attitude toward the Indians, see Francis Paul Prucha, "Andrew Jackson's Indian Policy: A Reassessment," *Journal of American History* 56 (December 1969): 527–39, and Binder, *The Color Problem*, pp. 136–56.

18. *Correspondence of Andrew Jackson*, ed. John Spencer Bassett, 7 vols. (Washington: Carnegie Institution of Washington, 1926–35), 1:494.

Behind Jackson's urging of Indian removal was a genuine concern to place the red men in a region where they would be free of white encroachment and jurisdictional disputes between the state and federal governments, and thus able to move steadily toward civilization at their own pace. His goal was to "exercise a parental control over their interests and possibly perpetuate their race."[19]

To call Jackson an "Indian-hater" as many persons have done or to assume that he had racist views is to mistake the tenor of the man and his times. In his "Farewell Address" on March 4, 1837, the retiring President summed up his views on the Indians and their removal to the West. He noted the happiness of the states that had been relieved of the burden of Indian nations in their midst, but he asserted that the Indians were now in a situation where "we may well hope that they will share in the blessings of civilization and be saved from . . . degradation and destruction," placed beyond the reach of injury where the "paternal care of the General Government will hereafter watch over them and protect them."[20]

The image of the Indian held by men like Jefferson, Cass, and Jackson—that the red man was barbaric but redeemable—had important consequences for American Indian policy. Granted the basic equality of the Indian with the white, the fundamentally same manhood and ultimate destiny, a ruthless destruction was out of the question. If circumstances made the man, then it was up to humanitarians and philanthropists to ameliorate the circumstances. If this could not be done when the Indians were in close and often irritating contact with aggressive white frontiersmen, then it must be done in some remote region to which the Indians could be removed.

Assimilation of the Indian into the white society was hoped for and expected, and Jefferson naively thought it could be accomplished in a single generation by proper education of the young. When the pressure of white advance to the West seemed about to crush the Indians before they were civilized enough to cope with it, removal to the west of the Mississippi seemed to be the only expedient that would both satisfy the whites and give the Indians the time they needed to effect a saving transformation in their ways. Once the Indians were in the West and before the movements to Oregon and California disrupted again the status in the West, the government continued its humane, though to a large extent misguided, attempts to instill into the Indians

---

19. Ibid., 4:81.
20. Richardson, *Messages and Papers of the Presidents,* 3:294.

the virtues of industry, enterprise, and thrift, and thus to lead them to civilization and Christianity.

That such attempts were necessary, worthwhile, and feasible was universally assumed by the government officials and their humanitarian allies in—as they phrased it—"the great work."

To these men of optimistic spirit we can add Horace Greeley, even though he might at first seem to be an incongruous companion. America's most prominent and influential newspaper editor, Greeley was an Easterner (he was born in New Hampshire in 1811 and worked in New England, Pennsylvania, and New York), but he was an enthusiastic promoter of western development. A special interest of his was a railroad to the Pacific, and in 1859 he left his desk and his family and set out on an arduous transcontinental journey to see for himself what sort of country a railroad would have to cross. The book he wrote, called *An Overland Journey, from New York to San Francisco in the Summer of 1859,* was a series of dispatches containing his shrewd observations of what he saw along the route. One dispatch, dated Denver, June 16, 1859, is headed "Lo! The Poor Indian!" and in it Greeley set down in his lucid prose what he thought about the Indians he had met as he traversed the prairies and the plains.[21]

He did not like them—for they hardly exhibited the solid virtues he espoused: hard work, and thrift, and wringing a living from the soil. "The Indians are children," he wrote. "Their arts, wars, treaties, alliances, habitations, crafts, properties, commerce, comforts, all belong to the very lowest and rudest ages of human existence. Some few of the chiefs have a narrow and short-sighted shrewdness, and very rarely in their history, a really great man, like Pontiac or Tecumseh, has arisen among them; but this does not shake the general truth that they are utterly incompetent to cope in any way with the European or Caucasian race. Any band of schoolboys, from ten to fifteen years of age, are quite as capable of ruling their appetites, devising and upholding a public policy, constituting and conducting a state or community, as an average Indian tribe."[22]

He could see, he said, why the whites who lived in close proximity to the Indians did not view them with the poetical visions of Cooper or Longfellow. He was convinced that if the Indian would not cultivate

21. Horace Greeley, *An Overland Journey, from New York to San Francisco in the Summer of 1859* (New York: C. M. Saxton, Barker and Company, 1860), pp. 149–56.
22. Ibid., p. 151.

the earth, he could not survive. "To the prosaic observer," he noted, "the average Indian of the woods and prairies is a being who does little credit to human nature—a slave of appetite and sloth, never emancipated from the tyranny of one animal passion save by the more ravenous demands of another." But what bothered him most was the fact that the Indian men were not working. "As I passed over those magnificent bottoms of the Kansas which form the reservations of the Delawares, Potawatomies, etc., constituting the very best corn-lands on earth," he wrote, "and saw their owners sitting around the doors of their lodges at the height of the planting season and in as good, bright planting weather as sun and soil ever made, I could not help saying, 'These people must die out—there is no help for them. God has given this earth to those who will subdue and cultivate it, and it is vain to struggle against His righteous decree.' "[23]

At first glance the picture looked hopeless, for Greeley saw no possibility of rehabilitating or civilizing the Indian men. "There is little probability that the present generation of 'braves' can be weaned from the traditions and the habits in which they find a certain personal consequence and immunity from daily toil, which stand them instead of intelligence and comfort," he declared from his lofty heights. "Squalid and conceited, proud and worthless, lazy and lousy, they will strut out or drink out their miserable existence, and at length afford the world a sensible relief by dying out of it."[24]

But Greeley did not give up all hope. The Indian *women* worked—and in them he saw "the germ of renovation for their race." In fact, he quickly advanced a plan for their salvation that was about what the Jeffersonians had in mind. He wanted to instruct the women, and even more especially the children, into being good, hard-working, industrious, thrifty Americans. "Let a farm and garden be started so soon as may be," he advocated as his plan for an Indian tribe, "and vegetables, grain, fruits given therefrom in exchange for Indian labor therein, at all times when such labor can be made available." His great hope, however, was in a school for the children. "Of course, the school, though primarily industrial," he insisted, "should impart intellectual and religious instruction also, wisely adapted in character and season to the needs of the pupils, and to their perception of those needs. Such an enterprise, combining trade with instruction, thrift with philanthropy, would gradually mould a generation after its own spirit—would teach

23. Ibid., p. 152.
24. Ibid., p. 153.

them to value the blessings of civilization before imposing on them its seeming burdens; and would, in the course of twenty years, silently transform an indolent savage tribe into a civilized christian community. There may be shorter modes of effecting this transformation, but I think none surer."[25]

For Greeley, work was the panacea. If the Indian would not labor, he should suffer for it. "The Indian likes bread as well as the white," he concluded; "he must be taught to prefer the toil of producing it to the privation of lacking it. This point gained, he will easily be led to seek shelter, clothing, and all the comforts of civilized life, at their inevitable cost; and thus his temporal salvation will be assured. Otherwise, his extermination is inexorably certain, and cannot long be postponed."[26]

Jefferson, Cass, Jackson, and Greeley all believed ultimately that the Indian could be saved, that he could be taught, induced, or forced to work and thereby be transformed. By education and example, the Indian would move from a nomadic savage state through Jefferson's progressive stages of culture to civilization. It was the humane and Christian duty of the government to help him on his way.

Not all Americans were so sure. One who belonged to a more pessimistic school was the eminent American historian Francis Parkman. His conclusions sprang from his own image of the Indian.[27]

Parkman was a romantic, brought up on the noble savages of Cooper's novels and formed by the heroic stories of Sir Walter Scott. The forest and its denizens fascinated him, and from his earliest youth the lore of the woodland was his intimate concern. One of his friends said that Parkman as a young man "had Injuns on the brain." Parkman was no armchair historian. His canon of historical study called not only for a thorough mastery of the documents but firsthand acquaintance as well with the natural features and human inhabitants of the places he wrote about. Since he had set his mind to tell the history of the North American forest, he soon began to observe and study the Indians. He began in the East, traveling to Maine, for example, to visit the remnants of Indians in that state. To his disappointment, he found no help, for these red men had long passed beyond their aboriginal condition.

25. Ibid., pp. 153–55.
26. Ibid., p. 156.
27. See Russel B. Nye, "Parkman, Red Fate, and White Civilization," in Clarence L. F. Gohdes, ed., *Essays in American Literature in Honor of Jay B. Hubbell* (Durham: Duke University Press, 1967), pp. 152–63; Mason Wade, *Francis Parkman, Heroic Historian* (New York: Viking Press, 1942); and Francis Parkman, *The Oregon Trail*, ed. E. N. Feltskog (Madison: University of Wisconsin Press, 1969).

So Parkman went where he knew he would find primitive Indians. In 1846 he headed out to the Oregon Trail and for three weeks lived in a Sioux Indian village. There he lost completely the sentimental view he had acquired from Cooper's romantic novels and substituted a highly critical one. Though his fascination with the Indians continued, he now viewed them only as savages, nothing more. His disgust—sharpened by the dysentery he suffered while with the Sioux—was in part no doubt an overreaction to the unrealistic views he had held before and a reflection of his New England background with its virtues of hard work and thrift, but Parkman's subsequent writings treated the Indians harshly. The crudeness, the cruelty, and the licentiousness of the Indian camp had almost overwhelmed him, and their laziness and instability irked him. In his Oregon Trail journal he wrote on July 6, 1846: "An Ind.'s meanest trait is his unsatiable appetite for food and presents. They are irrepressible beggars, and at meals, no matter how slender the repast may be, chiefs and warriors surround us with eager eyes to wait for a portion, and this although their bellies may be full to bursting. If one wishes to see an Ind. village, send a notice that you will feast, and they will come a two days' journey for the sake of your cup of coffee. What a life! where the excitement of an enjoyment so trifling can tempt them to such pains-taking. In fact, the greater part of a trapper's or an Ind.'s life is mere vacancy—lying about, as I am now, with nothing to do or think of."[28]

"Ambition, revenge, envy, jealousy, are his ruling passions . . . ," Parkman wrote of the Indian in *The Conspiracy of Pontiac.* "A wild love of liberty, an utter intolerance of control, lie at the basis of his character, and fire his whole existence."[29] The historian found the Indians irrational, inconsistent, improvident, and unpredictable.

This picture of the Indian in his primitive condition might well have been accepted, in its general outlines at least, by Jefferson or Cass, but they would have disagreed strongly with Parkman's ultimate conclusions about the Indian's destiny. Whereas the Jeffersonian mind saw the Indians as malleable, amenable to amelioration by a change of circumstances brought about through education, private property, and an agricultural life, Parkman saw the Indians as too rigid to change. "Some races of men," he wrote, "seem moulded in wax, soft and melting,

28. *The Journals of Francis Parkman,* ed. Mason Wade, 2 vols. (New York: Harper, 1947), 2:453.
29. Francis Parkman, *The Conspiracy of Pontiac,* Frontenac edition, 2 vols. (Boston: Little, Brown and Company, 1905), 1:45.

at once plastic and feeble. Some races, like some metals, combine the greatest flexibility with the greatest strength. But the Indian is hewn out of a rock. You can rarely change the form without destruction of the substance. Races of inferior energy have possessed a power of expansion and assimilation to which he is a stranger; and it is this fixed and rigid quality which has proved his ruin. He will not learn the arts of civilization, and he and his forest must perish together."[30]

The Indian would not open his mind to any ideas of improvement nor organize his culture on any strong principle of cohesion. "To reclaim the Indians from their savage state," Parkman noted, "has again and again been attempted, and each attempt has failed. Their intractable, unchanging character leaves no other alternative than their gradual extinction, or the abandonment of the western world to eternal barbarism."[31] Civilization to such men brought destruction, not blessings. The Indian, Parkman concluded, was devoted to savagery. "His haughty mind is imbued with the spirit of the wilderness," he wrote, "and the light of civilization falls on him with a blighting power."[32]

But Parkman, fortunately, was not typical, and he was wrong. He overreached himself in righting the erroneous concept of the red men that he had been fed by men like Cooper. Even his contemporaries Herman Melville and Theodore Parker, men no less sensitive than himself, criticized him for his depiction of the Indian. His portrayal of the Indian as a barbaric, unchangeable creature—hewn out of rock— added inescapable drama to his writings, but it had little effect upon the course of Indian relations in America.

The future was with the Jeffersonians and their heirs. It is true, of course, that their ideals met strong resistance and that injustice often overshadowed humanitarian effort. It is true, also, that the men of the pre–Civil War era, with few exceptions, were blind to the positive values in the Indian cultures with which they came in contact. But official American policy toward the Indian had in it a persistent element that aimed at the amelioration of the Indian's condition, his education, civilization, Christianization, and ultimate assimilation into American society. The image of the Indian as a human being, with capabilities and a destiny no different from the whites, was the indispensable substructure upon which such policy was based. Whatever its source, whether from pure theorizing or from hard practical experience, the

30. Ibid., 1:48.
31. Ibid., 2:170.
32. Ibid., 1:3.

image of the Indian in pre–Civil War America depicting him as fundamentally equal and ultimately improvable had profound significance for the course of the nation's history.

6

The United States Army and the Fur Trade

The United States Army on the frontier was an early research interest of mine, which in recent years has given way almost entirely to study of Indian policy. Yet the two topics are intimately related, since hostilities between Indians and whites were such an important element in Indian-white contact, and it is often impossible to look at one without some consideration of the other. A particular example of the intermingling of the two—leaving aside all the Indian wars that have been the subject of innumerable historical accounts—was the call for military protection of the fur trade, which I treat in this essay. It shows the importance of the frontier army in one aspect of government policy regarding the Indians. The essay was written for presentation at the First American Fur Trade Conference, hosted in St. Paul, Minnesota, by the Minnesota Historical Society in 1965. An undocumented version of it appeared in The Westerners Brand Book *(Chicago) 27 (March 1970): 1–3.*

My tendency to see some success in government policies to vindicate American sovereignty in the West has been challenged by Roger L. Nichols, in "The Army and the Indians, 1800–1830: A Reappraisal, the Missouri River Example," Pacific Historical Review *41 (May 1972): 151–68. I don't think there is deep disagreement between us, except that I am saying the cup was half full, while he insists it was half empty.*

The United States Army was so intimately connected with the American fur trade that it is impossible to think of one without the other. The army was the agent of the national government in the protection and expansion of the trade and then in its regulation. And this was no small undertaking, for the fur trade was not just another business enterprise falling casually under the eye of the federal officials. It had a unique diplomatic dimension of tremendous importance, and the United States government formulated an explicit policy in its regard. The basis of the policy can be set forth in a number of propositions:

In the first place, the fur trade was a significant economic activity in America. The government wished to encourage it for the wealth that it contributed to the nation and wanted to prevent that wealth from being drained off into foreign hands.

In the second place, the fur trade determined control of the Indians. It was axiomatic that the Indians adhered to the nation to which they were tied by trade.

In the third place, if American traders did not establish satisfactory liaison with the Indians, the tribes would give their furs and their allegiance to the British, and American authority over the territory in which the Indians resided would be nugatory.

Finally, because of the hostility of many of the Indian tribes (stirred up, it was presumed, by British agents), American traders needed military protection if they were to expand or even to continue their activity.

The working out of these principles in practice can be seen most clearly in the quarter century after 1815. This was the era of exploding western expansion and of awakening nationalism, and on both counts the fur trade was crucial. Expansion could not proceed smoothly if Indian control was forfeited; nor could the seeds of American national spirit blossom if lesions in our dominion over the northwest regions were permitted.

The rights which the British had had to trade in United States territory—privileges which they made full use of and by which they kept alive strong Indian opposition to the Americans—were ended by the Treaty of Ghent. On paper the undermining of American authority over the fur trade and over the Indians within our territory was no longer possible, and when Congress in 1816 passed a law limiting the granting of licenses for the fur trade to United States citizens, all seemed secure. Diplomatic historians have been satisfied to accept the formal documents and have blithely asserted that by these acts troubles with the British traders ended.[1]

---

1. See A. L. Burt, *The United States, Great Britain, and British North America from the Revolution to the Establishment of Peace after the War of 1812* (New Haven: Yale University Press, 1940), p. 376, and Bradford Perkins, *Castlereagh and Adams: England and the United States, 1812–1823* (Berkeley: University of California Press, 1964), p. 231.

Quite the contrary! In the decade from 1815 to 1825, and well beyond, there was a continual campaign to keep British traders off American soil, to break their hold over the Indians, and thus to channel the fur trade and with it control of the Indians into American hands. While the diplomats sat back and viewed their work with satisfaction, the regular army was moving in force into the Great Lakes region and into the valleys of the upper Mississippi and the Missouri, to make sure that the United States gained in fact what it had already acquired in principle.

The first cries of alarm came from Detroit. In July 1815, the Governor of Michigan Territory, Lewis Cass, sent to the War Department a plan which he hoped would cause "a salutary reform in the state of Our Indian relations." He prefaced his proposition with a strongly worded attack upon the British traders, to whom he traced most of the difficulties between the Americans and the Indians. He believed that the British were about to renew their activities with increased energy and pointed to the large quantity of trade goods arriving at Malden and the increased numbers of agents and subordinate officers. "These unerring indications give us timely warning," he advised, "that the same measures are to be adopted, the same lying system continued (pardon the epathet, could all the facts be presented to you, you would say that no milder term could be used) and the same plan of filling our Indian Country with their Agents and Interpreters and traders, which have at all former periods kept the North Western frontiers in a state of feverish alarm." Cass urged the establishment of a strong military post at each of the three channels by which the British communicated with the Indians living in the United States—a post at Green Bay and another at Prairie du Chien to cut the most important of the lines, that running between the Great Lakes and the Mississippi by means of the Fox and Wisconsin rivers; a post at Chicago, to cut the channel by way of the Illinois River; and a post at the Grand Portage, to check the traffic from Lake Superior to the headwaters of the Mississippi.[2]

Military movements soon fulfilled much of Cass's plan. In 1816 an energetic advance up the Mississippi from St. Louis resulted in the establishment of Fort Armstrong on Rock Island and Fort Craw-

2. Lewis Cass to Alexander J. Dallas, July 20, 1815, in Clarence E. Carter, ed., *The Territorial Papers of the United States,* 26 vols. (Washington: Government Printing Office, 1934–62), 10:573-75.

ford at Prairie du Chien. And in the same year the War Department reestablished Fort Dearborn at Chicago and built Fort Howard at Green Bay. These military posts, with the Indian agencies set up in their shadow, enabled the United States to cut off British traders from an area they had once dominated and to exert a reasonable control over the Indians through the activities of the agents backed up by the threat of military force.

The United States after the War of 1812 had more in mind, however, than a defensive barrier to protect settlements from potentially hostile tribes. Nothing shows more clearly the national importance given to the expansion and protection of the American fur trade (with its concomitant expression of American sovereignty) than the western defense plans proposed by John C. Calhoun when he became Secretary of War in Monroe's cabinet.[3]

Calhoun proposed a dramatic extension of the American military frontier, with strong forts to be built at Sault Ste. Marie, at the mouth of the Minnesota River on the upper Mississippi, and at the mouth of the Yellowstone or at the Mandan Village on the upper Missouri. He stated his purpose unequivocally: "to cut off all intercourse between the Indians residing in our territory, and foreign traders or posts" and "to overawe the neighboring tribes"; or as he put it in other words, the object was "the protection of our northwestern frontier, and the greater extension of our fur trade." Calhoun asserted that when the posts were well established and garrisoned, "our northwestern frontier will be rendered much more secure than heretofore, and . . . the most valuable fur trade in the world will be thrown into our hands."

There was no doubt in Calhoun's mind that these ends could be achieved only by military force. He adverted to the Treaty of Ghent, to the Act of 1816, and to instructions sent to the Indian agents. "But it is obvious,"he said, "that the act and instructions can have but little efficacy to remedy the evil. Without a military force properly distributed the trade would still be continued." Calhoun would have liked to settle the difficulties through diplomatic channels, but until Great Britain would herself bring an end to all intercourse with the

3. The best expression of Calhoun's proposal is his report to the chairman of the House Committee on Military Affairs, December 29, 1819, *American State Papers: Military Affairs,* 2:33–34. The quotations in the next two paragraphs are from this source.

Indians in the United States, the military posts, he said, "put in our hand the power to correct the evil."[4]

There was more at stake than protection of a commercial enterprise. With an exuberant, almost flamboyant nationalism, Calhoun wrote of the proposed post on the Missouri: "The remoteness of the post will, in some respects, render it unpleasant to those who may be detailed for the service; but I am persuaded that the American soldier, actuated by the spirit of enterprize, will meet the privations which may be necessary with cheerfulness. Combined with the importance of the service, the glory of planting the American flag at a point so distant, on so noble a river, will not be unfelt. The world will behold in it the mighty growth of our republic, which but a few years since, was limited by the Alleghany; but now is ready to push its civilization and laws to the western confines of the continent."[5]

The military action envisaged in Calhoun's plan soon began. In the summer of 1819 the Fifth Infantry, which had been concentrated at Detroit, moved across the Lakes, across the Fox-Wisconsin waterway, and up the Mississippi. Under Henry Leavenworth the post that was later named Fort Snelling was begun at the mouth of the Minnesota River in the fall, to become one of the key forts in the West.

The expedition up the Missouri fared less well, but it was a grand affair while it lasted. Contracts were let for the transportation of the troops from St. Louis to the Mandan Village by steamboat, then an

4. Diplomatic channels were used to remonstrate against the British entertainment at Malden of Indians from the United States, although nothing seems to have been said about traders. On November 19, 1819, Secretary of State John Quincy Adams sent to the United States Minister, Richard Rush, letters from the Governor of Michigan Territory reporting the large numbers of Indians going to Malden for presents. The instructions to Rush read in part: "The President desires that you would communicate copies of this body of evidence to the British Government, with the assurance of his belief that on this very unfriendly course of proceedings, the intentions of His Royal Highness the Prince Regent have not been carried into effect. At the same time you will take occasion to remark, in the most conciliatory manner, that it could not but serve to promote the good understanding and harmony between the two countries, if orders should be given to all the British authorities in Canada, to supersede entirely for the future the practice of inviting any of the Indians residing within our Boundaries, to Malden, or any other places within the British jurisdiction, and that of distributing to them any presents whatever." Diplomatic Instructions, All Countries, vol. 8, pp. 364–65, Records of the Department of State, National Archives, Record Group 59.

5. Calhoun to Thomas A. Smith, March 16, 1818, *Correspondence of John C. Calhoun,* ed. J. Franklin Jameson, *Annual Report of the American Historical Association for the Year 1899,* vol. 2 (Washington, 1900), p. 136.

untried means of travel on the Missouri. With great expectations, but with seemingly endless delays, the troops under Henry Atkinson moved by stages up the river. When the steamboats played out, keelboats were pressed into service, but the expedition—so hopefully called the Yellowstone Expedition—was forced to encamp at the Council Bluffs, a little above present-day Omaha. Here a cantonment was erected for the more than eleven hundred men who made up the command. The Yellowstone Expedition got no farther. Congress withheld the funds necessary for further advance, and the fort built on the bluffs in 1820, called Fort Atkinson, became the most advanced outpost on the Missouri.

Fort Atkinson was more than eight hundred miles short of the Mandan Village and twelve hundred miles short of the mouth of the Yellowstone, and the fur-trading interests, their spokesman in the Senate, Thomas Hart Benton, and a variety of Indian agents and army officers continued to fight for a fulfillment of Calhoun's dreams. The bugaboo of British traders dealing with the Indians in the United States formed the basis for impassioned pleas for military protection of the upper Missouri River. How active the British were is problematical, but they were regularly blamed for any hostility which the Indians displayed toward the American traders.[6]

The death of two leaders of a party of the Missouri Fur Company at the hands of the Blackfeet and the defeat of William H. Ashley by the Arikaras in 1823 set off a special outcry.

Benjamin O'Fallon, the United States Indian agent at Fort Atkinson, wrote in intemperate language to his superior in July 1823: "I was in hopes that the British traders had some bounds to their rapacity—I was in hopes that during the late Indian war, in which they were so instrumental in the indiscriminate massacre of our people, they had become completely satiated with our blood, but it appears not to have been the case.—Like the greedy wolf, not yet gorged with the flesh, they guard over the bones—they ravage our fields, and are unwilling that we should glean them—although barred by the treaty of Ghent, from participating in our Indian trade, they presume [to do so, and] . . .

---

6. Contemporary reports on the fur trade make frequent reference to British activity as a cause of Indian hostility. See the documents in *Senate Document* no. 67, 20th Cong., 2d sess., ser. 181; *Senate Document* no. 90, 22d Cong., 1st sess., ser. 213; Appendix B, "Newspaper Articles, 1822–1830," Donald McKay Frost, *Notes on General Ashley, the Overland Trail, and South Pass* (Worcester: American Antiquarian Society, 1945); and Dale L. Morgan, *The West of William H. Ashley* (Denver: Old West Publishing Company, 1964).

becoming alarmed at the individual enterprise of our people, they are exciting the Indians against us."[7]

At the same time General Edmund P. Gaines, commanding the Western Division, wrote to the Secretary of War: "If we quietly give up this trade, we shall at once throw it, and with it the friendship and physical power of near 30,000 efficient warriors, into the arms of England, who has taught us in letters of blood (which we have had the magnanimity to forgive, but which it would be treason to forget) that this trade forms the rein and curb by which the turbulent and towering spirit of these lords of the forest can alone be governed. . . . To suffer outrages such as have been perpetrated by the Ricarees and Blackfoot Indians to go unpunished, would be to surrender the trade, and with it our strong hold upon the Indians, to England."[8]

More insistent than either the Indian agents or the army officers were the trading interests of Missouri themselves, and Senator Benton broadcast their petitions in a national arena. Benton in 1824 began to agitate for a permanent military post high up on the Missouri, between the mouth of the Yellowstone and the falls of the Missouri. His Committee on Indian Affairs questioned Richard Graham, Indian agent at St. Louis, and Joshua Pilcher, a partner in the Missouri Fur Company, about the trade. Both men insisted that the richest fur country in the world lay at the headwaters of the Missouri above the junction of the Yellowstone. Benton then put the question to them: "Can the fur trade of this region be secured to the citizens of the United States, without the aid of a military post at or beyond the Mandan villages?"

Graham answered categorically: "I think it cannot. If the hand of Government were extended to the protection of the fur trade of this country, it would be a source of immense wealth to the nation; but, without the protection of a military post above the Mandans, our traders would be compelled to withdraw themselves, and the whole of that rich fur region will be occupied by those from the Hudson's Bay Company, and our traders cut off from any participation of it above the Mandans." Pilcher's response was similar.[9]

On March 18, 1824, Benton introduced a bill authorizing commissioners to negotiate treaties of friendship with the Missouri River tribes and directing a military force "to be transported to, and stationed at"

7. Frost, *Notes on General Ashley,* pp. 83–84.
8. Gaines to John C. Calhoun, July 28, 1823, *American State Papers: Military Affairs,* 2:579.
9. *American State Papers: Indian Affairs,* 2:451–57.

some suitable point on the upper Missouri. It is interesting to note that Benton entitled his bill, a bill "to enable the President to carry into effect the treaty made at Ghent, the 24th of December, 1814, excluding foreigners from trade and intercourse with Indian tribes within the United States, and to preserve the fur trade within the limits of the said United States."[10] Not all of the Senate, however, was as convinced of the need as was Benton. His provision for establishing a post was stricken out, and the title of the bill was changed. The most that he could get was authorization for a military escort to accompany the Indian commissioners.[11] This was at least something, and Henry Atkinson, who with Benjamin O'Fallon was appointed commissioner, took along a military command of 476 men. The troops impressed the Indian tribes with whom councils were held and managed to move 120 miles beyond the mouth of the Yellowstone before low water forced them back.[12]

Atkinson and O'Fallon discovered no British influence in the area they covered. The British traders had shifted westward toward the rich beaver of the Rockies, and Atkinson declared that no protection was needed for American traders below the falls of the Missouri and that beyond that point no post was feasible because of the difficulties of supply. He now believed that "an occasional show of an imposing military force in an Indian country" was more effective than a permanent garrison of troops among them, and he suggested an expedition of three hundred to four hundred troops every three or four years to the falls of the Missouri.

Thus ended for the time American military efforts to serve the fur traders of the Missouri. The companies in the Rockies had to shift for themselves and furnish their own protection as it was required. In fact, the advanced post at Council Bluffs was broken up in 1827 and a new post farther down the river, Fort Leavenworth, guarded the gateway to the West. The Santa Fe trade—in part a fur trade—got some intermittent support from military escorts on the trail, but it, too,

10. *Senate Journal,* 18th Cong., 1st sess., ser. 88, p. 239; *Annals of Congress,* 18th Cong., 1st sess., pp. 432–45.
11. *Senate Journal,* 18th Cong., 1st sess., ser. 88, pp. 281, 432; *Annals of Congress,* 18th Cong., 1st sess., pp. 450–61.
12. A summary account of the Atkinson-O'Fallon expedition is in Hiram M. Chittenden, *The American Fur Trade of the Far West,* 3 vols. (New York: Francis P. Harper, 1902), 2:608–18. A more recent study is Roger L. Nichols, *General Henry Atkinson: A Western Military Career* (Norman: University of Oklahoma Press, 1965), pp. 90–108.

despite the loud cries of western interests, had to look out for itself. The old refrain did not immediately die away, but special reports solicited in 1831 on the condition of the fur trade showed more interest in reducing the tariffs on trade goods than in military protection for the traders.[13]

Essential as military protection may have been for the preservation and extension of the fur trade, it soon turned out that the traders and the army were in bitter conflict.

The Indian trade was governed by a series of federal enactments initiated in 1790 and gradually expanded, known as the Indian trade and intercourse laws. These set up a licensing system to control the persons entering the Indian country for trade, and in the course of the decades limited the traders to designated sites and restricted or prohibited the introduction of whiskey into the Indian country. The Indian agents were responsible for the enforcement of the laws, but these men had no power, and the laws after 1796 provided explicitly that the military force of the United States might apprehend any person found in the Indian country in violation of the intercourse acts.[14]

The matter of the whiskey trade was given special attention. The law of 1802 gave the President discretionary power in limiting or preventing the liquor traffic, and traders were forbidden to vend liquors. In 1822 a supplement to the law gave the President authority to direct Indian agents and military officers "to cause the stores and packages of goods of all traders to be searched, upon suspicion or information that ardent spirits are carried into the Indian countries." If liquor was found, the goods of the trader were to be forfeited, his license canceled, and his bond put in suit.[15] In 1832 all discretionary authority ended, as Congress provided that "no ardent spirits shall be hereafter introduced, under any pretence, into the Indian country."[16]

It was in the attempt to enforce these laws that the army crossed swords with the traders. The traders were governed—one might better

13. *Senate Document* no. 90, 22d Cong., 1st sess., ser. 213.

14. A full discussion of these regulations is in Francis Paul Prucha, *American Indian Policy in the Formative Years: The Indian Trade and Intercourse Act, 1790–1834* (Cambridge: Harvard University Press, 1962).

15. *United States Statutes at Large*, 3:682–83.

16. Ibid., 4:564.

say driven—by their avidity for profits, and they dealt ruthlessly with all who stood in their way. The army officers, on the other hand, were motivated by a dedication to the federal laws that regulated the Indian trade, and they developed an aversion—amounting almost to an obsession—to those who seemed to care little about the laws or about the rights of the Indians. In the minds of the army officers a sharp distinction seemed to be drawn between the trade itself, which they looked upon with favor, and the traders, whom they often deprecated as scoundrels. At the same time that the army was promoting the expansion of the American fur trade as a sort of national mission, it was condemning and fighting the intrigue and machinations of the very men it was so laboriously protecting.

The Indian propensity for whiskey was the crux of the problem and made the introduction of liquor into the trade extremely difficult to stop. As Thomas L. McKenney, the head of the Indian Office, was forced to admit: "The source of all the difficulty is to be found in the necessity which the traders esteem themselves to be under to carry spirituous liquors into the Indian country; and it is from this source that so much wretchedness and so many evils proceed. . . . The trader with the whiskey, it must be admitted, is certain of getting most furs."[17]

The army officers took their duty seriously. Their alertness in searching the stores of traders suspected of carrying liquor no doubt kept down the flow into the Indian country. The officers at Fort Leavenworth, athwart the passageway up the Missouri, were more than attentive to duty. When Kenneth McKenzie, the American Fur Company's agent on the upper Missouri, tried to take liquor up the river in the spring of 1833, it was seized at Fort Leavenworth. "We have been robbed of all our liquors," McKenzie wrote. "They kicked and knocked about everything they could find and even cut through our bales of blankets which had never been undone since they were put up in England."[18] The distinguished foreign naturalist Maximilian, Prince of Wied, complained that the officers at the fort would scarcely allow him to take along a small portion of brandy in which to preserve his specimens of natural history.[19] By similar action the officers at Fort

17. McKenney to James Barbour, February 14, 1826, *American State Papers: Indian Affairs*, 2:659–60.
18. Chittenden, *American Fur Trade*, 1:357–58.
19. Reuben Gold Thwaites, ed., *Early Western Travels, 1748–1846*, 32 vols. (Cleveland: Arthur H. Clark Company, 1904–1907), 22:254.

Crawford and Fort Snelling tried to stanch the flow on the Mississippi, and those at Fort Smith, on the Arkansas.

It was really an impossible task. The frontier was too long and the ways of the traders too devious for the limited number of troops to patrol all the lines of access into the Indian country. The small traders—irresponsible, in many cases depraved—lived off clandestine intercourse with the Indians, supplying them with whiskey and some trade goods and reaping a harvest of furs in return. They trusted to their wits to escape the vigilance of the army and if apprehended in one spot quickly reappeared in another, enjoying a game of hide-and-seek with the law enforcers. More important, the agents of the American Fur Company mounted a frontal attack upon the army officers who searched their stores and confiscated their liquor. Army officers and Indian agents were haled into court by the fur company on charges of trespass and illegal seizure of goods.[20]

Whatever the outcome may have been in a given case, the threat of civil action against army officers was a deterrent to effective enforcement. The American Fur Company was powerful, it stood behind its traders, and it had the support of the local courts and judges, who did not take kindly to the army officers and what the frontiersmen considered their arbitrary, if not tyrannical, action. It was usually an uneven match. The army officers and Indian agents were isolated and ill-supported by far-off Washington, and whenever the interests of the American Fur Company were at stake, the officers suffered harassment, inconvenience, and often financial loss. It came to be the accepted thing that the officers would get into trouble by enforcing the acts, that the offenders brought to trial for violation of the laws would escape conviction in the frontier courts, and that the men apprehending them would be subjected to a civil prosecution for faithful discharge of their official duties. It is little wonder that Colonel Zachary Taylor concluded bitterly: "Take the American Fur Company in the aggregate, and they are the greatest scoundrels the world ever knew."[21]

A number of army officers recommended martial law for the Indian country, and some suggested a tightly regulated monopoly of the fur trade which would eliminate the evils arising from competition between traders for the furs and affections of the Indians, but this medicine was too strong for Americans to accept. The problems remained as long as the fur trade was important.

20. Prucha, *American Indian Policy in the Formative Years,* pp. 102–38.
21. Quoted in Kenneth W. Porter, *John Jacob Astor, Business Man,* 2 vols. (Cambridge: Harvard University Press, 1931), 2:756.

The army was the watchdog of the fur trade. It patrolled the Indian country to keep out interlopers and to pacify the Indians, and in so doing proclaimed and established the sovereignty of the new nation in the West. But it kept one eye on the very traders it was sent to protect, to make sure that they too stayed within the pale of the law. This is understandable enough, for the army was the agent, not of the traders, but of the nation, and for the nation the fur trade was not an end in itself, but a means for the protection and expansion of national sovereignty and grandeur.

7

Lewis Cass and American Indian Policy

The Detroit Historical Society in 1948 inaugurated an annual Lewis Cass Lecture devoted to the history of Detroit and the State of Michigan. When I was asked to give the lecture in 1966, I thought that no topic would be more appropriate than Lewis Cass himself. Certainly no person was more important in the long territorial history of Michigan than Cass, who served as territorial governor from 1813 to 1831. From his seat of government in Detroit, he devoted much of his time and energy to Indian affairs. Although he was criticized by his contemporary political opponents, Cass, I think, did a creditable job in his concern for Indian matters. When the lecture was published in pamphlet form, no documentation was included. In this reprinting I have added appropriate footnotes, so that an interested reader can trace my sources.

Lewis Cass was one of the master architects of American Indian policy. For nearly a quarter of a century, first as Governor of Michigan Territory from 1813 to 1831, then as Secretary of War in Jackson's cabinet from 1831 to 1836, he was extraordinarily active in the period when guidelines for dealing with the Indians were being drawn. No man had a greater sustained influence on this critical, complex, and confusing segment of American national policy.[1]

Printed source: *Lewis Cass and American Indian Policy* (Detroit: Wayne State University Press, 1967).

1. Studies on Cass and Indian affairs include Andrew C. McLaughlin, "The Influence of Governor Cass on the Development of the Northwest," *Papers of the American Historical Association* 3 (1889): 311–27, and Elizabeth Gaspar Brown, "Lewis Cass and the American Indian," *Michigan History* 37 (September 1953): 286–98. [A recent study is Ronald Gregory Miriani, "Lewis Cass and Indian Administration in the Old Northwest, 1815-1836" (Ph.D. diss., University of Michigan, 1974).]

Cass began his duties at Detroit after success as a young lawyer in Ohio and after valiant service in the War of 1812. When he started his long tour as governor, the war had not yet ended, and the frontier which he took charge of was suffering from the ravages of conflict and living under the threat of new outbreaks. The Indians, who were active allies of the British, demanded the greatest share of his attention, as they continued to do even when peace returned with the Treaty of Ghent.

Cass's initial Indian policy was one of simple expediency, dictated by the circumstances on the northwest frontier. His goal was to sever the allegiance which the Indians had long had to the British. This was to be done by negotiation if possible, by force if necessary. With the memory of Indian atrocities still so vivid, it was no time for what he called "the humane but chimerical plan of civilizing them" and his reports on Indian affairs were hard-headed and practical. When he submitted to the War Department in September 1814 an estimate of presents for the Indians, he spoke out frankly to justify what he feared might be considered an excessive demand for funds. There was no sentimental attachment to noble savages in Cass's message; he hoped only to maintain peace in the most economical way. "However we may despise them [the Indians]," he argued, "it is the part of true wisdom to consult their prejudices, to draw physical strength from their intellectual weakness, and to attach them to us through the medium of their affections and interest, or to compel them to join us by a display of our strength. The only question is, by which of these methods, by presents and gentle treatment or by force and fear we may expect with the most economy to attain our object."[2]

Cass was not dealing with the Indians in a vacuum, isolated as Michigan Territory seemed. He was in direct competition with the British at Malden across the Detroit River, and he chose to fight the British with their own weapons. The Indians were more attracted to the British than to the Americans because the British had plied them with presents. The same policy on the American side would obtain the same result, Cass felt, and he was determined to adopt it. He asked boldly for thirty or forty thousand dollars to be shrewdly distributed in "handsome presents" to the principal chiefs. It was a large sum in that day, but as Cass pointed out, no more than the cost of a couple companies of

2. Cass to John Armstrong, September 3, 1814, in Clarence E. Carter, ed., *The Territorial Papers of the United States,* 26 vols. (Washington: Government Printing Office, 1934–62), 10:476.

troops and considerably more advantageous. "If the Indians are convinced we mean to treat them liberally," he concluded, "I have no
doubt of their heartily joining [us]. The Expence at all Events will be
but temporary; a few Years will so diminish their numbers as to render
their hostility harmless and their friendship useless."[3]

Cass got his forty thousand dollars, and though his views about
Indian motivation softened somewhat through the years, the distribution of presents to conteract the British remained a basic principle of
his Indian policy.

The alternative—punitive expeditions against the Indians—Cass regarded as "expensive in the onset and uncertain in the result." He
preferred to appeal to what he called the Indians' "strong passion for
wealth," by which he was convinced the United States could maintain
peace more surely and more cheaply than by resort to physical force.[4]
But he was not averse to the use of the army as a preventive measure,
and stationing of regular army troops in his territory became a second
principle in his early Indian policy.

In the summer of 1815 Cass noted the arrival of new agents and the
accumulation of goods for Indian presents at Malden, and he feared a
renewal of operations by the British among the Indians of the Northwest. To prevent this baleful influence he proposed stopping up the
channels through which the British traders introduced their goods into
the United States. He wanted to establish a military post at Green Bay
and another at Prairie du Chien to block the great Fox-Wisconsin
passageway from the Lakes to the Mississippi. A post at Chicago would
achieve the same purpose for the Illinois River, and one on Lake
Superior would close the way of the Grand Portage. A large part of this
proposal soon became reality. In 1816 Fort Dearborn was reestablished
and Forts Howard and Crawford were built at Green Bay and Prairie du
Chien, but these military forces were not sufficient to satisfy Cass.[5]

As reports of unrest among the Indians created new alarm in the
spring of 1818, Cass fired off to the Secretary of War another of his
forthright statements. He painted a dramatic picture of the territory—
thin strips of settlement along the principal streams, with no compact
settlements which might protect themselves. "An interminable forest
approaches within a Mile of every house in the Territory," he said, "and
this forest equally serves to prevent discovery, and to retard pursuit."

3. Ibid., p. 479.

4. "Recommendations by Governor Cass on Indian Posts," enclosed in Cass to
A. J. Dallas, July 20, 1814, Carter, *Territorial Papers,* 10:582.

5. Cass to Dallas, July 20, 1815, ibid., pp. 575–76.

He spoke of the posts on the Lakes as "advanced guards, to discover and repel the first symptoms of attack," but without adequate garrisons they would be useless. "We owe our peace and safety," he declared, "solely to a display of physical force and . . . this weakest and most exposed frontier of the whole Union, unless protected by troops and Garrisons, could not for one hour resist the efforts of the Indians."[6]

Cass had more in mind than immediate protection of his people. He hoped ultimately to prevent Indian depredations by building up the settlements of the territory to the point where they would no longer invite attack and would indeed be strong enough to repel any Indian aggression. But meanwhile, Cass noted in 1819, the attacks of the Indians created uneasiness and disquietude and would "check if not entirely prevent migration to the Country, and stop our progress in improvement and population." The answer, of course, was a display of military force which would reassure the people in the East, who were "extremely sensitive upon the subject of Indian alarms," and encourage them to emigrate to Michigan.[7]

Cass continued to sing the same song, for a heavy influx of population into Michigan was slow in coming. "I consider this frontier the weakest and most exposed in the Union," he wrote again in 1825, as he demanded more troops for Detroit. And when the Winnebago scare in 1827 drew Cass west to see what could be done to restore tranquillity, he criticized the War Department for having evacuated Fort Crawford and insisted that the post be reoccupied. "We shall have no permanent peace, till there is a strong force here," he wrote from Prairie du Chien. "I speak from an intimate knowledge of the country, and of the feelings and situation of the Indians."[8]

A third principle of Cass's policy was the sound regulation of what he and his contemporaries referred to as the "Indian Department." This phrase was a catch-all label for the men who handled Indian affairs: the officials in the War Department, the Governor himself as *ex officio* Superintendent of Indian Affairs for his territory, the agents

6. Cass to John C. Calhoun, April 17, 1818, ibid., pp. 745–46.
7. Cass to Calhoun, January 6, 1819, ibid., pp. 808–9; Cass to Calhoun, May 27, 1819, ibid., pp. 827–31.
8. Cass to the Secretary of War, March 20, 1825, ibid., 11:664; Cass to James Barbour, July 4, 1827, ibid., p. 1095.

assigned to specified Indian tribes, interpreters, and a variety of black-smiths, gunsmiths, boatmen, and casual employees. This Indian Department was charged with considerable financial responsibility, for it dispersed presents and annuities to the Indians; and exact accounting for the funds and goods was a continual headache. Furthermore, it had large political, or diplomatic, responsibilities in preventing the intrusion of foreign agents and traders, supervising the activities of licensed traders, and in a hundred and one ways upholding the rights of the American government and displaying its justice and humanity in the Indian Country. One of the saddest aspects of developing American Indian policy in the first decades of our nation's existence was the disarray in the structure and operation of the Indian Department. The organization and duties grew piecemeal, and one wonders, looking back, why everything did not just collapse. One important reason was Lewis Cass.

Cass had a well-ordered mind, associated no doubt with his bent for law, and aside from the disastrous effect a disorderly Indian Department would have on Indian relations, he could not brook a slipshod organization. From the very first days of his tenure of office Cass gave critical attention to the work of the Indian agents. As early as September 1814, he had printed in Detroit a two-page broadside entitled "Regulations for the Indian Department." In it he spelled out thirty-three specific rules to govern the purchasing of Indian presents, the distribution of annuities, the duties of agents and interpreters, and the pay and rations of the agents. The War Department was quick to bless the move. "Your regulations for the Government of the Indian Department are approved of," Secretary of War Monroe wrote Cass at the end of October, "and it requires only a strict and honest execution of them by the several Agents, to place that Department on a sound and good foundation."[9]

The need for agents deep in the Indian Country soon became apparent to Cass. On July 10, 1815, he urged the War Department to establish Indian agencies at Green Bay, at Chicago, and at Mackinac Island to watch the movements of the Indians, gain their confidence, and supply their immediate wants.[10] The War Department set up these agencies and in 1817 placed under Cass's direction the agency at Fort Wayne, Indiana, and Piqua, Ohio, as well.

---

9. "Regulations for the Indian Department," Detroit, 1814, fascimile reproduction by Meriden Gravure Company; Secretary of War to Cass, October 24, 1814, Carter, *Territorial Papers*, 10:495.

10. Cass to Dallas, July 10, 1815, ibid., pp. 566–67.

Good men to staff the agencies were another of Cass's concerns. One of the principal reasons why the Indians were dissatisfied with the United States, he insisted, was the employment of unsuitable persons in the Indian Department. He wanted to employ a man "of character, Standing & talents whose intercourse with the Indians has been such as to give him correct ideas with respect to their views and feelings" and to send him out to the various agencies to hold councils with the tribes. And he proposed that interpreters be kept constantly traveling through the Indian Country to advance American views and to apprehend unlicensed traders.[11]

Cass watched closely the operations of his agents, and the correspondence between his office and the agencies was voluminous. How much he expected of the agents can be seen in his directions to Henry R. Schoolcraft when the latter was appointed to the new agency at Sault Ste. Marie in 1822.

Your jurisdiction will extend over a very extensive & a very important frontier, where the Indians are exposed to an undue share of foreign influence, and where the indications of a hostile feeling to the United States have not been equivocal. To withdraw them from their accustomed intercourse and associations, mildly but firmly to support the rights and enforce the laws of the United States, to render them every service compatible with your own interest and with that just economy, which is necessary, carefully to license the traders & to scrutinize their conduct and punish any infractions of the laws, & to act as a vigilant sentinel at an advanced post are among your most important & obvious duties.[12]

The wisdom and care of Cass did not go unnoticed by the War Department. When Peter B. Porter became Secretary of War in 1828 and discovered to his dismay the confusion in Indian matters for which he was responsible, he turned to Cass at Detroit and to William Clark at St. Louis for help. He called the two Indian superintendents to Washington and asked them to draw up a detailed and orderly set of regulations for the whole federal Indian Department. Cass accepted the charge with alacrity, and he and Clark drew up three significant documents which treated exhaustively of Indian matters. The first was a

11. Cass to Dallas, July 20, 1815, ibid., p. 581; Cass to William H. Crawford, December 15, 1815, ibid., p. 611.

12. Cass to Henry R. Schoolcraft, July 1, 1822, ibid., 11:250. The full scope of Cass's correspondence with the agents who were under his supervision can be seen in Records of the Michigan Superintendency of Indian Affairs, National Archives, Record Group 75.

proposed bill of fifty-six sections to codify general dealings with the Indians. Much of it was merely a transcription of previous laws, but with the document was a paragraph-by-paragraph commentary on the proposals. This is difficult reading, yet nothing gives a better view of Cass's mind on Indian policy. A second document, entitled "Regulations for the Government of the Indian Department," provided detailed procedures for carrying out the proposed law. The third item was a bill to consolidate into one law all provisions concerning payment of annuities to the Indian tribes.[13]

Porter submitted the proposals to Congress with the recommendation that they be speedily enacted. Although nothing happened, as was so often the case, the work was by no means wasted, for when Congress did act five years later, much of the Cass-Clark report was incorporated into the legislation. In the meantime, Cass as Secretary of War added still more to the formulation of a practical system for managing Indian affairs by his annual reports and his instructions to agents and commissioners. When in 1834 the Committee on Indian Affairs of the House of Representatives drew up a new trade and intercourse act and an act for organizing the Indian Department, both of which became law on June 30, Cass took an active part. The chairman of the committee asked for his advice, and Cass responded in his usual full and efficient manner by going in person to work with the committee.[14]

Cass's proposals and policies were influenced by his general views about the Indians and about the responsibilities that the United States had toward them. Admittedly, Cass's opinions of the Indians were less than complimentary. When viewing them simply as an enemy, as he did in his first days in Detroit, he could speak in the harshest terms. When viewing them as a primitive and uncivilized people, he could speak with the disdain of a superior being. But Cass was an enlightened man of his times, and there was in him a strong, sincere, and persistent streak of humanitarianism. He accepted the position that the white man, so largely responsible for the unhappy state of the Indians, owed the Indians "a great moral debt," and that everything possible should be done to uplift the condition of the miserable savages.

13. The work of Cass and Clark is discussed in Francis Paul Prucha, *American Indian Policy in the Formative Years: The Indian Trade and Intercourse Acts, 1790–1834* (Cambridge: Harvard University Press, 1962), pp. 252–56; the report itself is in *Senate Document* no. 72, 20th Cong., 2d sess., ser. 181.

14. Prucha, *American Indian Policy in the Formative Years,* pp. 259–60.

When the pressure of hostile threats subsided, Cass worked earnestly to better the lot of the Indians. How fully the Indians were fitted to partake of the blessings of American civilization Cass did not know. "But that we can greatly ameliorate their condition, that we can reclaim them from the pursuits of the chase to the labours of agriculture, and render them useful to themselves without being dangerous to us," he declared in 1816, "admits of no doubt and presents little difficulty." In a long exposition on Indian affairs which he sent to the Secretary of War after much careful thought in November 1816, Cass began with this statement about the Indians: "Our first and principal duty is to reclaim them as far as practicable, from the savage situation in which they are placed, and to impart to them as many of the blessings of civilized life, as their manners and customs and inveterate prejudices will permit." He goes on for six pages to outline a system of education, agricultural training, and persuasive good example.[15]

Cass never lost this honest concern for the well-being of the Indians, but at times he sounded as though he intended to civilize them whether they wanted it or not. "The time has arrived when we should be known to the Indians by every humane and benevolent exertion," he wrote in 1821; "and certainly on a fair retrospect of their former situation and on a correct view of their present social & moral degradation, they have a right to expect much. In fact we must think for them. We must frequently promote their interest against their inclination, and no plan for the improvement of their condition will ever be practicable or efficacious, to the promotion of which their consent must in the first instance be obtained."[16]

At times he had doubts about the possibilities of success. He considered it impossible to change the habits of Indians who had attained maturity and placed his hope in the rising generation, which might be properly educated in time. "A few years will settle this important question," he noted in 1826; "and we have no doubt, that on small reservations, and among reduced bands, where a spirit of improvement has already commenced, its effects will be salutary and permanent. But

15. Cass to Crawford, June 6, 1816, Records of the Michigan Superintendency, Letterbooks, vol. 1, p. 227; A System for the Regulation of Indian Affairs, 1816, Ayer Collection (Ayer NA 601), Newberry Library, Chicago. [The memoir of Cass has been printed in Francis Paul Prucha and Donald F. Carmony, "A Memorandum of Lewis Cass: Concerning a System for the Regulation of Indian Affairs," *Wisconsin Magazine of History* 52 (Autumn 1968): 35–50.]

16. Cass to Calhoun, April 6, 1821, Carter, *Territorial Papers,* 11:117.

we confess that, under other circumstances, our fears are stronger than our hopes."[17]

In Cass's mind, the biggest problem in ameliorating the condition of the Indians was liquor, and he opposed its introduction into the Indian Country, where it all too obviously corrupted the morals and manners of the Indians. Furthermore, if the Indians were sober, Cass felt that they could handle their own affairs and would be in little danger from unscrupulous traders. He went so far as to declare: "The entire exclusion of spiritous liquors from the Indian Country is . . . the only measure, which it is necessary for the Government to adopt with a view to secure the Indians from the frauds of trade." His proposals with Clark in 1829 recommended exclusion of liquor from the trade, and no doubt his influence was felt when Congress finally in 1832 absolutely prohibited liquor in the Indian Country.[18]

As long as discretion was permitted, however, Cass did not pursue a doctrinaire attitude. When it seemed to him, as it did in 1818 and 1823 for example, that the survival of American trade in competition with the British along the northern border demanded the use of liquor, he authorized the agents to permit its entry insofar as it was necessary.[19]

To some men of his time a panacea for all Indian troubles was the elimination of private traders, who were blamed for the pernicious influences affecting the Indians. Beginning in Washington's administration, in fact, the federal government had set up a system of government trading posts known as factories, which were intended to eliminate the abuses in the Indian trade by squeezing out the private traders. By the time that Cass became involved in Indian affairs, the factories had had a firm beginning and were an established part of American policy. Within his jurisdiction there were factories at Chicago, Green Bay, and Prairie du Chien.

But Cass was not a supporter of the factory system. "I am as well convinced as I can be of any fact," he wrote to the Secretary of War in his first extensive statement on Indian matters (September 3, 1814),

17. Lewis Cass, "Indians of North America," *North American Review* 22 (January 1826): 115.

18. Cass to Calhoun, September 14, 1818, "The Fur Trade in Wisconsin, 1812–1825," *Wisconsin Historical Collections* 20 (1911): 85–86; Prucha, *American Indian Policy in the Formative Years,* p. 254.

19. Prucha, *American Indian Policy in the Formative Years,* pp. 111–14.

"that in our intercourse with the Indians we have adopted too much the ideas of trading speculation.—Our trading factories, and our economy in presents have rendered us contemptible to them. The Government should never Come in contact with them, but in cases where its Dignity, its strength or its liberality will inspire them with respect or fear." Cass voiced no criticism of the "zeal, intelligence, and integrity" with which the factories were administered, but he declared, "believing as I do that the system itself is radically incorrect I cannot but recommend its abolition." There was plenty of private capital available for the trade, and the factories, he continued to insist, reduced respect for the United States in the minds of the Indians. Cass later admitted that his views on the matter were "rather speculative than practical," that the abolition of the factories might prove injurious to the United States and to the Indians, and that "it may sometimes be more expedient to continue a doubtful system rather than hazard effects which can neither be foreseen nor controlled." We may presume, however, that when the factory system was finally abolished in 1822, Cass shed no tears, although he objected strenuously to the proposal to foist off on him as presents for the Indians the unsalable materials left at the factories when they closed.[20]

Cass, then, did not show the bitter opposition to traders that appears in the writings of those who supported the factory system. In fact, one of the severest criticisms leveled against Cass by his detractors was that he was a tool of the American Fur Company, the most powerful of the traders in Michigan Territory. That Cass was friendly toward the company cannot be denied. When its agents wanted some special consideration in the trade, they counted on the influence of Cass to aid them, and they continued to count him on their side when any conflict over licenses, whisky, or trading sites arose. Charges that Cass accepted bribes, however, are without foundation. It was simply that Cass saw the need for American traders and believed that the American Fur Company was doing good work. When attacks were made upon the character and conduct of the company, Cass came to its support. "I have discovered in the views & proceedings of that company no indication of a feeling unfriendly to the United States," he wrote in 1821 to

20. Cass to Armstrong, September 3, 1814, Carter, *Territorial Papers,* 10:476; Cass to Calhoun, September 14, 1818, *Wisconsin Historical Collections,* 20:82–86; Cass to Calhoun, October 1, 1818, Records of the Michigan Superintendency, Letterbooks, vol. 3, p. 43; Cass to Calhoun, July 18, 1822, Carter, *Territorial Papers,* 11:254.

the Secretary of War, "and those gentlemen who conduct its operations, & who are known to me, are certainly too high minded to use the
means, which may be in their power, for any purposes incompatible
with the interest of the Country, or the just expectations of the Government." The monopoly with which the American Fur Company was
charged, Cass attributed to the "influence of capital, skill & enterprize." He asserted that the Company enjoyed no special privileges and
that "wealth and industry & skill must & should find their reward."[21]
There are plenty of indications in the letters of the agents of the
American Fur Company that that great organization was not always as
high-minded as Cass naïvely assumed. But Cass the New Englander
rejoiced to see economic rewards go to those who labored so diligently
and so shrewdly.

The principles for dealing with the Indians which Cass and the
government incorporated into their Indian policy—presents, military
protection, an organized Indian Department, and efforts to civilize the
Indians—were not the ultimate solution to the "Indian problem." In
the long run, or so it seemed clear to American statesmen of the time,
the Indians would be replaced by the whites in possession of the American continent. Cass's views on the matter were representative. He assumed, more or less as a matter of course, that the Indians would have
to give up the land that they did not make good use of, to make room
for the more efficient Americans. To some extent the Indians might be
absorbed into the mainstream of white civilization, but more likely
they would have to be progressively pushed westward as the need of
whites for land increased.

Cass developed a scientific interest in the Indians, their culture, and
their language. He sent out printed questionnaires to his agents to collect data, and he soon became something of an authority on Indian
life and manners. But his views of the Indians reflected the white
culture of which he was a part and to a large extent his New England
heritage with its emphasis on thrift, sobriety, and hard work. Some of
his statements about the Indians and their culture make uncomfortable
reading today. "They have no sciences," he wrote in 1826, "and their
religious notions are confused and circumscribed. They have little
property, less law, and no public offences. They soon forget the past,

21. Cass to Calhoun, October 26, 1821, ibid., pp. 156–57.

improvidently disregard the future, and waste their thoughts, when they do think, upon the present."[22] When he compared the Indian culture with the white, he left little doubt about which should carry the day. Take these paragraphs, for example, from his article in the *North American Review* for April 1827:

A principle of progressive improvement seems almost inherent in human nature. Communities of men, as well as individuals, are stimulated by a desire to meliorate their condition. There is nothing stationary around us. We are all striving in the career of life to acquire riches, or honor, or power, or some other object, whose possession is to realize the day dreams of our imaginations; and the aggregate of these efforts constitutes the advance of society.

But there is little of all this in the constitution of our savages. Like the bear, the deer, and buffalo of his own forests, an Indian lives as his father lived, and dies as his father died. He never attempts to imitate the arts of his civilized neighbors. His life passes away in a succession of listless indolence, and of vigorous exertion to provide for his animal wants, or to gratify his baleful passions. He never looks around him, with a spirit of emulation, to compare his situation with that of others, and to resolve on improving it. . . .

Under such circumstances, what ignorance, or folly, or morbid jealousy of our national progress does it not argue, to expect that our civilized border would become stationary, and some of the fairest portions of the globe be abandoned to hopeless sterility. That a few naked wandering barbarians should stay the march of cultivation and improvement, and hold in a state of perpetual unproductiveness, immense regions formed by Providence to support millions of human beings?[23]

Cass had no qualms about this process at all, so long as the Indians were justly reimbursed for whatever possessory right they had in the land, and so long as the agreements made in the treaties with the Indians were faithfully fulfilled. Cass was himself an aggressive participant in treating with the Indians for land cessions, and one of his contributions to the development of the Northwest was the progressive clearing of the land of its Indian title. This was in the beginning a piecemeal sort of operation. "Favourable moments must be embraced for this

22. Cass, "Indians of North America," pp. 53–120, gives an extensive view of Cass's opinions; the quotation is from p. 79.

23. Cass, "Policy and Practice of the United States and Great Britain in Their Treatment of Indians," *North American Review* 24 (April 1827): 391–92.

purpose as they occur," Cass wrote at the beginning of 1819, assuming that it was "an object with the Government to effect the removal of the Indians to the West side of the Mississippi as speedily as circumstances will permit, or by gradual cessions of Territory to confine them within reasonable limits."[24]

Cass was far from proposing a ruthless dispossession. In a treaty concluded with the Chippewas in 1819, he justified his failure to gain a wholesale removal at the minimal price by insisting that he had not been sent "to ascertain the lowest possible sum for which the miserable remnant of those, who once occupied our Country, are willing to treat, and to seize with avidity the occasion to purchase." He spoke of the debt owed the Indians and counseled patient forbearance. In the end the whites would prevail anyway, for as game was destroyed by the advancing white settlements, the country would become useless to the Indians and could be acquired at a low price by the Americans. Cass, moreover, was opposed to extinguishing Indian titles prematurely. Land retained by the Indians was "Indian Country" and as such was subject to the federal laws governing trade and intercourse with the Indians. Traders could be regulated, whiskey prohibited, and encroaching settlers removed. When the Indian title was transferred, the gates were opened to a flood of "enterprising adventurers."[25]

Although the acquisition of Indian land was going steadily forward, in 1825 President Monroe proposed a comprehensive removal policy by which the Indians would be urged to exchange all their lands in the East for lands west of the Mississippi. There they would be beyond the deleterious influence of their white neighbors and no longer an irritant to the states by their claims of independent nationhood. There they could be protected by the federal government and free to proceed at a leisurely pace on their march toward civilization. With Monroe's special message to Congress on the matter of Indian removal in January 1825, and the increasing pressure brought upon the southern Indians by the State of Georgia, the new proposal became an important topic of the day. Cass could not help but consider it when he wrote extended

24. Cass to Calhoun, January 6, 1819, Carter, *Territorial Papers,* 10:808–9.
25. Cass to Calhoun, September 30, 1819, ibid., pp. 864–65; Cass to Calhoun, November 11, 1820, ibid., 11:70.

articles on Indian matters in the *North American Review* in January 1826 and again in April 1827.[26]

At that time he was notably cautious about a wholesale program of removal. In 1826 he spoke highly of the originators of the plan. "But we are seriously apprehensive," he remarked, "that in this gigantic plan of public charity, the magnitude of the outline has withdrawn our attention from the necessary details, and that, if it be adopted to the extent proposed, it will exasperate the evils we are all anxious to allay." He spoke of the Indians' attachment to their old districts, the problems of adjusting to a new country, and the necessity of a "cordon of troops" to keep hostile tribes apart in their congested new homes. In his 1827 article he moved very little from this position. Despite discussions about removal in Congress and in the public press, he said, "the general opinion on its practicability and consequences is yet unsettled." He cast aside as unworthy of consideration the expense of the project and asked only what effect it would produce on the Indians themselves. "The magnitude of the subject is imposing," he said, "and its possible consequences appalling. Doubts and difficulties surround the question, and we do not here introduce it, that we may prejudge or even discuss it."[27]

Political developments finally made Cass's decision for him. When Andrew Jackson became President, a new impetus was given to the removal policy. Rather than a suggestion to be weighed and debated, as under Monroe and Adams, removal under Jackson became a point of positive administration policy. Politically minded men could no longer easily remain neutral in the matter. Whatever misgivings Cass might still have harbored about the policy in all its ramifications, he now had to declare for one side or the other. The decision, of course, was in Jackson's favor. In the *North American Review* for January 1830, Cass announced his wholehearted espousal of the administration policy and argued at length in its support.[28]

Critics of the removal policy did not fail to notice Cass's change of mind, and he was severely castigated for what appeared to be jumping on the Jackson bandwagon. It is impossible, of course, to establish

26. On the removal policy, see Prucha, *American Indian Policy in the Formative Years*, pp. 224–44.

27. Cass, "Indians of North America," pp. 116–18; Cass, "Policy and Practice of the United States and Great Britain," p. 409.

28. Cass, "Removal of the Indians," *North American Review* 30 (January 1830): 62–121.

the precise motivation behind Cass's new position, but it is clear that he did not do an about-face, as his critics implied. Rather, he now adopted unequivocally a policy toward which he had long been leaning. But whatever the reason, Cass soon became the official spokesman for Jackson's policy, when he assumed the office of Secretary of War.

In his first report as Secretary, November 21, 1831, Cass issued a strong statement justifying removal. He reviewed once more the history of the Indians in contact with the whites and concluded:

> A change in residence, therefore, from their present positions to the region west of the Mississippi, presents the only hope of permanent establishment and improvement. . . . If they remain, they must decline, and eventually disappear. Such is the result of all experience. If they remove, they may be comfortably established, and their moral and physical condition meliorated. It is certainly better for them to meet the difficulties of removal, with the probability of an adequate and final reward, than, yielding to their constitutional apathy, to sit still and perish.[29]

Subsequent reports repeated the same message. Cass endeavored to make removal as attractive to the Indians as possible, and he never quite understood why the Indians did not more readily accept what was for their own good. He met repeatedly with Cherokee delegations to explain the administration policy. He worked earnestly to fulfill the pledges made to the Indians in regard to their new home and outlined a policy to protect the Indians in the West. And he instructed the commissioners sent to examine the western country to find favorable districts for the Indians. Yet in the end he was exasperated by the adamant position of the Indians. "It was hoped that the favorable terms offered by the Government would have been accepted," he wrote to the Governor of Georgia. "But some strange infatuation seems to prevail among these Indians. That they cannot remain where they are and prosper is attested as well by their actual condition as by the whole history of our aboriginal tribes. Still they refuse to adopt the only course which promises a cure or even an alleviation of the evils of their present condition."[30]

---

29. *House Executive Document* no. 2, 22d Cong., 1st sess., ser. 216, p. 30.

30. Cass to Wilson Lumpkin, December 24, 1832, in Records of the Office of Indian Affairs, Letters Sent, vol. 9, pp. 486–89, National Archives, Record Group 75; Prucha, *American Indian Policy in the Formative Years,* pp. 246–47.

How shall we evaluate Cass and his Indian policy? His great virtue and the reason for his success was beyond question his honesty and his sense of justice, however limited the latter might seem according to our present standards. He may have held the Indians in low regard, but this never permitted him to deceive them or to cheat them. He won the Indians' respect, too, by his firmness and his courage. The firmness was a set policy. "I have found in my intercourse with the Indians, that firm and vigorous representations seldom fail in their effects," he wrote in 1822, and the Indians came to know that they did not have to fear dissimulation in Cass's dealings with them.[31] The courage was part of his personal make-up. His going alone into an Indian camp at Sault Ste. Marie in 1820 to tear down a British flag is the most famous example of Cass's daring. But it was indicative of his whole approach to Indian affairs. Cass stated explicitly the principles to which he adhered and the rights of the United States which he defended—and the Indians admired him for it. Nor did the wilderness hold any terrors for the Governor. He would set forth on a thousand-mile canoe trip into unknown and possibly hostile lands with as little hesitation as we might entrain for a nearby city on a business trip. He made every effort to know the land which was his domain and the people whom he governed. He did not make his decisions or formulate his policies in an ivory tower.

It has long been customary to speak of Lewis Cass's dealings with the American Indians in superlatives. One wonders at times if his biographers have not, a bit unconsciously perhaps, slipped off into hagiography and have seen the halo of the saint but not the warts that so strikingly marked the man.

The warts were undoubtedly there. Cass's understanding of the Indians and their culture was clouded by his own cultural outlook, which it never occurred to him to question. His friendship with the American Fur Company led him to lean too heavily in its favor in his official actions. His lack of firsthand knowledge of the civilization of the southern Indians, whose removal he pushed as Secretary of War, seriously weakened his arguments for removal. It is such aspects of his character, however, that make him come alive, make us realize that he was a real man confronting real problems in practical political situations, and not a plaster idol.

Yet it is ultimately the halo that holds our attention. Lewis Cass was a great man in his relations with the Indians. Without him the nation—and the Indians—would have been much the poorer.

31. Cass to Calhoun, July 9, 1822, *Wisconsin Historical Collections*, 20:264–65.

8

Indian Removal and the Great American Desert

*When I first began teaching in the history department of Marquette
University, I presented a paper on my researches on Indian policy to a
history faculty seminar. One of the professors asked me how I could
take such a positive view of the government's policy since it was clear
that when explorers returned with word of a Great American Desert
in the West, the government decided that the region would be a suitable
place to dump the eastern Indians. His question struck me because I
could not recall seeing any indication of such an attitude in the great
mass of sources I had recently studied. I took up the point in my next
summer's research, testing in every way possible the professor's question. I discovered, indeed, that his perception was a common one,
expressed almost universally in college textbooks, but I could find no
contemporary evidence to support it. In the process I learned a good
deal about the Great American Desert, about Indian removal policy,
and about how American textbooks are written.*

*I was pleased with the reaction to the article. John D. Hicks, in a
generous note, said, "I think you make a good case. We have all gone
along with Paxson's analysis all too carelessly." Ray Allen Billington
reversed his position in the new edition of his widely used textbook,*
Westward Expansion, *and other authors modified their statements. But
some writers continue to sing the old refrain.*

In 1820 Major Stephen H. Long of the United States Topographical
Engineers explored lands west of the Mississippi. From Council Bluffs
on the Missouri River he moved west, crossed the plains through what
is now Nebraska, headed south along the foothills of the Rockies, and

Printed source: *Indiana Magazine of History* 59 (December 1963): 299–322.

returned east following the Canadian River through present-day Oklahoma. The report of this expedition, published in 1823, proclaimed that most of the territory between the meridian of Council Bluffs and the Rocky Mountains was "almost wholly unfit for cultivation, and of course uninhabitable by a people depending upon agriculture for their subsistence."[1] Two years after the appearance of this report President James Monroe, following a proposal set forth by Secretary of War John C. Calhoun, officially adopted a policy of removing the Indian tribes in the East to unoccupied lands west of the Mississippi. These two events some American historians have been wont to join together in their interpretation of the Indian removal policy.

The common explanation of the removal policy presented by today's writers of general histories of the United States and of the westward movement may be stated, not unfairly, as follows. The Indians in the East, forming enclaves within the advancing white settlement, were becoming an increasingly greater problem. The whites coveted the Indian lands, and the contact between the two races was becoming more and more detrimental to the Indians, who acquired the white man's vices but not his virtues. Then came word of the nature of the trans-Mississippi West. If the West was indeed a great desert, useless to the whites, why not dispose of the bothersome Indians by moving them out into the plains. "The concept of a 'Permanent Indian Frontier,' where red men would be forever removed from the path of advancing white settlements," writes one authority on westward expansion, "dawned on officials as soon as government explorers made them aware of western geography. The region west of the 95th meridian, pathfinders agreed, was an arid waste unsuited to habitation. . . . Federal officials saw a possible solution to the vexing race problem in the explorers' tales. If all Indians east of the Mississippi were moved to the Great American Desert their valuable lands would be opened to settlement, friction between the two races removed, and natives protected from the sins and diseases of white men."[2] Another historian remarks in his textbook: "Luckily for the whites the solution of the problem

1. Edwin James, *Account of an Expedition from Pittsburgh to the Rocky Mountains Performed in the Years 1819 and '20,* 2 vols. and atlas (Philadelphia: H. C. Carey and I. Lea, 1822–23), 2:361. A three-volume edition of James's work was published in London in 1823. The London edition is reprinted in Reuben G. Thwaites, ed., *Early Western Travels, 1748–1846,* 32 vols. (Cleveland: Arthur H. Clark Company, 1904–1907), vols. 14–17.
2. Ray Allen Billington, *Westward Expansion: A History of the American Frontier,* 2d ed. (New York: Macmillan Company, 1960), p. 470.

of the Indians appeared obvious and easy." After noting that there was general belief in the "Great American Desert," he continues: "In view of the apparent unavailability of the Far West for white settlement it seemed reasonable to send the Indians to that part of the country."[3] A third textbook speaks of the "country reputed to be desert" as offering "a splendid opportunity to dispose of the Indians,"[4] and a fourth notes that "in the vast stretch of territory popularly regarded as the 'Great American Desert' . . . the displaced Indian tribes were supposed to live in isolation from the whites. . . ."[5]

For readers accustomed to thinking of American governmental policy toward the Indians in the blackest of terms, this account of the removal policy makes good sense. When still another historian notes that removal was in large part carried out by Andrew Jackson and describes him as a "veteran Indian fighter" who "accepted fully the brutal creed of his fellow Westerners that 'the only good Indian is a dead Indian,'"[6] the pieces of the picture fall comfortably into place.

Certain pertinent questions, however, need to be asked about the picture so assembled. Where did the officials who formulated the Indian

---

3. Robert E. Riegel, *America Moves West*, 3d ed. (New York: H. Holt Company, 1956), pp. 304–5.

4. Robert E. Riegel and David F. Long, *The American Story*, 2 vols. (New York: McGraw-Hill, 1955), 1:257.

5. Richard Hofstadter, William Miller, and Daniel Aaron, *The American Republic*, 2 vols. (Englewood Cliffs, N.J.: Prentice-Hall, 1959), 1:472. Similar statements concerning the relationship between Indian removal and the western desert may be found in Frederic L. Paxson, *History of the American Frontier, 1763–1893* (Boston: Houghton Mifflin Company, 1924), pp. 276–77; Roy M. Robbins, *Our Landed Heritage: The Public Domain, 1776–1936* (Princeton: Princeton University Press, 1942), p. 51; John D. Hicks and George E. Mowry, *A Short History of American Democracy* (Cambridge, Mass.: Houghton Mifflin Company, 1956), p. 214; Thomas D. Clark, *Frontier America: The Story of the Westward Movement* (New York: Charles Scribner's Sons, 1959), pp. 468, 475; Henry Bamford Parkes, *The United States of America: A History* (New York: Alfred A. Knopf, 1959), p. 195; T. Harry Williams, Richard N. Current, and Frank Freidel, *A History of the United States*, 2 vols. (New York: Alfred A. Knopf, 1959), 1:370; Alvin M. Josephy, Jr., *The Patriot Chiefs* (New York: Viking Press, 1961), p. 187; Bayrd Still, ed., *The West: Contemporary Records of America's Expansion Across the Continent, 1607–1890* (New York: Capricorn Books, 1961), p. 8. It is difficult to explain why such statements are repeated in so many books, since scholarly monographs and articles dealing with Indian removal or with the Great American Desert do not indicate any relationship between the two.

6. Thomas A. Bailey, *The American Pageant: A History of the Republic*, 2d ed. (Boston: D. C. Heath, 1961), p. 269.

removal policy think the Great American Desert was located? What area west of the Mississippi did they allot to the transplanted tribes? Were these two areas the same? Was it the intent of federal officials to settle the Indian on useless land? And did the contemporary critics condemn the removal policy because it would force the Indians out into the desert?

That there was common belief in the existence of the Great American Desert there can be no doubt. Historians and geographers have unearthed the surveys of explorers and have pointed to the popularization of these reports in the atlases and school geographies of the time.[7] It is necessary, however, to re-examine the data to determine with some exactness, if it is possible, just where the Great American Desert existed according to the belief of men in the 1820s and 1830s. Was everything west of Missouri and Arkansas considered desert—as some modern authors might lead us to believe—or was the desert area more precisely circumscribed?

The genesis of the desert idea and its spread among the public are established facts. Lieutenant Zebulon M. Pike, who journeyed across the plains in 1806–1807, reported that the area "may become in time equally celebrated as the sandy desarts [sic] of Africa" and predicted that white settlers would halt at "the borders of the Missouri and Mississippi, while they leave the prairies incapable of cultivation to the wandering and uncivilized aborigines of the country."[8] Pike's observations, however, had little influence either on cartographers or on the

7. A detailed account of the idea of the Great American Desert is given in Ralph C. Morris, "The Notion of a Great American Desert East of the Rockies," *Mississippi Valley Historical Review* 13 (September 1926): 190–200. See also Frank W. Blackmar, "The History of the Desert," *Transactions of the Kansas State Historical Society* 9 (1906): 101–14; Walter Prescott Webb, *The Great Plains* (Boston: Ginn and Company, 1931), pp. 152–60; Henry Nash Smith, *Virgin Land: The American West as Symbol and Myth* (Cambridge: Harvard University Press, 1950), pp. 174–83. The author found very helpful an unpublished paper, "The Cartographical History of the 'Great American Desert,'" by Guy-Harold Smith, professor of geography, Ohio State University, Columbus. A copy of the paper was kindly furnished the author by Professor Smith. [A more recent detailed study is Richard H. Dillon, "Stephen Long's Great American Desert," *Proceedings of the American Philosophical Society* 111 (April 1967): 93–108. See also Roger L. Welsch, "The Myth of the Great American Desert," *Nebraska History* 52 (Fall 1971): 255–65, and Roger L. Nichols, "Stephen Long and Scientific Exploration on the Plains," ibid. 52 (Spring 1971): 51–64.]

8. Zebulon M. Pike, *An Account of Expeditions to the Sources of the Mississippi and through the Western Parts of Louisiana* . . . (Philadelphia: C. and A. Conrad and Company, 1810), Appendix to part 2, p. 3. The London edition,

public mind. The first edition of his work, published in Philadelphia, is remarkable for the disorder of its material, and the London edition, although somewhat improved by the editor, is not much more satisfactory. In neither edition do the maps carry any notation of desert.

It is Stephen H. Long who must be credited with establishing the belief in the Great American Desert. In 1820 he produced a large manuscript map with the following inscription: "To the Hon. John C. Calhoun, Secy of War, This Map of the Country situated between the Meridian of Washington City and the Rocky Mountains, exhibiting the route of the late Exploring Expedition commanded by Maj. Long, together with other recent surveys and explorations by himself & others. . . ."[9] This map has the words GREAT DESERT entered on what is now the panhandle of Texas and the region immediately to the north. It was the first map to refer to or delineate the Great American Desert, and it became the progenitor of several decades of maps of the West.

The data on Long's expedition reached the public chiefly through the report of Edwin James, a member of Long's party, who published an account of the expedition in Philadelphia in 1823 and another edition in London later in the same year.[10] James described the area west of the 96th meridian as prairie country, with a scarcity of wood and water which would "prove an insuperable obstacle in the way of settling the country." But the epithet *desert* he reserved for a more restricted area—the region five hundred to six hundred miles wide at the base of the Rocky Mountains.[11] In the Philadelphia edition of James's work the map of the United States was printed as two plates, one showing the "Eastern Section," the other the "Western Section"; the name GREAT AMERICAN DESERT appears on the latter (see Plate II). In the London edition the area was designated simply GREAT DESERT, following almost exactly the manuscript map of Long.[12] Both

---

entitled *Exploratory Travels through the Western Territories of North America,* was published in 1811. One of the most complete editions of Pike's journals is Elliott Coues, ed., *The Expeditions of Zebulon Montgomery Pike,* 3 vols. (New York: Francis P. Harper, 1895). [An excellent scholarly edition is Donald Jackson, ed., *The Journals of Zebulon Montgomery Pike with Letters and Related Documents,* 2 vols. (Norman: University of Oklahoma Press, 1966).]

9. The original map is preserved in the Cartographic Branch of the National Archives, Washington, D.C.

10. See note 1. The Philadelphia edition appeared in two volumes of text with a separate volume of plates and maps dated 1822.

11. James, *Account,* 2:361, 386.

12. The map of the United States was printed as one plate in the London edition; it is reproduced in Thwaites, *Early Western Travels,* 14:30.

printings carry the annotation on the map, "The Great Desert is frequented by roving bands of Indians who have no fixed places of residence but roam from place to place in quest of game."

The popular map makers of the day copied from Long, James, and perhaps from each other. And they are remarkably uniform in their portrayal of the Great American Desert. One of the earliest atlases to mark the desert was that of Henry C. Carey, *A Complete Historical, Chronological, and Geographical American Atlas,* published in Philadelphia in 1822. Its general map of the United States shows no desert, but Plate 35, entitled "Map of Arkansa [sic] and other Territories of the United States, Respectfully inscribed to the Hon. J. C. Calhoun, Secretary of War, By S. H. Long Major T. Engineers," shows GREAT DESERT west of the 100th meridian, equidistant north and south of the Arkansas River (see Plate III). It carries the additional legend about the roving bands of Indians. The identical map was printed in the 1823 edition of Carey's *Atlas* and in the 1827 edition as well. The 1827 edition also shows GREAT AMERICAN DESERT on its general map of the United States.

The atlases of William C. Woodbridge present much the same information. His 1823 *School Atlas* shows no desert marked on its plate of North America and its map of the United States does not extend far enough to the west to show the area in question. But his *Modern Atlas, on a New Plan, to Accompany the System of Universal Geography,* in its editions of 1824 and 1829, shows the desert on the plate of the United States.[13] In both of these editions the words GREAT AMERICAN DESERT run in a broad sweep from northwest to southeast, beginning in what is now the northeast corner of Colorado and running down into north central Oklahoma. This brings the legend farther east than in any of the other contemporary atlases. One is forced to conclude, however, that the unusual sweep of the lettering was not due to any special geographical knowledge or conviction, but to the necessity of avoiding an inset map which covered much of the area designated desert in other atlases. Indeed, in the 1829 edition of the atlas the plate of North America shows GREAT AMERICAN DESERT in its usual position west of the 100th meridian, astride the Arkansas River (see Plate I). Woodbridge's maps of the United States carry the notation: "The desert is traversed by herds of Buffaloes & wild horses & inhabited only by roving tribes of Indians."

13. Woodbridge's atlases were published in Hartford. The plates in question bear the copyright date 1821.

The United States map (see Plate IV) published in 1835 by Thomas G. Bradford in *A Comprehensive Atlas, Geographical, Historical & Commercial*,[14] follows the same tradition. In large open capitals it indicates GREAT AMERICAN DESERT running north to south, beginning almost at the Canadian border and ending in the southwest corner of Oklahoma. For the most part the lettering runs along the 102nd meridian marked on the map. The maps printed in *Smith's Atlas*, 1839, add further clarification to the contemporary concept of the Great American Desert because the area is neatly stippled on the map, so that there can be few doubts about the limits intended.[15] The "Map of the United States and Texas" shows an irregular oblong area divided into roughly equal parts by the Arkansas River and lying between the 101st and the 105th meridians, extending as far south as the Red River. A similar area is marked out on the "Map of North America," but in less detail owing to the scale of the map. The same plates were used again in the 1844 edition of the atlas. *Mitchell's School Atlas,* published in revised edition in 1840, shows stippled areas of desert, which are almost identical with those in Smith's works, both on the map of the United States (see Plate V) and on the map of North America.[16]

It is clear, therefore, that during the decades of the 1820s and 1830s, when Indian removal on a large scale was planned and carried out, the Great American Desert occupied a precise and generally agreed upon position on the available maps. It was the area east of the Rockies, varying in length from north to south in the different atlases, but generally extending about two hundred miles north and the same distance south of the Arkansas River—in other words, from the northern boundary of present-day Colorado to the base of the Texas panhandle. The area designated, except for an occasional tail of the printing, is west of the 100th meridian and in some cases west of the 101st.[17]

The contemporary descriptions of the region designated as the Great

14. Thomas G. Bradford, *A Comprehensive Atlas, Geographical, Historical & Commercial* (Boston: J. H. Wilkins and R. B. Carter, 1835).

15. Roswell C. Smith, *Smith's Atlas* (Hartford: Spalding and Storrs, 1839).

16. Samuel A. Mitchell, *Mitchell's School Atlas,* rev. ed. (Philadelphia: Thomas, Cowperthwait and Company, 1840).

17. Morris speaks of "the notion of a great American desert, extending westward through the entire width of the United States from approximately the one hundredth meridian to the Rockies." Morris, "Notion of a Great American Desert," p. 190. The belief in the Great American Desert existed well beyond the middle of the nineteenth century. For the later history of the myth, see the works cited in note 7.

American Desert leave no doubt that it was considered desolate country, fit only for buffalo, wild horses, and roving Indians. Although the official reports were moderate in language and attempted a careful description of the various sections, distinguishing to some extent between prairie lands and the more arid region to the west, popular accounts were less discriminating. In 1828, for example, *Niles' Weekly Register* carried a little item on the desert, which drew ultimately upon the scientific reports of Long, but which presented the data in more extravagant language for popular consumption:

AMERICAN DESERT. There is an extensive desert in the territory of the United States, west of the Mississippi, which is described in Long's Expedition to the Rocky Mountains. It extends from the base of the Rocky Mountains 400 miles to the east, and is 500 from north to south. There are deep ravines in which the brooks and rivers meander, skirted by a few stunted trees, but all the elevated surface is a barren desert, covered with sand[,] gravel, pebbles, &c. There are a few plants but nothing like a tree to be seen on these desolate plains, and seldom is a living creature to be met with. The Platte, the Arkansas, and other rivers flow through this dreary waste.[18]

If Monroe and Adams and Jackson intended to move the Indians from their verdant lands in the East into "this dreary waste," their plans were despicable indeed. But was that their intention?

The idea of removing the Indians to the vast wilderness west of the Mississippi originated long before very much was known about the character of the region.[19] Thomas Jefferson in 1803 thought that the Louisiana Purchase might well be used by the Indians, and before his term of office ended the notion of exchanging lands in the East for those in the West was introduced cautiously among the Indians.[20] Such a movement, of course, would please the white settlers, who were anxious to be rid of the Indians, and the legislature of Tennessee in 1803 politely suggested to Congress that the Louisiana Purchase offered a fine opportunity to move the Indians out of Tennessee

18. *Niles' Weekly Register* 35 (September 27, 1828): 70.

19. A detailed account of the origin and development of the removal policy is Annie H. Abel, "The History of Events Resulting in Indian Consolidation West of the Mississippi," *Annual Report of the American Historical Association for the Year 1906,* 2 vols. (Washington, 1908), 1:233–450.

20. Secretary of War to Return J. Meigs, March 25 and May 5, 1808, Office of the Secretary of War, Letters Sent, Indian Affairs, vol. 5, pp. 364, 377, National Archives, Record Group 75.

altogether.[21] It cannot be argued from these designs, however, that the intent was to force the Indians onto useless lands, or for that matter onto lands less valuable than those they were asked to surrender. Although some scattered accounts of the trans-Mississippi West were available, accurate detailed information at the time was meager. One thing was clear, however: the country in the West was terribly large and whites would not be able to fill it for generations.

The removal suggestions of 1803 came to naught. After the War of 1812, however, the agitation was renewed, and President James Monroe and John C. Calhoun worked earnestly for a change in the Indian situation. Either the Indians would have to adopt the white man's way of life or move beyond the Mississippi out of the way of the whites. A treaty was signed with the Cherokees in 1817, by which some of the eastern holdings of the nation were exchanged for lands in Arkansas, and the commissioners dealing with the Indians north of the Ohio in 1818 were urged to be liberal in their offerings to induce the Indians to move west of the Mississippi.[22] Then the increasing pressure of Georgia upon the Cherokee lands within the state gave new impetus to the removal policy in the 1820s, and President Monroe became definitely committed to it as the only alternative to the destruction of the Indians. Although he opposed the extreme demands of the Georgians for the expulsion of the Cherokees, Monroe became convinced that removal was the only salvation for the Indians and recommended the policy in his special message to Congress in March 1824, and again in his annual message in December. Finally on January 27, 1825, Monroe sent to Congress a new special message on removal, insisting upon a liberal policy that would satisfy both Georgia and the Indians.[23]

This final message of Monroe on removal was based upon the report drawn up by Calhoun, dated January 24, 1825. Since Calhoun's report is cited as an official plan to dispose of the Indians by burying them in

21. Robert H. White, ed., *Messages of the Governors of Tennessee,* 5 vols. (Nashville: Tennessee Historical Commission, 1952–59), 1:153–54.

22. James Monroe, first annual message, December 2, 1817, James D. Richardson, comp., *A Compilation of the Messages and Papers of the Presidents,* 10 vols. (Washington: Government Printing Office, 1896–99), 2:16; C. Vandeventer to Lewis Cass, June 29, 1818, Office of the Secretary of War, Letters Sent, Indian Affairs, vol. D, pp. 176–77, National Archives, Record Group 75.

23. *Senate Document* no. 63, 18th Cong., 1st sess., ser. 91; Richardson, *Messages and Papers,* 2:261, 280–83.

the Great American Desert,[24] it must be looked at closely. Where precisely did Calhoun recommend that the Indians be sent? To begin with, he divided the eastern Indians into two groups. The smaller group consisted of those living in the northern parts of Indiana and Illinois, in Michigan, New York, and Ohio. These Calhoun wanted to move into the region west of Lake Michigan and north of Illinois—that is, into the present state of Wisconsin. In support of this recommendation, he advanced the following arguments:

> The climate and the nature of the country are much more favorable to their habits than that west of the Mississippi; to which may be added, that the Indians in New York have already commenced a settlement at Green Bay, and exhibit some disposition to make it a permanent one; and that the Indians referred to in Indiana, Illinois, in the peninsula of Michigan, and Ohio, will find in the country designated kindred tribes, with whom they may be readily associated. These considerations, with the greater facility with which they could be collected in that portion of the country, compared with that of collecting them west of the Mississippi, form a strong inducement to give it the preference.[25]

Obviously, there is no question of Long's Great American Desert here.

For the southern tribes and those in southern Illinois and Indiana—the great bulk of the eastern Indians—Calhoun recommended lands lying west of Arkansas and Missouri. Calhoun speaks of the area only in general terms as a "sufficient tract of country west of the State of Missouri and Territory of Arkansas." There are no details in the report about the nature of the country to which the Indians would be sent, most likely because Calhoun expected that lands would be assigned the Indians which they themselves had examined and declared satisfactory. He emphasized that "no arrangement ought to be made which does not regard the interest of the Indians as well as our own."[26] This concern to satisfy the Indians was echoed in Monroe's message. The President proposed to convey to each tribe "a good title to an adequate portion

---

24. Billington, *Westward Expansion*, p. 470; Hicks and Mowry, *Short History of American Democracy*, pp. 214–15; Paxson, *History of the American Frontier*, pp. 276–77; Riegel, *America Moves West*, p. 305; Riegel and Long, *The American Story*, 1:257; Robbins, *Our Landed Heritage*, p. 51.

25. *American State Papers: Indian Affairs*, 2:543.

26. Ibid., pp. 543–44.

of land to which it may consent to remove," and asserted that the full plan of removal—new lands, a stable government in the West, and added protection against white encroachment—would undoubtedly induce the Indians to relinquish their old lands and move west.[27]

These official documents, it is true, cannot be expected to set forth explicitly an intention to dispose of the Indians by removing them to worthless lands which the whites would never want, but the documents are not intelligible if read in that sinister light. Nor do subsequent developments in the removal program give any evidence that the plan of the government was to move the Indians out to the Great American Desert.

Monroe's proposals were not enacted by Congress in 1825, although Thomas Hart Benton pushed through the Senate a bill incorporating the basic elements of Calhoun's report.[28] Little, likewise, was done in the following administration; John Quincy Adams adhered to Monroe's removal policy for want of any better solution to the Indian problem.[29] Adams' Secretary of War, James Barbour, however, advocated removal of the Indians as individuals rather than as tribes and in a long report of February 3, 1826, to the chairman of the House Committee on Indian Affairs outlined his removal plans, the first point of which was to set aside the country west of the Mississippi and between Lakes Michigan and Huron and the Mississippi for the exclusive use of the Indians. He apologized a bit for including the area east of the Mississippi, but argued that he was merely following the earlier suggestion of Calhoun, that the Indians then occupied the area, and that "from its natural features, [it] is not desirable at present for the habitation of our citizens." There was a note of genuine concern for the Indians throughout the report, as Barbour candidly recounted the evils and injustice in previous dealings with the Indians. He made no reference to the quality of the land in the West, but the assumption was implicit in the report that the land would be suitable for the Indians as they approached civilization. Barbour's main design was to prevent future conflicts between the Indians and the whites over the land, such as were then raging in Georgia. "The principal recommendation of this plan, next to the advantages to be gained by ourselves," he wrote, "is, that the future residence of these people will be forever undisturbed; that

27. Richardson, *Messages and Papers,* 2:281.

28. *Senate Journal,* 18th Cong., 2d sess., ser. 107, pp. 124, 130, 164, 185, 187.

29. *Memoirs of John Quincy Adams, Comprising Portions of His Diary from 1795 to 1848,* ed. Charles Francis Adams, 12 vols. (Philadelphia: J. B. Lippincott and Company, 1875–77), 7:113.

there, at least, they will find a home and a resting place; and being exclusively under the control of the United States, and, consequently, free from the rival claims of any of the States, the former may plight its most solemn faith that it shall be theirs forever; and this guaranty is therefore given."[30] The Indians west of the Mississippi would be forever secure in possession of the land—not because the whites would never want it, but because the Indian title would be absolute and guaranteed.

Barbour's proposals were heartily seconded by William Clark, Superintendent of Indian Affairs at St. Louis and one of the best informed, most sympathetic, and most influential Indian officials. Clark, in March 1826, noted the changed relationship between the United States and the Indians, that the red men were no longer a hostile threat to be put down by war but had become instead "objects of pity and commiseration." He wanted the Indians to be educated and instructed in agricultural pursuits and the ways of civilization, a possibility only if the Indians could be removed from the existing contacts and conflicts with the whites. As for the territory to which the Indians would be moved, Clark had the following comment:

> . . . the country west of Missouri and Arkansas, and west of the Mississippi river, north of Missouri, is the one destined to receive them. From all accounts, this country will be well adapted to their residence; it is well watered with numerous small streams and some large rivers; abounds with grass, which will make it easy to raise stock; has many salt springs, from which a supply of the necessary article of salt can be obtained; contains much prairie land, which will make the opening of farms easy; and affords a temporary supply of game.[31]

With proposals for removal heavy in the air, the House of Representatives requested of the Secretary of War, in the middle of December 1826, specific information on particular questions relative to the removal policy and the Indians' reactions to it. A number of the points of inquiry had a direct bearing on the nature of the country to which the Indians were to move. The House resolution asked, among other things, whether the Indians were "acquainted with the nature and situation of the country to which they are to be removed; and to what particular district or districts of country West of the Mississippi, they

30. *American State Papers: Indian Affairs,* 2:646–49.
31. Ibid., p. 653.

ought, in his opinion, to be removed."[32] Barbour turned the questions over to Thomas L. McKenney, head of the Office of Indian Affairs and a key figure in Indian policy making. McKenney in his answers gave an honest picture of the state of information available to the planners at the moment. He admitted frankly the lack of knowledge about the nature of the land to which the Indians were to be removed and insisted that the lands be examined and proved suitable before they were allotted to the Indians. And it was land suitable for agricultural pursuits which concerned him, since the advocates of removal hoped to induce the Indians to change to agricultural subsistence in their new homes. There was no question here of finding land suitable for nomadic hunters. In McKenney's long reply there is not the slightest hint that he thought of the area in question as the Great American Desert.

McKenney answered the congressional queries point by point: "The Indians are not 'acquainted' with either 'the nature or situation of the country to which it is proposed to remove them.' The 'particular district of country' which has been looked to, for the permanent home of the Indians who should emigrate west of the Mississippi, is that which lies north of the river Arkansas, and west of the State of Missouri; but, as no examination of it has been made, with a view to its occupancy by the tribes now in the States east of the Mississippi, it cannot be known 'what particular district or districts of country west of the Mississippi they ought to occupy.'" McKenney asserted that the first step should be an actual examination of the western country to determine "its extent and fitness for a last home for the most unfortunate of human beings." He thought it "not unreasonable" that if the land in the West could be examined and judged suitable by a deputation of the Indians themselves, the Indians would be willing to accept removal.[33]

The examination of the western territory with a view to locating the Indians progressed slowly, but there was no intention of sending the Indians to land they had not judged suitable for their needs. Congress in May 1828 appropriated $15,000 for an exploration of the country west of the Mississippi and authorized the appointment of commissioners to accompany the Indians.[34] The commissioners in their reports described the territory as far as they had examined it and set forth both advantages and disadvantages. In general, however, the reports

32. *House Journal,* 19th Cong., 2d sess., ser. 147, p. 66.
33. *American State Papers: Indian Affairs,* 2:699–702.
34. *United States Statutes at Large,* 4:315.

were favorable. One of the commissioners—Isaac McCoy, a Baptist missionary and long-time friend of the Indians—declared that "the country under consideration is adequate to the purpose of a permanent and comfortable home for the Indians; and whatever may be the obstacles which at present oppose, they may nevertheless be located there without recourse to any measure not in accordance with the most rigid principles of justice and humanity."[35] George B. Kennerly, who led the expedition composed of deputations of the Choctaws, Chickasaws, and Creeks, reported, "There is a sufficient quantity of well timbered and watered land on the Arkansas and its tributaries for the whole of the southern Indians, if a proper distribution be made."[36]

Not much could be accomplished, however, until Congress acted to authorize a large-scale removal and to provide the funds this would require. Numerous bills were introduced and reports submitted as pressure on the southern Indians mounted. A strong argument for removal continued to be the assertion that by moving the Indians to lands which were outside any state or organized territory, the question of conflict of claims to the land would cease since the federal government could and would guarantee the Indians' rights to the western lands without danger of state interference.[37]

When Andrew Jackson became president, the forces working for removal of the Indians took on new energy and after long and bitter debate in Congress the Removal Bill became law on May 28, 1830.[38] Work then began in earnest to draw up treaties of removal with the Indians, to direct the actual migration, and to mark out the districts in the West to be allotted to each group.

The situation was complex and confusing and, to facilitate the settlement of the Indians in the West, Congress authorized in July 1832 the appointment of three commissioners with extensive powers to investigate the territory, to select tracts of land for the incoming Indians, and to adjudicate conflicting claims.[39] Secretary of War Lewis Cass gave the commissioners a long set of instructions, in which he urged them to make arrangements that would satisfy the Indians and thus preserve peace in the area. The commissioners were instructed

---

35. *House Report* no. 87, 20th Cong., 2d sess., ser. 190, p. 24.

36. Ibid., p. 25.

37. Report of House Committee on Indian Affairs, February 8, 1829, ibid., pp. 1–3.

38. *United States Statutes at Large,* 4:411–12. The debates appear in *Register of Debates,* 21st Cong., 1st sess., pp. 305–67, 580–98.

39. *United States Statutes at Large,* 4:595–96.

particularly to welcome the Indian delegations sent out to investigate the land and to see that they were satisfied. "You will perceive," Cass told the three men, "that the general object is to locate them all in as favorable positions as possible, in districts sufficiently fertile, salubrious & extensive, & with boundaries, either natural or artificial, so clearly defined, as to preclude the possibility of dispute. There is country enough for all, & more than all. And the President is anxious, that full justice should be done to each, & every measure adopted be as much to their satisfaction, as is compatible with the nature of such an arrangement." The commissioners were asked to transmit to the War Department all the information they could procure respecting the territory into which the Indians were to move.[40]

The commissioners submitted a report from Fort Gibson, dated February 10, 1834. The country acquired from the western Indians for the purpose of providing land for the Indians coming from the East the commissioners declared to be "very extensive," running from the Red River to 43°30' north latitude, and from the western boundary of Missouri and Arkansas to the 100th meridian. The climate, they reported, did not "materially vary from the climate, in the corresponding degrees of latitude, in the Atlantic States, some distance in the interior from the seaboard," and the soil, was of great diversity such "as generally is found in the States bordering on the Mississippi." The commissioners reported considerable game but predicted that it would soon be destroyed as the eastern Indians moved in. "The question then arises," they wrote, "'is the country able to furnish them a support in any other way; and particularly is it calculated for the purposes of agriculture?' And this question the commissioners answer unhesitatingly in the affirmative. They are of opinion that there is a sufficiency of good first rate soil, now belonging to those tribes who already have lands assigned to them, and in sufficient quantity still undisposed of, to assign to such tribes as may hereafter choose to remove here, to support them, if they will settle down like our white citizens and become agriculturists."[41]

Other reports on inspection of the lands proposed for the eastern Indians were of like tenor. A treaty with the Delaware Indians for removal west of Missouri provided that the lands be inspected and agreed upon before the treaty would take effect.[42] The agent appointed to

40. *House Executive Document* no. 2, 22d Cong., 2d sess., ser. 233, pp. 32–37.
41. *House Report* no. 474, 23d Cong., 1st sess., ser. 263, pp. 82–84.
42. Charles J. Kappler, ed., *Indian Affairs: Laws and Treaties,* vol. 2, *Treaties* (Washington: Government Printing Office, 1904), pp. 304–5.

accompany the Indians in their tour was again Isaac McCoy. His report to the Secretary of War in April 1831 described in some detail the lands extending about two hundred miles west of the Missouri and Arkansas lines. "I beg leave, sir, to state distinctly," he reported, "that I am confirmed in an opinion often expressed, that the country under consideration may safely be considered favorable for settlement: the distance, on an average of two hundred miles from the State of Missouri and Territory of Arkansas, water, wood, soil, and stone, are such as to warrant this conclusion." McCoy noted that the Delawares were so anxious to move to the new tract that they did not wait for the United States aid promised in the treaty. This, McCoy asserted, furnished *"the best comment on the suitableness of that country for the permanent residence of the Indians."*[43]

In a treaty signed at Chicago on September 26, 1833, the Chippewa, Ottawa, and Potawatomi tribes were granted a tract of land in western Iowa in exchange for their lands east of the Mississippi, with the commonly included proviso that they were to send a delegation first to inspect the land.[44] The agent who accompanied the group kept a journal of the expedition, and his comments on the excellence of the country were numerous and enthusiastic. "The country over which we passed today," he wrote in a typical passage, "is quite rolling—generally prairie but numerous groves of fine timber present themselves in every direction. This country is equal in point of beauty & fertility to any in the U. States."[45]

By 1834 areas west of the Mississippi had been allotted to the various Indian tribes. A map of these areas, entitled "Map of the Western Territory, &c." (see Plate VI), was prepared in the War Department at the request of the House Committee on Indian Affairs. It shows definitively the lands to which the Indians were to be removed. In addition to Iowa, which was still largely Indian country, the lands to be occupied by the Indians form a block of territory lying adjacent to Missouri and Arkansas. The strips of land designated for the Osages, Cherokees, Creeks, and Choctaws extend west to the limit of United States territory—that is, to the eastern boundary of the Texas panhandle at the 100th meridian—in order to give the tribes "outlets" to

---

43. *Senate Document* no. 512, vol. 2, 23d Cong., 1st sess., ser. 245, pp. 435–36. Italics are in the original.

44. Kappler, *Treaties,* p. 402.

45. William Gordon Journal, 1835, Potawatomi, Records of the Commissary General of Subsistence, National Archives, Record Group 75.

the west. The lands of the other tribes are huddled in smaller allotments along the Missouri border. There is a dotted line on the map running north and south from the Platte to the Red River, approximately two hundred miles west of the Arkansas and Missouri boundaries, which is labeled "Western boundary of habitable Land." All the districts except for the outlets of the Osages, Cherokees, Creeks, and Choctaws lie to the east of this line. None of the areas falls within the region commonly designated on the maps of the day as the Great American Desert.[46]

Although the removal policy was carried out with determination, critics of the program were not lacking. As aggression against the southern Indians increased and as the movement in Congress in 1829 and 1830 to pass a removal bill gained momentum, the outcry against forcing the Indians to move reached great heights. Senator Theodore Frelinghuysen of New Jersey, Senator Peleg Sprague of Maine, and others made long speeches in defense of Indian rights, and the press was filled with articles condemning the Jackson policy.

What did these loud and determined critics have to say about the lands in the West to which the Indians were to be removed? Did they condemn Jackson's policy on the ground that the Indians were to exchange good land in the East for desert country in the West? It is remarkable how seldom this question entered into the argument. Senator Sprague, it is true, condemned the policy of moving the Indians "to a distant and an unsubdued wilderness" and "to frowning forests, surrounded with naked savages."[47] But his concern was about moving the Cherokees away from the farms they had already improved and developed to new land where they would have to begin anew rather than about any reputed desert characteristics of the land.

The great argument against removal rested on the guaranteed rights of the Indians to the lands they occupied in the East and on the force of existing treaty obligations. The innumerable memorials which poured into Congress from the North and Northeast had as their plea that the rights of the Indians to their lands in the East be protected. The memorials did not argue about the quality of land to be given the Indians in the West. Had there been indications that the Jackson administration intended to send the Indians into worthless desert land, it is inconceivable that this fact would not have been pounced upon by the administration's critics.

46. *House Report* no. 474, following p. 131.
47. *Register of Debates*, 21st Cong., 1st sess., p. 356.

The most important spokesman against removal in 1829 and 1830 was the Reverend Jeremiah Evarts, secretary of the American Board of Commissioners for Foreign Missions, in Boston. The missionaries of the American Board had been prominent in the Cherokee nation and strongly supported the Indians in their refusal to move. Evarts, as the most articulate spokesman of the group, published a series of articles under the name "William Penn" in which he exhausted the arguments against Jackson and the Georgians. These articles appeared first in the *National Intelligencer* and then were circulated widely in book form.[48] Only in the final article, Number XXIV, did Evarts advert to the land in the West. He described it as prairie land, not as desert; and he questioned its suitableness for the Indians because of the lack of streams and timber. "The vast prairies of the west will ultimately be inhabited," he remarked. "But it would require all the wealth, the enterprise, and the energy, of Anglo-Americans, to make a prosperous settlement upon them." Because the land *was* habitable, however, Evarts argued that the removal plan would settle nothing permanently:

> Another removal will soon be necessary. If the emigrants become poor, and are transformed into vagabonds, it will be evidence enough, that no benevolent treatment can save them, and it will be said they may as well be driven beyond the Rocky Mountains at once. If they live comfortably, it will prove, that five times as many white people might live comfortably in their places. Twenty-five years hence, there will probably be 4,000,000 of our population west of the Mississippi, and fifty years hence not less than 15,000,000. By that time, the pressure upon the Indians will be much greater from the boundless prairies, which must ultimately be subdued and inhabited, than it would ever have been from the borders of the present Cherokee country.[49]

This was remarkable prescience. It is also a clear indication that Evarts did not think the Indians were being moved to a sterile wasteland.

What conclusion, then, is to be drawn about the relationship between the concept of the Great American Desert and Indian removal?

The idea of removal—that is, the exchange of lands in the East for lands in the West—originated in Jefferson's administration, when the

---

48. Jeremiah Evarts, *Essays on the Present Crisis in the Condition of the American Indians* (Boston: Perkins and Marvin, 1829).

49. Ibid., pp. 98. 100.

Louisiana Purchase made the scheme feasible. The plan then developed slowly. Removal treaties were signed from 1817 on, with the urgency for removal increasing as the desire of the whites for eastern lands increased. In the 1820s the agitation reached new heights because of the action of Georgia and other southern states to force the Indians from their land holdings in those states. The Cherokee action in adopting a new constitution, which emphasized their sovereignty within the state of Georgia, and the discovery of gold on the Indian lands brought matters to a head, and after some delay Congress in 1830 enacted legislation which provided the means for carrying out the removal policy that had been adopted by President Monroe and supported by his successor, John Quincy Adams. The adoption and speeding up of the program in the 1820s was occasioned by events in the East—not in the West. The idea of the great desert found in the reports of Long's explorations had nothing to do with the origin or the development of the removal policy.

When the time came to make definite allotments of land for the eastern Indians, considerable pains were taken to investigate the nature of the West in order to make sure that it offered suitable resources for the Indians. Delegations of the Indians were sent to look at the land for themselves before accepting the allotments. Sympathetic friends of the Indians who had firsthand contact with the region reported favorably on its suitability. Opponents of removal offered little criticism of the policy on the basis of giving the Indians poor land in return for what they relinquished in the East. Nowhere did Long's report enter into the discussion.[50]

Nor did the land allotted to the emigrating Indians *in fact* fall within the area generally conceived at the time to be an uninhabitable desert. If this was due to conscious policy, the idea that the Indians were deliberately disposed of in the desert loses all credibility. If this happened only by chance, because of lack of accurate knowledge about the West or because of failure to consider this aspect of the question at all, the officials who engineered removal cannot be accused of intentionally removing the Indians to a useless wilderness.

There is no doubt that the removal policy brought hardship and injustice to the Indians. The red men were forced to move from their cherished ancestral lands, to which their rights had been clearly guaranteed. But the removal plan was never a scheme to dump the Indians into the desolate wastes of the Great American Desert.

[50. See a reference to Long cited in Ronald N. Satz, *American Indian Policy in the Jacksonian Era* (Lincoln: University of Nebraska Press, 1975), p. 27.]

Plate I

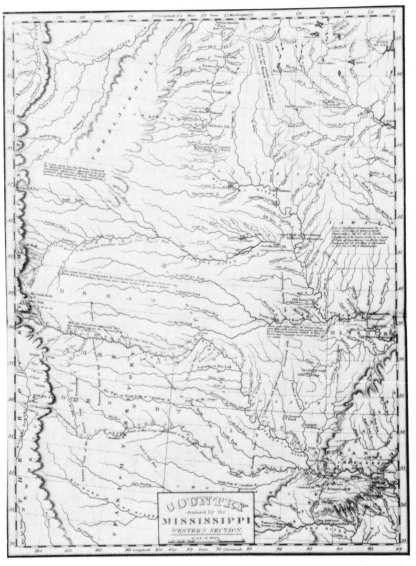

Plate II

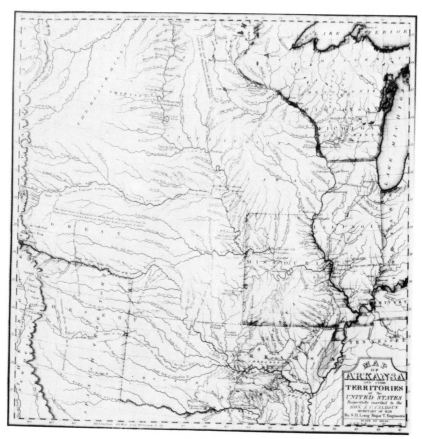

Lilly Library, Indiana University

Plate III

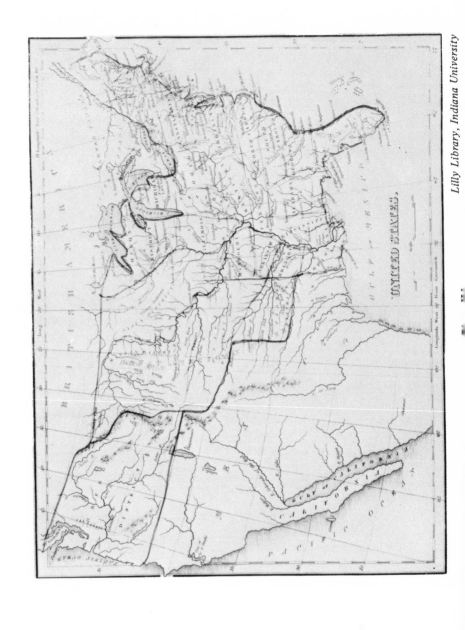

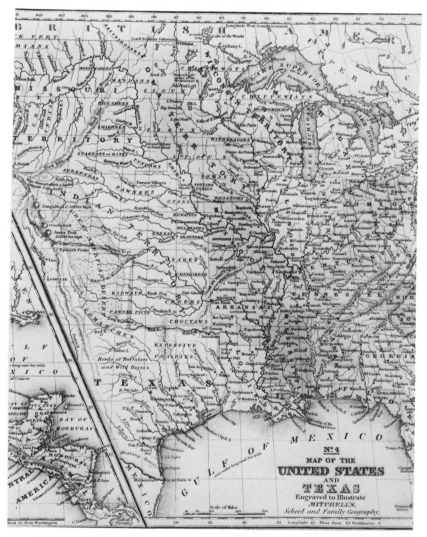

Plate V

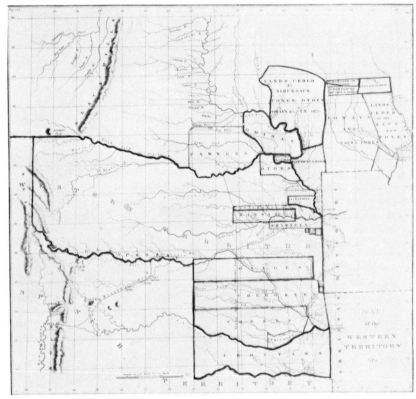

Plate VI

9

Thomas L. McKenney
and the New York Indian Board

Indian removal in the Jackson era was a national question that was greatly agitated by both pro- and anti-Jackson forces. One significant element in the controversy that has interested me a great deal was the strong position taken by religious men and societies, for such activity showed the tremendous impact that religious beliefs had—or sought to have—on public issues of the day. The religious opposition to removal was broadcast widely through the works of Jeremiah Evarts, secretary of the American Board of Commissioners for Foreign Missions, but much less attention has been paid to religious groups favoring removal. One of these was the New York Indian Board discussed in this essay.

I discovered that it was difficult, if not impossible, to separate the religious motivation behind preservation and improvement of the Indians through removal from political considerations and from the personal ambitions of Thomas L. McKenney, the force behind the Board. McKenney was a complicated character, about whom we have recently come to know a good deal, thanks in large part to the biography by Herman J. Viola, Thomas L. McKenney: Architect of America's Early Indian Policy, 1816–1830 *(Chicago: Swallow Press, 1974). The essay, I think, contributes to an understanding of the man and of the great complexity of the removal question.*

In the 1820s Indian affairs in the United States were reaching a crisis. The hope that had once been entertained for civilizing the aborigines and incorporating them into the main stream of American society had grown dim and in the minds of many had flickered out altogether. By 1825 President James Monroe was recommending removal of the

Printed source: *Mississippi Valley Historical Review* 48 (March 1962): 635-55.

Indians to the West as the only means of saving them from destruction.[1] From that date on the relative condition of the Indians worsened, the drive for clearing the eastern states of the tribes gained momentum, and politicians and the public began to turn the removal question into a factional dispute.

The conflict was clearest in Georgia, where the Cherokees clung tenaciously to their ancestral lands.[2] When the Cherokees sent a delegation to Washington in 1829 to complain about the encroachments of Georgia, President Andrew Jackson, who had long questioned the propriety of considering the Indian tribes as independent nations, gave them no encouragement. Jackson sided with the Georgians, who declared that they could not permit an *imperium in imperio* within their boundaries, and the hapless Cherokees were told bluntly by Secretary of War John H. Eaton that they could expect no succor from the federal government. Eaton urged the Cherokees to accept the inevitable and remove to the West, where questions of jurisdiction and sovereignty would no longer plague them and where the United States could firmly protect them without dangerous involvement in questions of state rights.[3]

Eaton's message to the Cherokees, a forthright statement of the Jacksonian position, was immediately challenged by northern humanitarians who came to the aid of the beleaguered Cherokees. Of these defenders of the Indians, the missionaries of the American Board of Commissioners for Foreign Missions were in the forefront. With headquarters in Boston, and largely Congregational and Presbyterian in

1. Message of January 27, 1825, James D. Richardson, comp., *A Compilation of the Messages and Papers of the Presidents, 1789–1897,* 10 vols. (Washington: Government Printing Office, 1896–99), 2:280–83.

2. For information on the Georgia-Cherokee controversy, see Annie H. Abel, "The History of Events Resulting in Indian Consolidation West of the Mississippi," *Annual Report of the American Historical Association for the Year 1906,* 2 vols. (Washington, 1908), 1:233–450; Charles C. Royce, "The Cherokee Nation of Indians: A Narrative of Their Official Relations with the Colonial and Federal Government," *Fifth Annual Report of the Bureau of Ethnology, 1883–1884* (Washington, 1887), pp. 121–378; Ulrich B. Phillips, "Georgia and State Rights: A Study of the Political History of Georgia from the Revolution to the Civil War, with Particular Regard to Federal Relations," *Annual Report of the American Historical Association for the Year 1901,* 2 vols. (Washington, 1902), 2:3–224; Thomas V. Parker, *The Cherokee Indians, with Special Reference to Their Relations with the United States Government* (New York: Grafton Press, 1907).

3. John H. Eaton to the Cherokee Delegation, April 18, 1829, Office of Indian Affairs, Letters Sent, vol. 5, pp. 408–12, National Archives, Record Group 75.

membership, this group had been active in establishing missionary schools among the Cherokees. Their school at Brainerd in southeastern Tennessee had been founded in 1817 and was the most flourishing of the Indian schools. When Congress in 1819 authorized an annual appropriation of $10,000 to support educational establishments among the Indians, the American Board became the largest beneficiary. By 1829 it had twenty-one schools among the Five Civilized Tribes, compared with seven for all other denominations combined, and zealous missionaries of the American Board like Samuel Worcester and Elizur Butler wielded great influence among the Cherokee leaders.[4]

When Georgia began to move in earnest against the Cherokees, the missionaries of the American Board sparked a great outcry. Using strongly moral and religious arguments, in keeping with the nature of the group, they defended the right of the Indians to stay unmolested on their lands.[5] The American Board spoke with knowledge and conviction, and as the crisis sharpened the Jackson administration realized that it could not afford to let all of the voices of religion and righteousness speak out against removal. The administration, too, must enlist a group of religious leaders to carry to the public the arguments of the Jackson party, under the aegis of humanity and justice and Christian concern for the Indian.

The instrument developed for the purpose by the Jacksonians was the Indian Board for the Emigration, Preservation, and Improvement of the Aborigines of America, formally organized in New York on July 22, 1829. The instigator and chief architect of the Indian Board was Thomas L. McKenney, who since 1824 had headed the Office of Indian Affairs within the War Department.

McKenney was perhaps the best informed man in the United States on Indian affairs. From 1816 to 1822 he had directed the operations of the government trading factories as superintendent of Indian trade, and he had used the office as a focus for Indian matters. His voluminous correspondence shows a deep and genuine concern for bettering the conditions of the Indians and protecting them in their rights. After his appointment to the Office of Indian Affairs he continued his

    4. Report of Thomas L. McKenney, November 17, 1829, *Senate Document* no. 1, 21st Cong., 1st sess., ser. 192, pp. 176–77.
    5. The opposition of the missionaries to removal had been noted for some time, and Secretary of War Peter B. Porter in his annual report of 1828 had inveighed against the missionaries for opposing the determined policy of the War Department. Report of the Secretary of War, November 24, 1828, *Senate Document* no. 1, 20th Cong., 2d sess., ser. 181, p. 22.

zealous work, ably handling the Indian business of the War Department and promoting Indian interests. McKenney looked with great hope upon the efforts undertaken by the government to civilize and educate the Indians and thus prepare them for entry into the white man's society. He shared and had outspokenly advanced the opinion that the Indians were making great forward strides. He liked to cite figures of increasing enrollments in Indian schools as sure evidence of the progress being made, and he accepted optimistically the glowing reports sent back by the missionaries. To him there seemed to be no doubt about the speedy incorporation of the Indians into the states and territories where they dwelt.[6]

But McKenney had changed his mind after an extensive tour of the frontier in 1827. What he had seen convinced him of the degradation of large numbers of Indians; and he could no longer believe in the imminence of their pulling abreast of the whites in civilization. Convinced that the survival of the Indians depended upon their separation from the whites, he joined those working for the removal of the Indians to the West—an emigration that was to be voluntary, though promoted and aided by the government, and to be followed up by protection of the Indians in their new home and new energetic steps to improve them there.[7]

Because of his conviction as to what the condition of the Indians demanded and his key government position, McKenney was an ideal man to enlist support for the Jacksonian removal program. He was, moreover, a man well received in church circles because of his own religious temperament and his long and active support of missionary activities among the Indians. At the same time, however, his position in the Jackson administration was not secure. He was known to have been an ardent supporter of John C. Calhoun, and he had received clear intimations of the president's opposition to him and of the offer of his position to other men; on his own admission it was only the active support of Secretary of War Eaton that kept him in office.[8] The enlistment of church support for removal at this critical juncture may well have seemed to McKenney an excellent opportunity to ingratiate

6. McKenney's position is fully expounded in Office of Indian Trade, Letters Sent, and Office of Indian Affairs, Letters Sent, National Archives, Record Group 75. See also Thomas L. McKenney, *Memoirs, Official and Personal* (New York: Paine and Burgess, 1846).

7. Report of McKenney, March 22, 1830, *Senate Document* no. 110, 21st Cong., 1st sess., ser. 193.

8. McKenney, *Memoirs,* pp. 206, 223.

himself more firmly with Eaton and perhaps with the President as well.

The precise origin of the plan to organize church support for the Jacksonian program is not clear. The proposal may have come from Jackson, or from Eaton, or from McKenney himself, but there is no doubt that the work was done by McKenney.[9] At an earlier date McKenney had hoped to persuade the American Board itself to declare in favor of a positive program for preserving the Indians. In a private letter of March 23, 1827, to Jeremiah Evarts, the secretary of the American Board, he pointed out the necessity of stirring Congress to action. "Every good man should interfere," he wrote, "and voices should be raised from every corner of the land where Justice and Humanity can be found to exist." McKenney recognized the necessity, furthermore, of stimulating the voices; his letter to Evarts was intended to engage him in the work of "collecting and embodying" the voice of the people. "To be effectual," he declared, "it must be general; & it must be loud." He proposed that Evarts use the existing organization of agents and local auxiliaries affiliated with the American Board to carry out the work and urged that memorials be sent to Congress from all parts of the country and that committees of respectable and influential men be sent to Washington to promote the matter with the members of Congress.[10] Although McKenney made his appeal as one Christian to another, leaving "politicks out of the question," he seemed unable to stir Evarts to the kind of action he desired, and the events of the following months ranged the two men on opposite sides of the removal question.

Rejected by the Congregationalists and Presbyterians of the American Board in Boston, McKenney turned next to the Episcopalians. To offset the influence of the Boston group, he appealed to Bishop John H. Hobart of New York.[11] What McKenney now had in mind, and what he outlined for the approval of the Bishop, was an association aimed

9. McKenney asserted in his *Memoirs* (pp. 224–25) that the Indian Board was the spontaneous work of the clergymen themselves, who merely turned to him for aid. The contemporary letters contradict such an interpretation.

10. McKenney to Jeremiah Evarts, March 23, 1827, Papers of the American Board of Commissioners for Foreign Missions, Houghton Library, Harvard University. Material from this collection is used with permission of the American Board.

11. McKenney to John H. Hobart, April 7, 1829, copy in Papers of the American Board of Commissioners for Foreign Missions. The quotations are from this text of the letter.

specifically and solely at the rescue of the Indians and the improvement of their condition, a group that would not be distracted from this work by concern for other projects such as foreign missions. He noted, he said, a prejudice in Congress and among the public against missionaries, whether foreign or domestic. "A union, then, of attempts to benefit the Indians, with either of those branches of Philanthropy, must tend to weaken the disposition in the public mind, which would otherwise be strong, and active (if rightly cherished) in favor of our Indians." The missionary groups, furthermore, it was believed, generally opposed the government's policy of emigration and hindered the government from adopting more active and energetic measures to aid the Indians.

McKenney proposed to Hobart the organization in New York of an association designed exclusively to promote "the security, preservation, and happiness of our Indians." The group should stand behind the government's policy of removal as the first step in saving the Indians and should stir up public opinion in support of the measure, sending committees to Washington to let Congress know what the will of the people really was. The association, furthermore, should make it its business to go among the Indians and persuade them of the wisdom of emigration, promising them an ever-enduring new home, protection, and assistance. If such a group could be organized, unconnected with other benevolent schemes, it could not fail to redeem the Indians, carry out the policy of the government, and satisfy the "ever restless wishes of several powerful states." If he were an emperor, McKenney declared, he would set aside a portion of country for the aborigines and there protect and improve them. This was a fanciful supposition, he admitted, but it was not necessary to be an emperor to accomplish the goal. There was a power at hand "greater than could be exerted even by the crown or the sceptre"—public opinion. And New York was the place to begin.

To his great disappointment, no active support was immediately forthcoming from Bishop Hobart. McKenney remained undaunted, however, and while continuing to hope that the Episcopalian clergymen in New York would eventually come to his side he turned to the Dutch Reformed Church. Here he found the cooperation he was seeking in the Reverend Eli Baldwin and a small group of clergy and laymen.

On May 21, 1829, with the permission and, presumably, the blessing of the Secretary of War, McKenney sent to Baldwin a copy of Eaton's address to the Cherokees and a copy of a long letter he himself had written to Jeremiah Evarts on May 1. In the letter to Evarts, McKenney had fired the opening round in his campaign, for it was less an attempt to convince Evarts than to make an open stand against the position of the American Board and its missionaries. The two documents contained in some detail the administration's position. Baldwin was to use them in his efforts to organize an association in New York which would have "for its exclusive object the colonization and preservation of our Indians." The arguments set forth in his letter to Evarts, McKenney hoped, would be enough to rouse into action the good people of New York.[12]

The position that McKenney was thus beginning to propagandize in earnest was summed up in three basic propositions. The first of these was an avowal that the states had the right to assert and exercise jurisdiction over the Indians within their limits and an explicit declaration that the federal government would not and could not interfere with the exercise of such authority. This was the stand Jackson and Eaton had taken in regard to the Cherokees in Georgia. The second was a strong conviction that the best interests of the Indians themselves required their removal beyond the Mississippi. There the Indians would be assigned suitable lands which would be guaranteed to them and on which they would be protected. The United States would furnish them the aid necessary to emigrate, to become established comfortably in their new home, and to improve their condition. The third was a solemn assurance that the removal would be voluntary. No force would be used, but every effort would be made to convince the Indians of their plight and to induce them to move.

McKenney was heartened by Baldwin's favorable response to his appeal and at the end of June outlined for him in more detail the action that was demanded. If Bishop Hobart declined to associate formally in the movement, the Dutch Reformed clergy must press forward without him, for a small beginning was all that was required. If a board could be set up, it would serve as a parent organization, in McKenney's vision. Other groups presenting their services to the President could then be referred to the parent board, and successive additions would be made, "until the power would be resistless, and carry all before it." At the end of his letter, McKenney urged Baldwin to present the plan again to Bishop Hobart. *"He is a host,"* McKenney concluded, "and your two Churches whether formally, or informally united, I would consider adequate to carry this great measure through.

12. McKenney to Eli Baldwin, May 21, 1829, Office of Indian Affairs, Letters Sent, vol. 5, pp. 439–40.

All this ought to be ripe before the meeting of the next Congress. There is no time to be lost."[13]

Baldwin, more hesitant in nature than the effusive McKenney and less sure of what needed to be done, got under way slowly. It was clear that not much would be accomplished without the active intervention of McKenney. There was hope of getting the support of General Stephen Van Rensselaer, perhaps the wealthiest and socially most prominent man in the state, but Baldwin was not sure that Van Rensselaer would attend the meetings of the group unless invited by McKenney himself. And for the meetings which Baldwin proposed to call—first "a small meeting of our most influential and pious Citizens" and then a larger public meeting at which a constitution might be adopted—McKenney's presence was considered indispensable. McKenney was asked, too, to outline the duties of the association to be formed. Things generally looked favorable, Baldwin reported to McKenney on July 7, "still I am by no means sanguine. Much depends upon your influence."[14]

McKenney did what he could to bolster Baldwin's resolve by complimenting him on his work and emphasizing its importance. He promised, also, to come to New York to take an active part in the proceedings as soon as he could get the permission of the Secretary of War to leave his office.[15] Meanwhile Baldwin went ahead in organizing his friends. On July 10, he and ten others—laymen and clergy of the Dutch Reformed Church—met "for the purpose of considering whether some measures cannot be adopted and pursued, for the salvation of the Indians within the United States." The letters of McKenney to Baldwin were read, as well as Eaton's address to the Cherokees, McKenney's letter to Evarts, and a letter from Van Rensselaer pledging his interest and support. The group adopted a resolution formally approving the administration's policy of removal as expressed in Eaton's address and appointed a committee (consisting of Baldwin, McKenney, and the Reverend Jacob Brodhead) to draw up a constitution.[16]

McKenney was well pleased with the progress and sent more words

13. McKenney to Baldwin, June 27, 1829, ibid., vol. 6, pp. 30–32.

14. Baldwin to McKenney, July 7, 1829, Office of Indian Affairs, Letters Received, Miscellaneous.

15. McKenney to Baldwin, July 9, 1829, Office of Indian Affairs, Letters Sent, vol. 6, pp. 45–46.

16. *Documents and Proceedings Relating to the Formation and Progress of a Board in the City of New York, for the Emigration, Preservation, and Improvement, of the Aborigines of America* (New York: Vanderpool and Cole, 1829), pp. 20–21; Baldwin to McKenney, July 11, 1829, Office of Indian Affairs, Letters Received, Miscellaneous.

of encouragement and more directions as to what he considered the work of the board to be, and soon he was on hand in New York to take a personal part in the organization and proceedings of the Indian Board.[17] On Sunday evening, July 19, he met with Baldwin and others at Baldwin's home and discussed with them the proposed association and constitution. He was careful to insist that "all that could be tortured into a resemblance of bigotry or sectarianism" be excluded from the constitution, so that the document would in no way sound partisan. He reported enthusiastically on the character of the men with whom he was dealing and emphasized to the Secretary of War—through whom, no doubt, he expected the word to reach the President—that the group was solidly behind Jackson. "I confess I never had such hopes of the Indians before," McKenney wrote after this first meeting. "I am utterly mistaken if this body of men (there are in it three churches— Dutch reformed—Episcopal—& Presbyterian) does not carry *all before it.*"[18]

On Wednesday evening, July 22, the Indian Board was formally organized and the constitution adopted. Stephen Van Rensselaer, although not present at the meeting, was elected president of the Board; five vice-presidents were chosen; and Eli Baldwin was named corresponding secretary.[19] The constitution itself was admirably short and to the point. Its preamble was a brief statement of the plight of the Indians in their present circumstances, coupled with the assertion that the only hope for their survival lay in removal. The official designation of the association was to be "The Indian Board, for the Emigration, Preservation, and Improvement of the Aborigines of America." The Board was to consist of not more than thirty acting members, one-half of whom were to be from New York City. Officers were provided for and provisions were made for filling vacancies in the Board. Authority was given the Board to elect honorary members, who were to have "the privileges of members, with the exception of a right to vote."

The core of the constitution lay in three articles which set forth the objects of the organization:

ARTICLE IV. This Board engages to afford to the emigrant Indians, all the necessary instruction in the arts of life, and in the duties of religion.

17. McKenney to Baldwin, July 13, 1829, Office of Indian Affairs, Letters Sent, vol. 6, pp. 46–48.
18. McKenney to John H. Eaton, Tuesday [July 21, 1829], Office of Indian Affairs, Letters Received, Miscellaneous.
19. *Documents and Proceedings,* pp. 21–24.

ARTICLE V. This Board is pledged to co-operate with the Federal Government of the United States, in its operations in Indian Affairs; and at no time to contravene its laws.

ARTICLE VI. This Association invite the citizens of the United States, without respect to sect or party, religious or political, to co-operate with them in this benevolent enterprise.[20]

McKenney's hand could be seen throughout. "The scheme rests entirely & in every part," he wrote to Eaton, "on the Govt policy, looking 1st to the *emigration*; 2d the *preservation,* & third the *improvement* of the Indians.* The study was to make it conform in all respects to the views of the Executive, fully concurring in the leading one, viz—*emigration* as being essential to the two last." To McKenney's mind, the Indian Board and its platform would satisfy everyone. The southern states would hail it because it promoted the removal of the Indians; the northern and eastern states would unite behind the scheme because they could not fail to be convinced that the Indians could not be preserved where they were. Conviction was supposed to come from reading Eaton's letter to the Cherokees, which McKenney hoped to see widely circulated. McKenney's optimistic tone in his letters to Eaton was symptomatic of his temperament but was perhaps intended as well to keep the administration solidly behind the venture. "These people are *resolved*," he concluded. "Nothing can turn them aside. They are tremendous in power, & look, to me, as if they could move the world. It is a body of great men—guided by virtue, & the good of man. I flatter myself when you shall see the entire proceedings you will look upon them in the light in which I see them."[21]

McKenney knew well that the removal measure was becoming a hot political question, but it was his hope that the Indian Board might appear to be above politics, with only the interests of the Indians at heart. As church-affiliated men, the members might be free from charges of partisan politics and thus gather universal support. Nevertheless, in his desire to impress Eaton and the President with the sterling character of the men who had gathered together to support removal, McKenney penned a special letter to Eaton, which he was careful to mark "Private." The nonpartisan purity of the enterprise, or at least of McKenney's part in it, was somewhat besmirched by this forthright admission:

20. Ibid., pp. 22–23.

21. McKenney to Eaton, Wednesday Evening [July 22, 1829], Office of Indian Affairs, Letters Received, Miscellaneous.

I think these *divines* are the most thorough going Jacksonites in the nation. I found myself in the midst of a hot-bed—and really, from considerations of policy, found it necessary, knowing their *object* to be pure, & to embrace only the rescue of the Indians, to suggest, for the sake of giving power to the undertaking, & relieving it from all liability of being *suspected* as being a political machine, that a general invitation should be worked up, & *in the constitution,* to *all* Citizens, without respect to *sects,* or *parties,* to unite &c. It was adopted. A merrier, or better tempered, or happier set of folks it would be hard to find.[22]

After the adoption of the constitution and the formal organization of the Indian Board, the work of the great cause could get started. But what was this work to be? Obviously, the Board was in no position to do anything to aid the emigration of the Indians directly; it had no suitable organization, no funds, no missionary personnel. Its first task and its fundamental purpose for being was to create, stimulate, and broadcast public opinion in favor of voluntary emigration. Since it could not do its work in the confines of Baldwin's study, it would now have to take its message to the public.

At a meeting on July 28, attended by fifteen men, preliminary steps were taken. First, a public meeting was set for August 5, to be held in the church of the Reverend Alexander McLeod, one of the Board's vice-presidents, at which McKenney would deliver an address. Second, the secretary was directed to prepare a memorial for presentation to Congress at its next session. Third, the secretary was instructed to send a copy of the constitution and an account of the origins and proceedings of the Board to President Jackson, soliciting his approval and cooperation.[23]

Before the public meeting could take place McKenney fell ill. Yet even from his sickbed he kept Eaton closely informed of the progress of events in New York. He wanted to make no move without step-by-step approval by the Secretary of War and veered dangerously close to sycophancy in his expressions of desire to do the Secretary's bidding. Despite postponement of the meeting to wait for McKenney's recovery, interest did not slacken. "There is a deep anxiety felt here," McKenney reported to Eaton, "and no inconsiderable anxiety is experienced to know the nature of this association & its objects; & to learn the *true*

22. Enclosure in letter cited in note 21.
23. *Documents and Proceedings,* pp. 24–25.

grounds of the policy discussed. Some appear to think the Executive means to *oppress* the Indians; some think one thing & some think another—& all think something."[24]

On August 12, after a week's delay, the public meeting was held with some six hundred persons present, according to McKenney's account, which may well have been an exaggeration. Baldwin himself reported: "The meeting was not large but the interest felt was manifest from the earnestness with which persons drew nearer to the stage, the better to hear the address, the Col's voice having lost some of its volume by his late indisposition." Before McKenney delivered his address—which ran for fifty minutes—Eaton's letter to the Cherokees and the constitution of the Indian Board were read to the assembly. McKenney's address restated his position and was delivered (as Baldwin noted) "in his usual style of elegance and perspicuity."[25] There can be little doubt that the audience got a clear picture of the position advanced by Eaton and Jackson and supported so eagerly by McKenney.

The next move was to get the hearing of a wider audience by distributing the address of McKenney and other pertinent documents in printed form. For the accomplishment of this objective, McKenney's continued presence in New York was essential, since he was the only one who had the whole matter in hand and who could intelligently correct the printer's proofs. Baldwin, moreover, had his parochial duties to perform, and the other members of the Board had scattered to carry on their everyday business. McKenney, who had intended to return to his office in Washington on Friday, August 14, asked Eaton for permission to stay until the proposed pamphlet was ready, for the Board was anxious in this first undertaking that "not a *jot* of any thing should be wrong." McKenney's enthusiasm had not been dampened. "*Every* thing looks encouraging," he told Eaton. "I doubt whether *any man,* after these matters get before the public, will have the hardihood to take ground against them. I think the blow is struck that will silence all opposers upon this branch of the clamors of the day."[26]

24. McKenney to Eaton, Monday [August 3, 1829], Office of Indian Affairs, Letters Received, Miscellaneous.

25. McKenney to Eaton, Thursday [August 13, 1829], ibid.; Baldwin to Eaton, August 14, 1829, ibid. McKenney's address is printed in *Documents and Proceedings,* pp. 28–43.

26. McKenney to Eaton, August 14, 1829, Office of Indian Affairs, Letters Received, Miscellaneous. Part of McKenney's enthusiasm came from his continuing expectation that other groups would flock to join the Dutch Reformed clergymen in the work of saving the Indians. He reported that the Moravians had pledged

There remained, however, one delicate matter to be taken care of: the payment for the printing and distribution of the Indian Board's pamphlet. To propagandize the principles and program of the Indian Board required money, and the Board had none. McKenney, who advised the printing of three thousand copies, again came to the rescue by calling upon the War Department to pick up the bill. "I have told the board," he advised the Secretary of War, "that I had no doubt you would aid them from the Civilization fund, (it being *legitimately* applicable to the object) in the preliminary, & *necessary* expenses attending its organization, & the publication of documents &c, in aid of civilization. I suppose 200$ will cover all. There is a plenty—perhaps 1000 dollars over the allotments for '29—which I kept to meet emergencies."[27]

Before releasing its pamphlet the Board desired a formal endorsement of the whole project from the President himself. Baldwin, on August 14, sent to Jackson a copy of the constitution of the Board and documents relating to its origin and its proceedings and asked meekly for the President's patronage.[28] In transmitting the papers to Eaton, who was to lay them before Jackson, McKenney was considerably more outspoken. He pressed Eaton for an immediate answer from the President directly (or from Eaton himself in the President's name) so that it might be included in the pamphlet. Nor did he hesitate to suggest what the President ought to say, insisting that a clear statement be issued which would silence the critics who feared that Jackson intended to drive the Indians out by force.[29]

Eaton replied in the name of the President on August 25 and expressed Jackson's gratification at the course pursued by the Indian

---

cooperation and he was sure the Methodists would join; the Baptists, he said, were "secured." The Baptists had been regular supporters of the policy of removal. It does not appear, however, that they or any of the other church groups took any formal part in the Indian Board.

27. McKenney to Eaton, August 14, 1829, and Baldwin to Eaton, August 14, 1829, Office of Indian Affairs, Letters Received, Miscellaneous. The $10,000 annual fund for civilizing the Indians was authorized in a law approved March 3, 1819. *United States Statutes at Large,* 3:516–17. The administration of the fund was included among McKenney's duties when Secretary of War John C. Calhoun set up the Bureau of Indian Affairs in 1824. *House Document* no. 146, 19th Cong., 1st sess., ser. 138, p. 6.

28. Baldwin to the President of the United States, August 14, 1829, *Documents and Proceedings,* pp. 44–45.

29. McKenney to Eaton, August 21, 1829, Office of Indian Affairs, Letters Sent, vol. 6, p. 70.

Board. After praising the Board for its principles of justice and humanity toward the Indians and making passing reference to the "many inaccuracies, both as to object and motive" which appeared in the public journals, he contributed an unequivocal statement on the use of force: "I beg leave to assure you, that nothing of a compulsory course, to effect the removal of this unfortunate race of people, has ever been thought of by the President, although it has been so asserted."[30]

With this endorsement of the Executive, the collection of documents was complete, and a forty-eight-page pamphlet entitled *Documents and Proceedings Relating to the Formation and Progress of a Board in the City of New York, for the Emigration, Preservation, and Improvement, of the Aborigines of America* was issued. It contained McKenney's letters to Baldwin of May 21 and to Evarts of May 1, Jackson's talk to the Creeks of March 23, Eaton's letter of April 18 to the Cherokees, McKenney's address of August 12, and Eaton's reply of August 25 to Baldwin, as well as minutes of the various meetings of the Board and certain routine correspondence. It was an important collection of documents and was the first comprehensive public expression of the administration's avowed policy in regard to Indian removal.

The reaction to the publication cannot be fully determined. Those who already sided with McKenney were of course happy with the pamphlet. Thus Heman Lincoln, secretary of a Baptist missionary association in Boston, wrote to congratulate McKenney on the New York address and to entreat him to come to Boston, where he could be sure of a most cordial reception.[31] In reply to Lincoln, McKenney penned another of his long epistles—the man seldom wrote a short letter—in which he expressed his hope that his exertions in aiding the Board would bear good fruit for the Indians. He emphasized the fact that he had acted in compliance with the wishes of Eaton and Jackson and that the proceedings of the Indian Board met the full approval of the President. He praised again the character of the men who made up the Board. "They are worthy of the cause; and the cause is worthy of them," he wrote. "And if any thing can convince the Indians as to what *is* best for them, in their present emergency, it must be to witness the efforts of *such* men, to save them. As wise men they see the cloud that hangs over our red Brothers, and have analized its elements, and

---

30. Eaton to Baldwin, August 25, 1829, *Documents and Proceedings,* pp. 45–48.

31. Heman Lincoln to McKenney, September 19, 1829, Office of Indian Affairs, Letters Received, Miscellaneous.

convinced of their destructive qualities, they as *good men* have come forward, voluntarily, without fee or reward, to advise and Counsel the Indians how to save themselves from the fury of the storm. Such disinterested benevolence, will not, it is hoped, be lost upon these people."[32]

Of singular importance was the use made of the *Documents and Proceedings* by Lewis Cass in an unsigned article which appeared in the *North American Review* in December 1829. Cass publicized the organization and work of the Indian Board and by summarizing, quoting, and paraphrasing at considerable length the main documents in the collection spread before a wide audience a favorable presentation of the administration's proposals.[33] Through Baldwin, McKenney was also able to publish in New York certain letters and documents which advanced the views of the Board. The New York *Evening Post,* a pro-Jackson paper, had published on June 19 the long letter of McKenney to Evarts, dated May 1; in the issue of October 7 it prominently displayed, with laudatory comments, the exchange of correspondence between Heman Lincoln and McKenney. The *Post* continued to support the Jackson policy and to print documents supplied to it by McKenney through Baldwin, who was identified by the papers as "a quarter of the highest respectability."

As the removal controversy waxed stronger, it became necessary for McKenney to refute publicly some of the charges made against his position. One such attack came from the *Cherokee Phoenix,* a newspaper published within the Cherokee Nation. The editors of the *Phoenix,* whose views were shared or reflected by the missionaries of the American Board of Commissioners for Foreign Missions, were far from favorable to McKenney's address to the Indian Board. One of the arguments for removal advanced by McKenney was that the great majority of the southern Indians were living in deplorable conditions and desired to emigrate in order to better their lot, but they were held back by threats and actual force by the few chiefs to whose advantage it was to stay in the East. The *Phoenix* took issue with McKenney on this point and flatly denied his assertion, declaring on the contrary that "the great body of the tribe are *not anxious to remove.*"[34] To forestall the spread of such arguments by his opponents, McKenney sent to Baldwin a

32. McKenney to Lincoln, September 28, 1829, Office of Indian Affairs, Letters Sent, vol. 6, pp. 97–101.
33. Lewis Cass, "Removal of the Indians," *North American Review* 30 (January 1830): 62–121.
34. *Evening Post* (New York), October 15, 1829.

number of documents from persons in the Indian territory that sub-
stantiated his assertions of the Indians' desire to emigrate and the use
of threats to stop those who wanted to go, and urged Baldwin to have
them published.[35] On October 15, these documents appeared in the
New York *Evening Post,* and more documents of the same nature
were published on November 5. When Cass's article appeared in the
North American Review, the *Post* extracted large sections of it for its
readers.[36]

There was, furthermore, an open controversy carried on by the New
York Indian Board against the writings and activities of Jeremiah
Evarts and the American Board of Commissioners for Foreign Missions.
A series of articles in the Washington *National Intelligencer,* written by
Evarts under the name "William Penn," had made much of the solemn
obligations assumed by the United States in its treaties with the Cherokees. Such arguments McKenney considered beside the point, since it
was then impossible for the Indians to live and prosper in contact with
the whites, no matter what ought to have been done in the past.[37] In
the middle of October, too, Baldwin reported to McKenney a meeting
of the American Board at Albany, at which the following resolution
was adopted: "The Committee feel bound, on this occasion, to declare,
that in their judgment, no Indians should be compelled to leave the
lands which they derived from their ancestors, of which they are in
peaceable possession, and which have been guaranteed to them by
solemn treaties." McKenney professed that he was "at a loss to com-
prehend the import, or bearing, of the resolution." He continued to
insist that there was no intention on the part of anyone—President,
Congress, or the people—to compel the Indians to remove. Every effort
would be made to convince the Indians that such a change was required, but if they could not be persuaded they would be left where
they were, no matter how dire the consequences.[38]

At a meeting of the New York Indian Board on October 22 a committee of seven men was appointed to carry the Board's memorial to

35. McKenney to Baldwin, October 8, 1829, Office of Indian Affairs, Letters
Sent, vol. 6, pp. 104–6.

36. *Evening Post* (New York), January 7, 9, 1830.

37. Jeremiah Evarts, *Essays on the Present Crisis in the Condition of the American Indians: First Published in the National Intelligencer, under the Signature of
William Penn* (Boston: Perkins and Marvin, 1829); McKenney to Lincoln, September 28, 1829, Office of Indian Affairs, Letters Sent, vol. 6, pp. 100–101.

38. Baldwin to McKenney, October 19, 1829, Office of Indian Affairs, Letters
Received, Miscellaneous; McKenney to Baldwin, October 23, 1829, Office of Indian Affairs, Letters Sent, vol. 6, p. 135.

Washington and to lobby for the removal plan with the members of
Congress. McKenney's views as to the best time to come were solicited,
and it was apparent that he was to be the guiding force in the whole
matter. More than that, Baldwin turned again to him for money to
sustain the operations of the Board. "May I assure the Committee," he
asked, "that their reasonable expenses will be paid?"[39] This request for
more financial aid was embarrassing to McKenney. He had sent the
Board funds for the publication of their pamphlet, but he could see no
way clear to assume more responsibility for the expenses of the Board,
which was supposed to appear before the public as an independent
group of religious men who had decided that the administration's program for the Indians was the only one that would serve the dictates
of justice and humanity. McKenney suggested instead that Baldwin
raise the money from the churches, in order to guard both the Indian
Board and the President from imputations which might be cast upon
them, especially since the other groups interested in the removal question bore their own expenses.[40]

A fundamental weakness of the Indian Board thus appeared. The
inherent enthusiasm of the members was not strong enough to sustain
much activity without the prodding and support of McKenney. Baldwin
replied to McKenney's suggestion: "It is impossible at the present stage
of our existence to appeal to the Churches for pecuniary aid with success, and the members of the Committee do not seem willing to give
their time, and bear their own expenses. It is therefore doubtful whether they will come on." Baldwin, however, was willing to make another
effort to collect funds if McKenney so advised.[41]

McKenney had termed the presence of the committee in Washington
"indispensable." The members should come as official bearers of the
memorial of the Board and arrive in the second or third week of the
congressional session. "First impressions are important," McKenney
insisted. "Others will be here, acting upon opposite principles. You
have a great work in hand—and great glory will attend your success."
But first the memorial had to be drawn up. This work, too, fell to Baldwin, who had no opportunity to consult with any of the members of
the Board on the subject. He relied, of course, on McKenney, sending

39. Baldwin to McKenney, October 22, 1829, Office of Indian Affairs, Letters
Received, Miscellaneous.
40. McKenney to Baldwin, October 27, 1829, Office of Indian Affairs, Letters
Sent, vol. 6, p. 138.
41. Baldwin to McKenney, November 26, 1829, Office of Indian Affairs, Letters Received, Miscellaneous.

him a rough draft of the memorial for his corrections. By the middle of February, Baldwin and three associates appeared in Washington with the memorial—at whose expense it is not possible to determine. They registered at a hotel on Pennsylvania Avenue and then called at McKenney's office. They expected to call on the chairmen of the congressional committees on Indian affairs, but their great dependence was still upon McKenney.[42]

The memorial of the Indian Board was presented in the House of Representatives on February 22, 1830, by Representative Campbell P. White, a Jackson Democrat from New York City, and in the Senate the following day by Senator Nathan Sanford, Democrat of New York.[43] It followed the customary form of such petitions, beginning with a highly rhetorical introduction which set forth the reasons for calling upon Congress:

> . . . the present degraded, scattered, and withering condition of our native Indians, is a matter of painful solicitude to the civilian, the philanthropist, and the Christian.
>
> Once they were numerous and independent; then the proud chief, with lofty crest and stately step, braved the Northern blast, and defied the foe; his spirit was buoyant as the wind, his soul was elevated, and his heart sincere. But, the subject of nameless misfortunes, his race has gone, or is now going, like the leaves of Autumn, and, we fear, without timely relief, will soon perish forever.

The solution called for, of course, was speedy and final removal. The memorial stated the desire of the Indian Board to cooperate in such a program and to afford instruction to the Indians; it repeated the invitation originally set forth in the Board's constitution to other citizens of the United States to join with it in promoting the plan; and it petitioned Congress for help in the form of necessary legislation.[44]

The presentation of the memorial was the last public act of the Board. The members of the committee hurried home to be about their personal duties, and instead of becoming the parent organization for a great public movement, gathering adherents from all parts of the country and carrying all before it, the Indian Board evaporated. The

42. McKenney to Baldwin, October 27, 1829, Office of Indian Affairs, Letters Sent, vol. 6, p. 138; Baldwin to McKenney, November 26, 1829, and Baldwin to McKenney, February 17, 1830, Office of Indian Affairs, Letters Received, Miscellaneous.

43. *House Journal,* 21st Cong., 1st sess., ser. 194, p. 322; *Senate Journal,* 21st Cong., 1st sess., ser. 191, p. 149.

44. *House Report* no. 233, 21st Cong., 1st sess., ser. 200.

American Board of Commissioners for Foreign Missions and other highly vocal opponents of removal became the voice of the churches on the Indian question.

Why did the New York Board fall apart? McKenney gave his own answer in his *Memoirs*. After describing in some detail the organization of the Indian Board and quoting the basic documents which displayed the purposes and policies of the organization, he continued: "The reader may feel anxious to know what were the fruits of the association, organized for these holy objects, and under such high auspices. I answer, *there were none!* So far as my knowledge extends, there went forth from that Board not a single influence towards the accomplishment of the great ends of its creation. It had being given to it, and life, but it was struck by paralysis!"[45] The paralysis McKenney had in mind was Jackson's determination to use force.

The question of compelling the Indians to move was a delicate one. The great argument of the opponents of the government policy was that removal meant removal by force, since the Indians did not wish to leave. McKenney had hoped to destroy such contentions by convincing the public that the use of force was no part of the administration's program. He himself reiterated the position again and again and he was sincerely attached to the principle. He would do anything he could to convince the Indians that their only salvation lay in emigration. "Seeing as I do the condition of these people," he said, "and that they are bordering on destruction, I would, were I empowered, take them *firmly* but *kindly* by the hand, and tell them they must go; and I would do this, on the same principle that I would take my own children by the hand, firmly, but kindly and lead them from a district of Country in which the plague was raging."[46] He would not force them to leave against their will. McKenney began to have doubts, however, about the convictions of Jackson and Eaton and the administration supporters in Congress on the point, and it was his contention in his *Memoirs* that when it became clear that the government would rely on force in removing the Indians, the foundations of the Indian Board gave way.[47]

McKenney's was an easy explanation, which put the blame on the Jackson administration and exonerated the Board. Actually, inherent weaknesses in the Board and its position consigned it to oblivion. With

45. McKenney, *Memoirs*, pp. 252–53.
46. McKenney to Baldwin, October 28, 1829, Office of Indian Affairs, Letters Sent, vol. 6, p. 140.
47. McKenney, *Memoirs*, p. 255.

the passage of the Indian Removal Act in May 1830, ostensibly the first purpose of the Board—the emigration of the Indians with government aid—had been realized. But the carrying out of the law might be accomplished by methods which the Board, if it was true to its principles, could not countenance. To continue to speak out in favor of removal was to place oneself in the Jackson camp and to fall under the opprobrium of the articulate groups which so roundly condemned the administration's actions. A supporter of the Indian Board had pictured the association in October 1829 as a middle voice between the extremists who declared that the Indians had no rights or title to their lands and could be harried out at will and the other extremists who wanted to "meet Georgia at the bayonet's point" if she dared to carry out her threats against the Indians.[48] This middle ground of seeking to persuade the Indians to exchange their territories voluntarily was less tenable after pressures began to be exerted on the Indians.

The secondary purposes of the Indian Board—to instruct the Indians in their new homes and to form a sort of parent group around which other supporters of the Indians could rally—were beyond the possibilities of the New York Board. The Board had no internal cohesion and no means to keep it viable. Its president, Van Rensselaer, was a mere figurehead who took no active part in either the organization or the proceedings of the group. The corresponding secretary, Baldwin, had his busy parochial duties to fill his time, while the other members of the association were dispersed and had responsibilities which made it impossible for them to devote the necessary time or energy to the Board. There was no personnel to devote time to the work of emigration, preservation, and improvement of the Indians. The bold promise of the Board's constitution "to afford to the emigrant Indians, all the necessary instruction in the arts of life, and in the duties of religion" was no more than a pious intention. Finances were neither provided for nor available.

The weaknesses of the New York Indian Board stand in vivid contrast to the strength of the American Board of Commissioners for Foreign Missions, which led the opposition. The American Board was a time-tested organization, with a full-time corresponding secretary to direct the world-wide missionary efforts of the group. It had a highly organized supporting structure of agents, associations, and auxiliaries in local congregations to gather funds and promote the work of the

48. *Magazine of the Reformed Dutch Church* (New Brunswick, N.J.) 4 (October 1829): 222.

parent organization, and it published its own *Missionary Herald*. Its missionaries were firsthand sources for data on conditions among the Indians. More important, the American Board and those who agreed with its stand on the Indian question advanced a policy which lent itself to an evangelical crusade. Their extreme position in support of Indian rights was dramatic and caught the attention and support of men and women in an age of religious and humanitarian ferment. Their demand for recognition of Indian rights took its place with agitation against the Sunday mails, the Sunday school movement, and proposals for temperance and for the colonization of the Negroes. The New York Indian Board could hardly have competed against such fervor with the best of organization.

It is clear, finally, that the Indian Board could not exist without McKenney. He was, after all, the father and inspiration of the association; without him it must inevitably disintegrate. After the passage of the Removal Act McKenney's interest in the Indian Board flagged, for he himself was hastening toward a break with Jackson. In his *Memoirs*, published in 1846 in justification of his career, McKenney emphasized his opposition to the use of force in Indian removal and strongly condemned the coercive actions of Jackson. His account points to the removal controversy as the cause of his break with the administration. There were probably more deep-seated causes, however, for McKenney as an ardent Calhoun supporter had incurred Jackson's suspicion if not enmity. His zealous initial promotion of Jackson's Indian policy through the Indian Board had failed to secure his position within the administration, and in August 1830, after expecting dismissal for many months, he finally received a curt note from the acting Secretary of War, informing him that his services were no longer required.[49] Cut off from all official relations with the government, McKenney severed his connections with the New York Indian Board, and with his withdrawal the Board collapsed.

49. P. G. Randoph to McKenney, August 16, 1830, Records of the Office of the Secretary of War, Letters Sent, Military Affairs, vol. 13, National Archives, Record Group 107; McKenney, *Memoirs*, pp. 255, 261–62.

10

Andrew Jackson's Indian Policy: A Reassessment

This essay was given as a paper at the meeting of the Organization of American Historians at Dallas in April 1968. The paper elicited a lively discussion from the floor; the remark I remember best came from a noted historian of the Jackson period, Edward Pessen, who said that the only conclusion he could reach after hearing the paper was that I meant it as satire. It was then that I came to realize for the first time the deep-seated antipathy toward Andrew Jackson that exists among many historians dealing with Indian policy.

My purpose in the paper was to examine the removal policy in the perspective of the times in which it was adopted. My goal was not to praise Jackson but to try to understand his endorsement of the policy. I hoped to do that in part by looking at the alternatives that might have been adopted as a solution to the Indian problem of the day, rather than to begin with the assumption that Jackson was an Indian-hater and an evil man. But even the hint of a reasonable word on Jackson's behalf was enough to cause great distress among some historians, an attitude of mind that prevented careful reading of what I had written. Edward Pessen is still unreconstructed (see the 1978 edition of his book Jacksonian America: Society, Personality, and Politics*), but I have received support for my position. At the very least, the essay has stirred up much discussion and, I believe, has forced other historians to take a more careful look at Andrew Jackson and Indian removal.*

A great many persons—not excluding some notable historians—have adopted a "devil theory" of American Indian policy. And in their demonic hierarchy Andrew Jackson has first place. He is depicted

Printed source: *Journal of American History* 56 (December 1969): 527–39.

primarily, if not exclusively, as a western frontiersman and famous Indian fighter, who was a zealous advocate of dispossessing the Indians and at heart an "Indian-hater." When he became President, the story goes, he made use of his new power, ruthlessly and at the point of a bayonet, to force the Indians from their ancestral homes in the East into desert lands west of the Mississippi, which were considered forever useless to the white man.[1]

This simplistic view of Jackson's Indian policy is unacceptable. It was not Jackson's aim to crush the Indians because, as an old Indian fighter, he hated Indians. Although his years in the West had brought him into frequent contact with the Indians, he by no means developed a doctrinaire anti-Indian attitude. Rather, as a military man, his dominant goal in the decades before he became President was to preserve the security and well-being of the United States and its Indian and white inhabitants. His military experience, indeed, gave him an overriding concern for the safety of the nation from foreign rather than internal enemies, and to some extent the anti-Indian sentiment that has been charged against Jackson in his early career was instead basically anti-British. Jackson, as his first biographer pointed out, had "many private reasons for disliking" Great Britain. "In her, he could trace the efficient cause, why, in early life, he had been left forlorn and wretched, without a single relation in the world."[2] His frontier experience, too, had convinced him that foreign agents were behind the raised tomahawks of the red men. In 1808, after a group of settlers had been killed by the Creeks, Jackson told his militia troops: "[T]his brings to our recollection the horrid barbarity committed on our frontier in 1777 under the influence of and by the orders of Great Britain, and it is presumable that the same influence has excited those barbarians to the late and recent acts of butchery and

---

1. Typical examples of this view are Oscar Handlin, *The History of the United States,* 2 vols. (New York: Holt, Rinehart and Winston, 1967–68), 1:455; T. Harry William, Richard N. Current, and Frank Freidel, *A History of the United States,* 2 vols. (New York: Alfred A. Knopf, 1964), 1:392; Thomas A. Bailey, *The American Pageant: A History of the Republic,* 3d ed. (Boston: D. C. Heath, 1966), p. 269; Dale Van Every, *Disinherited: The Lost Birthright of the American Indian* (New York: Morrow, 1966), p. 103; R. S. Cotterill, "Federal Indian Management in the South, 1789–1825," *Mississippi Valley Historical Review* 20 (December 1933): 347.

2. John H. Eaton, *The Life of Andrew Jackson, Major General in the Service of the United States: Comprising a History of the War in the South, from the Commencement of the Creek Campaign, to the Termination of Hostilities before New Orleans* (Philadelphia: M. Carey and Son, 1817), p. 18.

murder. . . .".[3] From that date on there is hardly a statement by Jackson about Indian dangers that does not aim sharp barbs at England. His reaction to the Battle of Tippecanoe was that the Indians had been "excited to war by the secrete agents of Great Britain."[4]

Jackson's war with the Creeks in 1813-14, which brought him his first national military fame, and his subsequent demands for a large cession of Creek lands were part of his concern for security in the West.[5] In 1815, when the Cherokees and Chickasaws gave up their overlapping claims to lands within the Creek cession, Jackson wrote with some exultation to Secretary of War James Monroe: "This Territory added to the creek cession, opens an avenue to the defence of the lower country, in a political point of view incalculable."[6] A few months later he added: "The sooner these lands are brought into markett, [the sooner] a permanant security will be given to what, I deem, the most important, as well as the most vulnarable part of the union. This country once settled, our fortifications of defence in the lower country compleated, all [E]urope will cease to look at it with an eye to conquest. There is no other point of the union (america united) that combined [E]urope can expect to invade with success."[7]

Jackson's plans with regard to the Indians in Florida were governed by similar principles of security. He wanted "to concentrate and locate the F[lorida] Indians at such a point as will promote their happiness and prosperity and at the same time, afford to that Territory a dense population between them and the ocean which will afford protection and peace to all."[8] On later occasions the same views were evident. When negotiations were under way with the southern Indians for removal, Jackson wrote: "[T]he chickasaw and choctaw country

3. *Correspondence of Andrew Jackson,* ed. John Spencer Bassett, 6 vols. (Washington: Carnegie Institution of Washington, 1926-35), 1:188.

4. Andrew Jackson to William Henry Harrison, November 30, 1811, ibid., p. 210. See also Jackson to James Winchester, November 28, 1811; Jackson to Willie Blount, June 4, July 10, and December 21, 1812; Jackson to Thomas Pinckney, May 18, 1814, ibid., 1:209, 226, 231-32, 250; 2:3-4.

5. For the part played by the desire for defense and security in the Treaty of Fort Jackson, see Jackson to Pinckney, May 18, 1814, ibid., 2:2-3, and Eaton, *Life of Jackson,* pp. 183-87. Eaton's biography can be taken as representing Jackson's views.

6. Jackson to James Monroe, October 23, 1816, *Correspondence,* 2:261.

7. Jackson to Monroe, January 6, 1817, ibid., p. 272. See also Jackson to Monroe, March 4, 1817, ibid., pp. 277-78.

8. Jackson to John C. Calhoun, August 1823, ibid., 3:202. See also Jackson's talk with Indian chieftains, September 20, 1821, ibid., p. 118.

are of great importance to us in the defence of the lower country[;] a white population instead of the Indian, would strengthen our own defence much." And again: "This section of country is of great importance to the prosperity and strength of the lower Mississippi[;] a dense white population would add much to its safety in a state of war, and it ought to be obtained, if it can, on any thing like reasonable terms."[9]

In his direct dealings with the Indians, Jackson insisted on justice toward both hostile and peaceful Indians. Those who committed outrages against the whites were to be summarily punished, but the rights of friendly Indians were to be protected. Too much of Jackson's reputation in Indian matters has been based on the first of these positions. Forthright and hard-hitting, he adopted a no-nonsense policy toward hostile Indians that endeared him to the frontiersmen. For example, when a white woman was taken captive by the Creeks, he declared: "With such arms and supplies as I can obtain I shall penetrate the creek Towns, untill the Captive, with her Captors are delivered up, and think myself Justifiable, in laying waste their villiages, burning their houses, killing their warriors and leading into Captivity their wives and children, untill I do obtain a surrender of the Captive, and the Captors."[10] In his general orders to the Tennessee militia after he received news of the Fort Mims massacre, he called for "retaliatory vengeance" against the "inhuman blood thirsty barbarians."[11] He could speak of the "lex taliones,"[12] and his aggressive campaign against the Creeks and his escapade in Florida in the First Seminole War are further indications of his mood.

But he matched this attitude with one of justice and fairness, and he was firm in upholding the rights of the Indians who lived peaceably in friendship with the Americans. One of his first official acts as major general of the Tennessee militia was to insist on the punishment of a militia officer who instigated or at least permitted the murder of an Indian.[13] On another occasion, when a group of Tennessee volunteers robbed a friendly Cherokee, Jackson's wrath burst forth: "that a sett of men should without any authority rob a man who is claimed as a

9. Jackson to John Coffee, August 20, 1826; Jackson to Coffee, September 2, 1826, ibid., p. 310, 312. See also Fred L. Israel, ed., *The State of the Union Messages of the Presidents, 1790-1966,* 3 vols. (New York: Chelsea House, 1966), 1:334.

10. Jackson to Blount, July 3, 1812, *Correspondence,* 1:230.

11. General Orders, September 19, 1813, ibid., pp. 319-20.

12. Jackson to David Holmes, April 18, 1814, ibid., p. 505.

13. Jackson to Colonel McKinney, May 10, 1802, ibid., p. 62.

member of the Cherokee nation, who is now friendly and engaged with us in a war against the hostile creeks, is such an outrage, to the rules of war, the laws of nations and of civil society, and well calculated to sower the minds of the whole nation against the united States, and is such as ought to meet with the frowns of every good citizen, and the agents be promptly prosecuted and punished as robers." It was, he said, as much theft as though the property had been stolen from a white citizen. He demanded an inquiry in order to determine whether any commissioned officers had been present or had had any knowledge of this "atrocious act," and he wanted the officers immediately arrested, tried by court-martial, and then turned over to the civil authority.[14]

Again, during the Seminole War, when Georgia troops attacked a village of friendly Indians, Jackson excoriated the governor for "the base, cowardly and inhuman attack, on the old woman [women] and men of the chehaw village, whilst the Warriors of that *village* was with me, fighting the battles of our *country* against the common enemy." It was strange, he said, "that there could exist within the U. States, a cowardly monster in human shape, that could violate the sanctity of a flag, when borne by any person, but more particularly when in the hands of a superanuated Indian chief worn down with age. Such base cowardice and murderous conduct as this transaction affords, has not its paralel in history and should meet with its merited punishment." Jackson ordered the arrest of the officer who was responsible and declared: "This act will to the last ages fix a stain upon the character of Georgia."[15]

Jackson's action as commander of the Division of the South in removing white squatters from Indian lands is another proof that he was not oblivious to Indian rights. When the Indian Agent Return J. Meigs in 1820 requested military assistance in removing intruders on Cherokee lands, Jackson ordered a detachment of twenty men under a lieutenant to aid in the removal. After learning that the officer detailed for the duty was "young and inexperienced," he sent his own aide-de-camp, Captain Richard K. Call, to assume command of the troops and execute the order of removal.[16] "Captain Call informs me," he wrote in one report to Secretary of War John C. Calhoun, "that much noise of opposition was threatened, and men collected for the

14. Jackson to John Cocke, December 28, 1813, ibid., p. 415.
15. Jackson to Governor of Georgia, May 7, 1818, ibid., 2:369–70.
16. Jackson to Calhoun, July 9, 1820, ibid., 3:29. See also Jackson's notice to the intruders, ibid., p. 26n.

purpose who seperated on the approach of the regulars, but who threaten to destroy the cherokees in the Valley as soon as these Troops are gone. Capt. Call has addressed a letter to those infatuated people, with assurance of speedy and exemplary punishment if they should attempt to carry their threats into execution." Later he wrote that Call had performed his duties "with both judgement, and prudence and much to the interest of the Cherokee-Nation" and that the action would "have the effect in future of preventing the infraction of our Treaties with that Nation."[17]

To call Jackson an Indian-hater or to declare that he believed that "the only good Indian is a dead Indian" is to speak in terms that had little meaning to Jackson.[18] It is true, of course, that he did not consider the Indians to be noble savages. He had, for example, a generally uncomplimentary view of their motivation, and he argued that it was necessary to operate upon their fears, rather than on some higher motive. Thus, in 1812 he wrote: "I believe self interest and self preservation the most predominant passion. [F]ear is better than love with an indian."[19] Twenty-five years later, just after he left the presidency, the same theme recurred; and he wrote: "long experience satisfies me that they are only to be well governed by their fears. If we feed their avarice we accelerate the causes of their destruction. By a prudent exertion of our military power we may yet do something to alleviate their condition at the same time that we certainly take from them the means of injury to our frontier."[20]

Yet Jackson did not hold that Indians were inherently evil or inferior. He eagerly used Indian allies, personally liked and respected individual Indian chiefs, and when (in the Creek campaign) an orphaned Indian boy was about to be killed by Indians upon whom his care would fall, generously took care of the child and sent him home to Mrs. Jackson to be raised with his son Andrew.[21] Jackson was convinced that the barbaric state in which he encountered most Indians had to

17. Jackson to Calhoun, July 26, September 15, 1820, ibid., pp. 30–31, 31n.

18. Note this recent statement: "President Jackson, himself a veteran Indian fighter, wasted little sympathy on the paint-bedaubed 'varmints.' He accepted fully the brutal creed of his fellow Westerners that 'the only good Indian is a dead Indian.'" Bailey, *American Pageant*, p. 269.

19. Jackson to Blount, June 17, 1812, *Correspondence*, 1:227–28.

20. Jackson to Joel R. Poinsett, August 27, 1837, ibid., 5:507.

21. See Jackson to Mrs. Jackson, December 19, 1813, ibid., 1:400–401; Eaton, *Life of Jackson*, pp. 395–96.

change, but he was also convinced that the change was possible and to an extent inevitable if the Indians were to survive.

Much of Jackson's opinion about the status of the Indians was governed by his firm conviction that they did not constitute sovereign nations, who could be dealt with in formal treaties as though they were foreign powers. That the United States in fact did so, Jackson argued, was a historical fact which resulted from the feeble position of the new American government when it first faced the Indians during and immediately after the Revolution. To continue to deal with the Indians in this fashion, when the power of the United States no longer made it necessary, was to Jackson's mind absurd. It was high time, he said in 1820, to do away with the "farce of treating with Indian tribes." [22] Jackson wanted Congress to legislate for the Indians as it did for white Americans.

From this view of the limited political status of the Indians within the territorial United States, Jackson derived two important corollaries. One denied that the Indians had absolute title to all the lands that they claimed. The United States, in justice, should allow the Indians ample lands for their support, but Jackson did not believe that they were entitled to more. He denied any right of domain and ridiculed the Indian claims to "tracts of country on which they have neither dwelt nor made improvements, merely because they have seen them from the mountain or passed them in the chase." [23]

A second corollary of equal import was Jackson's opinion that the Indians could not establish independent enclaves (exercising full political sovereignty) within the United States or within any of the individual states. If their proper status was as subjects of the United States, then they should be obliged to submit to American laws. Jackson had reached this conclusion early in his career, but his classic statement appeared in his first annual message to Congress, at a time when the conflict between the Cherokees and the State of Georgia had reached crisis proportions. "If the General Government is not permitted to tolerate the erection of a confederate State within the territory of one of the members of this Union against her consent," he said, "much less could it allow a foreign and independent government to establish itself there." He announced that he had told the Indians that "their attempt

22. Jackson to Calhoun, September 2, 1820, *Correspondence,* 3:31–32. See also Jackson to John Quincy Adams, October 6, 1821, and Jackson to Calhoun, September 17, 1821, *American State Papers: Miscellaneous,* 2:909, 911–12.

23. Israel, *State of the Union Messages,* 1:310. See also Jackson to Isaac Shelby, August 11, 1818, *Correspondence,* 2:388.

to establish an independent government would not be countenanced by the Executive of the United States, and advised them to emigrate beyond the Mississippi or submit to the laws of those States."[24] I have been unable to perceive any sufficient reason," Jackson affirmed, "why the Red man more than the white, may claim exemption from the municipal laws of the state within which they reside; and governed by that belief, I have so declared and so acted."[25]

Jackson's own draft of this first annual message presents a more personal view than the final public version and gives some insight into his reasoning. He wrote:

The policy of the government has been gradually to open to them the ways of civilisation; and from their wandering habits, to entice them to a course of life calculated to present fairer prospects of comfort and happiness. To effect this a system should be devised for their benefit, kind and liberal, and gradually to be enlarged as they may evince a capability to enjoy it. It will not answer to encourage them to the idea of exclusive self government. It is impracticable. No people were ever free, or capable of forming and carrying into execution a social compact for themselves until education and intelligence was first introduced. There are with those tribes, a few educated and well informed men, possessing mind and Judgment, and capable of conducting public affairs to advantage; but observation proves that the great body of the southern tribes of Indians, are erratic in their habits, and wanting in those endowments, which are suited to a people who would direct themselves, and under it be happy and prosperous.[26]

Jackson was convinced, from his observation of the political incompetence of the general run of Indians, that the treaty system played into the hands of the chiefs and their white and half-breed advisers to the detriment of the common Indians. He said on one occasion that such leaders "are like some of our bawling politicians, who loudly

24. Israel, *State of the Union Messages,* 1:308–9. Jackson dealt at length with this question in his message to the Senate, February 22, 1831. James D. Richardson, comp., *A Compilation of the Messages and Papers of the Presidents,* 10 vols. (Washington: Government Printing Office, 1896–99), 2:536–41. See also Jackson to Secretary of War [1831?], *Correspondence,* 4:219–20.

25. Draft of Second Annual Message, series 8, vol. 174, nos. 1409–10, Andrew Jackson Papers, Library of Congress. This statement does not appear in the final version.

26. Draft of First Annual Message, December 8, 1829, *Correspondence,* 4: 103–4.

exclaim we are the friends of the people, but who, when the[y] obtain their views care no more for the happiness or wellfare of the people than the Devil does—but each procure[s] influence through the same channell and for the same base purpose, *self-agrandisement.* "[27]

Jackson was genuinely concerned for the well-being of the Indians and for their civilization. Although his critics would scoff at the idea of placing him on the roll of the humanitarians, his assertions—both public and private—add up to a consistent belief that the Indians were capable of accepting white civilization, the hope that they would eventually do so, and repeated efforts to take measures that would make the change possible and even speed it along.

His vision appears in the proclamation delivered to his victorious troops in April 1814, after the Battle of Horseshoe Bend on the Tallapoosa River. "The fiends of the Tallapoosa will no longer murder our Women and Children, or disturb the quiet of our borders," he declared. "Their midnight flambeaux will no more illumine their Council house, or shine upon the victim of their infernal orgies. They have disappeared from the face of the Earth. In their places a new generation will arise who will know their duties better. The weapons of warefare will be exchanged for the utensils of husbandry; and the wilderness which now withers in sterility and seems to mourn the disolation which overspreads it, will blossom as the rose, and become the nursery of the arts."[28]

The removal policy, begun long before Jackson's presidency but wholeheartedly adopted by him, was the culmination of these views. Jackson looked upon removal as a means of protecting the process of civilization, as well as of providing land for white settlers, security from foreign invasion, and a quieting of the clamors of Georgia against the federal government. This view is too pervasive in Jackson's thought to be dismissed as polite rationalization for avaricious white aggrandizement. His outlook was essentially Jeffersonian. Jackson envisaged the transition from a hunting society to a settled agricultural society, a process that would make it possible for the Indians to exist with a higher scale of living on less land, and which would make it possible for those who adopted white ways to be quietly absorbed into the white society. Those who wished to preserve their identity in Indian

27. Jackson to Robert Butler, June 21, 1817, ibid., 2:299. See also Jackson to Coffee, June 21, 1817, and U.S. Commissioners to Secretary Graham, July 8, 1817, ibid., pp. 198, 300.

28. Proclamation, April 2, 1814, ibid., 1:494.

nations could do it only by withdrawing from the economic and political pressures exerted upon their enclaves by the dominant white settlers. West of the Mississippi they might move at their own pace toward civilization.[29]

Evaluation of Jackson's policy must be made in the light of the feasible alternatives available to men of his time. The removal program cannot be judged simply as a land grab to satisfy the President's western and southern constituents. The Indian problem that Jackson faced was complex, and various solutions were proposed. There were, in fact, four possibilities.

First, the Indians could simply have been destroyed. They could have been killed in war, mercilessly hounded out of their settlements, or pushed west off the land by brute force, until they were destroyed by disease or starvation. It is not too harsh a judgment to say that this was implicitly, if not explicitly, the policy of many of the aggressive frontiersmen. But it was not the policy, implicit or explicit, of Jackson and the responsible government officials in his administration or of those preceding or following his. It would be easy to compile an anthology of statements of horror on the part of government officials toward any such approach to the solution of the Indian problem.

Second, the Indians could have been rapidly assimilated into white society. It is now clear that this was not a feasible solution. Indian culture has a viability that continually impresses anthropologists, and to become white men was not the goal of the Indians. But many important and learned men of the day thought that this was a possibility. Some were so sanguine as to hope that within one generation the Indians could be taught the white man's ways and that, once they learned them, they would automatically desire to turn to that sort of life. Thomas Jefferson never tired of telling the Indians of the advantages of farming over hunting, and the chief purpose of schools was to train the Indian children in white ways, thereby making them immediately absorbable into the dominant culture. This solution was at first the hope of humanitarians who had the interest of the Indians at heart, but little by little many came to agree with Jackson that this dream was not going to be fulfilled.

Third, if the Indians were not to be destroyed and if they could not be immediately assimilated, they might be protected in their own culture on their ancestral lands in the East—or, at least, on reasonably large remnants of those lands. They would then be enclaves within the

29. Israel, *State of the Union Messages,* 1:310, 335, 354, 386–87.

white society and would be protected by their treaty agreements and by military force. This was the alternative demanded by the opponents of Jackson's removal bill—for example, the missionaries of the American Board of Commissioners for Foreign Missions. But this, too, was infeasible, given the political and military conditions of the United States at the time. The federal government could not have provided a standing army of sufficient strength to protect the enclaves of Indian territory from the encroachments of the whites. Jackson could not withstand Georgia's demands for the end of the *imperium in imperio* represented by the Cherokee Nation and its new constitution, not because of some inherent immorality on his part but because the political situation of America would not permit it.

The jurisdictional dispute cannot be easily dismissed. Were the Indian tribes independent nations? The question received its legal answer in John Marshall's decision in *Cherokee Nation v. Georgia,* in which the chief justice defined the Indian tribes as "dependent domestic nations." But aside from the juridical decision, were the Indians, in fact, independent, and could they have maintained their independence without the support—political and military—of the federal government? The answer, clearly, is no, as writers at the time pointed out. The federal government could have stood firm in defense of the Indian nations against Georgia, but this would have brought it into head-on collision with a state, which insisted that its sovereignty was being impinged upon by the Cherokees.

This was not a conflict that anyone in the federal government wanted. President Monroe had been slow to give in to the demands of the Georgians. He had refused to be panicked into hasty action before he had considered all the possibilities. But eventually he became convinced that a stubborn resistance to the southern states would solve nothing, and from that point on he and his successors, John Quincy Adams and Jackson, sought to solve the problem by removing the cause. They wanted the Indians to be placed in some area where the problem of federal versus state jurisdiction would not arise, where the Indians could be granted land in fee simple by the federal government and not have to worry about what some state thought were its rights and prerogatives.[30]

30. For the development of the removal idea, see Annie Heloise Abel, "The History of Events Resulting in Indian Consolidation West of the Mississippi," *Annual Report of the American Historical Association for the Year 1906,* 2 vols. (Washington, 1908), 1:233–450; Francis Paul Prucha, *American Indian Policy in the Formative Years: The Indian Trade and Intercourse Acts, 1790–1834* (Cambridge: Harvard University Press, 1962), pp. 224–49.

The fourth and final possibility, then, was removal. To Jackson this seemed the only answer. Since neither adequate protection nor quick assimilation of the Indians was possible, it seemed reasonable and necessary to move the Indians to some area where they would not be disturbed by federal-state jurisdictional disputes or by encroachments of white settlers, where they could develop on the road to civilization at their own pace, or, if they so desired, preserve their own culture.

To ease the removal process Jackson proposed what he repeatedly described as—and believed to be—*liberal* terms. He again and again urged the commissioners who made treaties to pay the Indians well for their lands, to make sure that the Indians understood that the government would pay the costs of removal and help them get established in their new homes, to make provision for the Indians to examine the lands in the West and to agree to accept them before they were allocated.[31] When he read the treaty negotiated with the Chickasaws in 1832, he wrote to his old friend General John Coffee, one of the commissioners: "I think it is a good one, and surely the religious enthusiasts, or those who have been weeping over the oppression of the Indians will not find fault with it for want of liberality or justice to the Indians."[32] Typical of his views was his letter to Captain James Gadsden in 1829:

> You may rest assured that I shall adhere to the just and humane policy towards the Indians which I have commenced. In this spirit I have recommended them to quit their possessions on this side of the Mississippi, and go to a country to the west where there is every probability that they will always be free from the mercenary influence of White men, and undisturbed by the local authority of the states: Under such circumstances the General Government can exercise a parental control over their interests and possibly perpetuate their race.[33]

The idea of parental or paternal care was pervasive. Jackson told Congress in a special message in February 1832: "Being more and more convinced that the destiny of the Indians within the settled portion of the United States depends upon their entire and speedy migration to the country west of the Mississippi set apart for their permanent residence, I am anxious that all the arrangements necessary to the complete execution of the plan of removal and to the ultimate security and

31. See, for example, Jackson to Coffee [September 1826?], *Correspondence*, 3:315–16.
32. Jackson to Coffee, November 6, 1832, ibid., 4:483.
33. Jackson to James Gadsden, October 12, 1829, ibid., p. 81.

improvement of the Indians should be made without further delay."
Once removal was accomplished, "there would then be no question of
jurisdiction to prevent the Government from exercising such a general
control over their affairs as may be essential to their interest and
safety."[34]

Jackson, in fact, thought in terms of a confederacy of the southern
Indians in the West, developing their own territorial government which
should be on a par with the territories of the whites and eventually
take its place in the Union.[35] This aspect of the removal policy, because
it was not fully implemented, has been largely forgotten.

In the bills reported in 1834 for the reorganization of Indian affairs
there was, in addition to a new trade and intercourse act and an act
for the reorganization of the Indian Office, a bill "for the establishment
of the Western Territory, and for the security and protection of the
emigrant and other Indian tribes therein." This was quashed, not by
western interests who might be considered hostile to the Indians, but
by men like John Quincy Adams, who did not like the technical details
of the bill and who feared loss of eastern power and prestige by the
admission of territories in the West.[36]

Jackson continued to urge Congress to fulfill its obligations to the
Indians who had removed. In his eighth annual message, in December
1836, he called attention "to the importance of providing a well-
digested and comprehensive system for the protection, supervision, and
improvement of the various tribes now planted in the Indian country."
He strongly backed the suggestions of the Commissioner of Indian
Affairs and the Secretary of War for developing a confederated Indian
government in the West and for establishing military posts in the Indian country to protect the tribes. "The best hopes of humanity in
regard to the aboriginal race, the welfare of our rapidly extending
settlements, and the honor of the United States," he said, "are all
deeply involved in the relations existing between this Government
and the emigrating tribes."[37]

Jackson's Indian policy occasioned great debate and great opposition
during his administration. This is not to be wondered at. The "Indian
problem" was a complicated and emotion-filled subject, and it called
forth tremendous efforts on behalf of the Indians by some missionary

34. Richardson, *Messages and Papers*, 2:565–66.
35. Jackson to Coffee, February 19, 1832, and Jackson to John D. Terrill,
July 29, 1826, *Correspondence*, 4:406, 3:308–9.
36. Prucha, *American Indian Policy in the Formative Years*, pp. 269–73.
37. Israel, *State of the Union Messages*, 1:465–66.

groups and other humanitarians, who spoke loudly about Indian rights. The issue also became a party one.

The hue and cry raised against removal in Jackson's administration should not be misinterpreted. At the urging of the American Board of Commissioners for Foreign Missions, hundreds of church groups deluged Congress with memorials condemning the removal policy as a violation of Indian rights; and Jeremiah Evarts, the secretary of the Board, wrote a notable series of essays under the name "William Penn," which asserted that the original treaties must be maintained.[38] It is not without interest that such opposition was centered in areas that were politically hostile to Jackson. There were equally sincere and humanitarian voices speaking out in support of removal, and they were supported by men such as Thomas L. McKenney, head of the Indian Office; William Clark, superintendent of Indian affairs at St. Louis; Lewis Cass, who had served on the frontier for eighteen years as governor of Michigan Territory; and the Baptist missionary Isaac McCoy—all men with long experience in Indian relations and deep sympathy for the Indians.

Jackson himself had no doubt that his policy was in the best interests of the Indians. "Toward this race of people I entertain the kindest feelings," he told the Senate in 1831, "and am not sensible that the views which I have taken of their true interests are less favorable to them than those which oppose their emigration to the West."[39] The policy of rescuing the Indians from the evil effects of too-close contact with white civilization, so that in the end they too might become civilized, received a final benediction in Jackson's last message to the American people—his "Farewell Address" of March 4, 1837. "The States which had so long been retarded in their improvement by the Indian tribes residing in the midst of them are at length relieved from the evil," he said, "and this unhappy race—the original dwellers in our land—are now placed in a situation where we may well hope that they will share in the blessings of civilization and be saved from that degradation and destruction to which they were rapidly hastening while they

38. See the indexes to the *House Journal,* 21st Cong., 1st sess., ser. 194, pp. 897–98, and the *Senate Journal,* 21st Cong., 1st sess., ser. 191, p. 534, for the presentation of the memorials. Some of the memorials were ordered printed and appear in the serial set of congressional documents. Jeremiah Evarts's essays were published in book form as *Essays on the Present Crisis in the Condition of the American Indians; First Published in the National Intelligencer, Under the Signature of William Penn* (Boston: Perkins and Marvin, 1829).

39. Richardson, *Messages and Papers,* 2:541.

remained in the States; and while the safety and comfort of our own citizens have been greatly promoted by their removal, the philanthropist will rejoice that the remnant of that ill-fated race has been at length placed beyond the reach of injury or oppression, and that the paternal care of the General Government will hereafter watch over them and protect them."[40]

In assessing Jackson's Indian policy, historians must not listen too eagerly to Jackson's political opponents or to less-than-disinterested missionaries. Jackson's contemporary critics and the historians who have accepted their arguments have certainly been too harsh, if not, indeed, quite wrong.

40. Ibid., 3:294. See the discussion in John William Ward, *Andrew Jackson: Symbol for an Age* (New York: Oxford University Press, 1955), pp. 40–41.

11

American Indian Policy in the 1840s: Visions of Reform

It had been suggested by Reginald Horsman ("American Indian Policy and the Origins of Manifest Destiny," University of Birmingham Historical Journal 11 [December 1968]: 128–40) that Indian policy in the early nineteenth century was in a sense a dress rehearsal for the Manifest Destiny that came into full flower in the 1840s. That idea intrigued me, and I undertook an investigation of what the federal government was doing in Indian affairs in that crucial decade, assuming that if Horsman was correct, I would find some relationship to expansionism. Perhaps I looked in the wrong places, but I discovered that in the 1840s Indian policy seemed to reflect, not expansionism, but the upsurge of American reform that so strongly marked the period. The decade furnishes a good example of the strong influence of American reform impulses on Indian-white relations in the United States. The essay was presented in October 1969 at the University of Kansas, as part of a conference on the Trans-Mississippi West honoring the historian George L. Anderson.

The decade of the 1840s was an interlude of relative quiet in American Indian relations, and it gave the federal government the opportunity to promote with sincerity and enthusiasm a program for the civilization and advancement of the Indian nations with whom it had long been in contact. By 1840 the removal of these eastern Indians to new homes west of the Mississippi had largely been accomplished, bringing to a culmination the removal policy that had been the answer to the "Indian problem" of the generation of James Monroe, John Quincy

Printed source: John G. Clark, ed., *The Frontier Challenge: Responses to the Trans-Mississippi West* (Lawrence: University Press of Kansas, 1971), pp. 81–110.

Adams, and Andrew Jackson. Now there stretched ahead an indefinite future in which the officials of the Indian Office envisaged the flowering of earlier attempts to ameliorate the condition of the Indians. In their visions these men shared in the vital optimism of their age. Betterment of all mankind seemed within easy reach, and concern for society's unfortunates (the delinquent, the insane, the indigent poor, the deaf, and the blind) appeared everywhere. Crusades for peace, for women's rights, for temperance, for education, and for abolition of slavery marched with reforming zeal and a strange naiveté through the land. Words like *benevolence, philanthropy,* and *perfectability* slipped easily from men's tongues. The plans for civilizing and Christianizing the Indians who had been removed from the main arena of American life partook of this evangelizing spirit. The Indian policy of the 1840s, indeed, must be considered in the light of what Arthur M. Schlesinger has called "the first great upsurge of social reform in United States history."[1]

Such a reform movement, of course, was not new, for there had always been voices raised on behalf of the Indians. Removal itself, its advocates within the federal government thought, was a humanitarian measure. They did not think that they were acting as harshly toward the Indians as their critics at the time and as later historians have claimed. Rejecting infeasible alternatives to solving the Indian problem, they sought to remove the red men from contact with white society and beyond the reach of jurisdictional disputes between the states and the federal government. The War Department put together what it considered a liberal offer to the Indians. In return for the agreement on the part of the Indians to give up their lands east of the Mississippi for comparable lands west of Missouri and Arkansas, the federal government

1. Arthur M. Schlesinger, *The American as Reformer* (Cambridge: Harvard University Press, 1950), p. 3. For surveys of the reforming spirit of the times, see Alice Felt Tyler, *Freedom's Ferment: Phases of American Social History to 1860* (Minneapolis: University of Minnesota Press, 1944), and Clifford S. Griffin, *Their Brothers' Keepers: Moral Stewardship in the United States, 1800–1865* (New Brunswick: Rutgers University Press, 1960). [See also Ronald G. Walters, *American Reformers, 1815–1860* (New York: Hill and Wang, 1978). A useful collection of contemporary essays is Walter Hugins, ed., *The Reform Impulse, 1825–1850* (Columbia: University of South Carolina Press, 1972).] The intellectual setting in which movements for bettering the conditions of the Indians must be placed is set forth in Perry Miller, *The Life of the Mind in America from the Revolution to the Civil War* (New York: Harcourt, Brace and World, 1965). See especially his remarks on benevolence, pp. 78–84. On reform in general, see David Brion Davis, ed., *Ante-Bellum Reform* (New York: Harper and Row, 1967).

offered to assume the costs of removal, to subsist the Indians for a year in the new land, and to provide substantial annuity payments. Beyond this simple exchange the United States committed itself to provide more general aid and protection. Altogether, the stipulations and pledges were thought to be so beneficial to the tribes that the Indian leaders could not refuse to accept removal.

President Monroe, in a special message to Congress on Indian removal delivered on January 27, 1825, set the general tone and pattern. He urged for the Indians "a well-digested plan for their government and civilization, which should be agreeable to themselves, would not only shield them from impending ruin, but promote their welfare and happiness." He recommended some sort of internal government for the tribes in the West, with sufficient power to hold the tribes together in amity and to preserve order, to prevent intrusion on the Indian lands, and to teach the Indians by regular instruction the arts of civilized life. "It is not doubted," he concluded, "that this arrangement will present considerations of sufficient force to surmount all their prejudices in favor of the soil of their nativity, however strong they may be."[2]

Andrew Jackson, in his first annual message on December 8, 1829, spoke in the same way. In the West, he asserted, the Indians "may be secured in the enjoyment of governments of their own choice, subject to no other control from the United States than such as may be necessary to preserve peace on the frontier and between the several tribes. There the benevolent may endeavor to teach them the arts of civilization, and, by promoting union and harmony among them, to raise up an interesting commonwealth, destined to perpetuate the race and to attest the humanity and justice of this Government."[3] Similarly, Lewis Cass, in his first annual report as Secretary of War, spoke of removal as presenting "the only hope of permanent establishment and improvement." He recommended instruction in the "truths of religion, together with a knowledge of the simpler mechanic arts and the rudiments of science," and he listed seven fundamental principles, which he asserted would constitute the best foundation both for American efforts and for Indian hopes. In addition to a solemn pledge that the land assigned to the Indians would be a permanent home and that an adequate force would be provided to suppress intertribal hostilities, he encouraged

2. James D. Richardson, comp., *A Compilation of the Messages and Papers of the Presidents, 1789–1897*, 10 vols. (Washington: Government Printing Office, 1896–99), 2:281–82.

3. Ibid., p. 458.

severalty of property, assistance in opening farms, and employment of persons to instruct the Indians. He spoke also of leaving the Indians free to enjoy their own institutions insofar as they were "compatible with their own safety and ours, and with the great objects of their prosperity and improvement."[4] The government clearly intended, therefore, to promote the civilization of the Indians in their new homes.

The 1840s were years for fulfillment of the promises. The men in charge of Indian affairs in that decade were convinced of the wisdom of the removal policy and eager to make it work for the Indians. "It will be the end of all," T. Hartley Crawford, the Commissioner of Indian Affairs appointed by President Van Buren, wrote after his first year in office, "unless the experiment of the Government in the Indian territory shall be blessed with success." He admitted that the outcome was uncertain, but he was not disheartened and he urged perseverance.[5]

As Crawford warmed to his job, he became bolder in his praise of removal as essential for Indian betterment. He considered other alternatives that might have been pursued—assimilation of Indians into the mass of white society and life as farmers on their lands in the East—and rejected them as infeasible. Removal to the West, he judged, was "the only expedient—the wisest, the best, the most practicable and practical of all." His view of the advantages to the Indians was idyllic, his goals utopian. The Indians, he prophesied, would find "a home and a country free from the apprehension of disturbance and annoyance, from the means of indulging a most degrading appetite, and far removed from the temptations of bad and sordid men; a region hemmed in by the laws of the United States, and guarded by virtuous agents, where abstinence from vice, and the practice of good morals, should find fit abodes in comfortable dwellings and cleared farms, and be nourished and fostered by all the associations of the hearthstone. In no other than this settled condition can schools flourish, which are the keys that open the gate to heaven and God." He foresaw for the Indians in their new western homes a great flowering of the solid Puritan virtues—"temperance and industry, and education and religion." Imbued with this attitude, he could not but urge the speedy removal of those Indians who had not yet migrated.[6]

4. Report of the Secretary of War, November 21, 1831, *House Executive Document* no. 2, 22d Cong., 1st sess., ser. 216, pp. 30–34.

5. Report of T. Hartley Crawford, November 25, 1839, *House Executive Document* no. 2, 26th Cong., 1st sess., ser. 363, p. 346.

6. Report of Crawford, November 28, 1840, *Senate Document* no. 1, 26th Cong., 2d sess., ser. 375, pp. 232-34.

These sentiments Crawford repeated year after year while he was Commissioner of Indian Affairs. A treaty with Wyandots in Ohio was looked upon as a means to promote their comfort and, as a consequence, their advance in morals, civilization, and Christianity, although the Commissioner was not so obtuse that he did not appreciate the advantages to the whites in obtaining the Wyandots' Ohio acres. Like so many others, from Thomas Jefferson on, he rejoiced that the duty of Americans toward the Indians coincided with their own interests. Removal from the lands that the whites wanted would bring to the Indians seclusion and protection from the contaminating influences of white civilization.[7]

Crawford's vision was reflected in the statements of the Secretaries of War. Joel R. Poinsett in 1840 spoke of removal as the only way, not only to civilize the red man, but to perpetuate his existence. John C. Spencer remarked two years later that the end of the removal process was in sight. "It is to be hoped that the red man will then be suffered to rest in peace," he concluded, "and that our undivided efforts will be bestowed in discharging the fearful responsibilities we have incurred to improve his intellectual and moral condition as the only means of rendering him happy here or hereafter."[8]

For the whites, the removal of the Indians from the East was an end in itself, since the lands they coveted could then be acquired and developed. For the Indians, on the other hand, removal was only a means to an end. Relocation was to make possible their civilization. The instrument that would bring all this about, the panacea for all the ills besetting the Indians, was education.

That the Indians were educable was a basic tenet of the reformers. It was admitted, of course, that the present state of the Indians was one of semibarbarism. The aborigines were indolent, a condition aggravated by the lack of individual property, which alone would give incentive to work. They were erratic, wandering from place to place without permanency of residence. They were warlike, for their culture elevated war into an advantage and violence into a virtue. Contrasted with the Americans, who extolled thrift, perseverance, enterprise, domestic peace, and Christian morality, the Indians were an inferior people, standing in the way of progress. But the unfortunate condition of the

7. Report of Crawford, November 16, 1842, *Senate Document* no. 1, 27th Cong., 3d sess., ser. 413, p. 379.

8. Report of Joel R. Poinsett, December 5, 1840, *Senate Document* no. 1, 26th Cong., 2d sess., ser. 375, p. 28; Report of John C. Spencer, November 26, 1842, *Senate Document* no. 1, 27th Cong., 3d sess., ser. 413, p. 190.

red men was not irremediable. The government officials did not believe in a racial inferiority that was not amenable to betterment. "It is proved, I think, conclusively," Crawford remarked of the Indian race, "that it is in no respect inferior to our own race, except in being less fortunately circumstanced. As great an aptitude for learning the letters, the pursuits, and arts of civilized life, is evident; if their progress is slow, so has it been with us and with masses of men in all nations and ages."[9] Circumstances and education alone made the difference between them and the whites; and Indian agents, missionaries, and traders contributed evidence that the red men were susceptible to improvement. There would be no racial obstacle to the eventual assimilation of the Indians into the political life of the nation.[10]

So, schools for Indians were advocated with great enthusiasm, befitting an age in which education was considered the "universal utopia."[11] The promotion of schools as the agency to swing the Indians from a state considered to be barbarous, immoral, and pagan to one that was civilized, moral, and Christian took on new exuberance when the Indians were safely ensconced in the West, where the "experiment" could be carried out unhindered. Indian schools, Commissioner Crawford asserted in 1839, formed "one of the most important objects, if it be not the greatest, connected with our Indian relations. Upon it depends more or less even partial success in all endeavors to make the Indian better than he is." The Commissioner hammered tirelessly at this same theme. "The greatest good we can bestow upon them," he said in 1842, "is education in its broadest sense—education in letters, education in labor and the mechanic arts, education in morals, and education in Christianity."[12]

The initial problem was how to intrigue the Indians, both the youths to be educated and their parents, into accepting the schooling. It was all too evident that simply duplicating white schools in the Indian country

9. Report of Crawford, November 25, 1844, *Senate Document* no. 1, 28th Cong., 2d sess., ser. 449, p. 315.

10. Report of Thomas H. Harvey, October 8, 1844, ibid., p. 435; Report of William Wilkins, November 30, 1844, ibid., p. 127.

11. The phrase is from a chapter heading in Arthur A. Ekirch, Jr., *The Idea of Progress in America, 1815-1860* (New York: Columbia University Press, 1944), p. 195.

12. Report of Crawford, November 25, 1839, *House Executive Document* no. 2, 26th Cong., 1st sess., ser. 363, p. 343; Report of Crawford, November 16, 1842, *Senate Document* no. 1, 27th Cong., 3d sess., ser. 413, p. 386. See also his report of November 28, 1840, *Senate Document* no. 1, 26th Cong., 2d sess., ser. 375, p. 242.

or sending Indian children to the East for formal education was not the whole answer. Learning in letters alone was not appreciated by the Indians and did not give any practical advancement to the young Indians, who became misfits within their own community. The answer, rather, lay in manual labor schools, whose full importance was made explicit by Crawford:

> The education of the Indian is a great work. It includes more than the term imports in its application to civilized communities. Letters and personal accomplishments are what we generally intend to speak of by using the word; though sometimes, even with us, it has a more comprehensive meaning. Applied to wild men, its scope should take in much more extensive range, or you give them the shadow for the substance. They must at the least be taught to read and write, and have some acquaintance with figures; but if they do not learn to build and live in houses, to sleep on beds; to eat at regular intervals; to plough, and sow, and reap; to rear and use domestic animals; to understand and practise the mechanic arts; and to enjoy, to their gratification and improvement, all the means of profit and rational pleasure that are so profusely spread around civilized life, their mere knowledge of what is learned in the school room proper will be comparatively valueless. At a future day, more or less remote, when those who are now savage shall have happily become civilized this important branch of Indian interest may be modified according to circumstances; but at present, when every thing is to be learned at the school, and nothing, as with us, by the child as it grows up, unconsciously and without knowing how or when the manual labor school system is not only deserving of favor, but it seems to me indispensable to the civilization of the Indians; and their civilization, with a rare exception here and there, is as indispensable to real and true Christianity in them.[13]

This apotheosis of white cultural traits and insistence upon them, willy-nilly, for the Indians is an overpowering indication of the ethnocentric viewpoint of the white reformers. Once the way of life was accepted, then more formal education in arts and letters would be seen to be advantageous, and the desire to attain it would motivate the Indians to attend and promote traditional schools. As civilization advanced, Christianity could be promoted, and moral improvement would

13. Report of Crawford, November 25, 1844, *Senate Document* no. 1, 28th Cong., 2d sess., ser. 449, p. 313.

follow. The desire for material well-being would stimulate industry, which would in turn accelerate the whole process. It was a wonderful white man's carrousel.

The practical model for the Indian Office planners was the Methodist mission school established in 1839 for the Shawnees at the Fort Leavenworth Agency, which seemed to embody all the characteristics demanded to accomplish the goal. In 1840 it had some fifty students, in about equal proportions of boys and girls, running in age from six to eighteen years. "They can nearly all read, many can compose and write sentences, and a number are acquainted with the rule of three," Crawford reported. "They are taught out of school to split wood, plough, mow, &c.; and when all the appliances are ready for use, will learn the mechanic arts. The girls have made the same average progress in letters, and are taught the various branches of housewifery." Two three-story brick buildings had been erected and a third was under way. There were houses for the principal and for the blacksmith, and a shop, a barn, and stables. Between five hundred and six hundred acres of land were fenced and in cultivation. "The spirit manifested in thus reclaiming the wild woods," the Commissioner noted, "has been extended to the much more important work of mental culture." Plans called for accommodations ultimately for two hundred students, at a yearly expense of not more than seventy dollars each. Crawford considered the school as "the strongest evidence I have yet seen of the probability of success, after all our failures, in the efforts made by benevolent and religious societies, and by the Government, to work a change in Indian habits and modes of life; while it is conclusive proof that these sons of the forest are our equals in capacity."[14] For its good work, and even more as a harbinger of greater things to come within the Indian territory, the school won praise from the highest sources. Manual labor schools for all the Indians became the goal of the War Department and the Indian Office.[15]

Two other principles, in connection with manual labor education, were adopted by the Indian Office. One of these, as was appropriate in

14. Report of Crawford, November 28, 1840, *Senate Document* no. 1, 26th Cong., 2d sess., ser. 375, p. 243. Crawford got his information from a report of John B. Luce, November 11, 1840, ibid., pp. 387–88. See also the reports on the beginning of the school in Report of the Commissioner of Indian Affairs, 1839, Appendix no. 38, *House Executive Document* no. 2, 26th Cong., 1st sess., ser. 363, pp. 433–34.

15. Report of W. L. Marcy, December 5, 1846, *Senate Document* no. 1, 29th Cong., 2d sess., ser. 493, p. 60; Report of W. Medill, November 30, 1846, ibid., p. 227.

a period that saw the first organized crusade for women's rights, was that Indian schools should teach girls as well as boys, if civilization was to be forwarded. When Crawford, early in his term of office, noted that more boys than girls were being educated, he asked, "Upon what principle of human action is this inequality founded?" And he set forth his argument in strong terms:

> Unless the Indian female character is raised, and her relative position changed, such an education as you can give the males will be a rope of sand, which, separating at every turn, will bind them to no amelioration. Necessity may force the culture of a little ground, or the keeping of a few cattle, but the savage nature will break out at every temptation. If the women are made good and industrious housewives, and taught what befits their condition, their husbands and sons will find comfortable homes and social enjoyments, which, in any state of society, are essential to morality and thrift. I would therefore advise that the larger proportion of pupils should be female.[16]

"The conviction is settled," he reiterated in 1841, "that the civilization of these unfortunate wards of the Government will be effected through the instrumentality of their educated women, much more than by their taught men."[17] Although the Commissioner's goals were never met, promotion of female education continued.

A second principle, gradually developed during the decade, was that Indian youths should be taught in the Indian country where they lived and not sent off to eastern schools. There had been a tradition of sending select Indian boys to white schools in the East, where it was supposed they could more quickly absorb the white man's civilization. The Cherokee leaders John Ridge and Elias Boudinot, for example, had been educated at Cornwall, Connecticut. The Choctaws had made arrangements with Richard M. Johnson of Kentucky, by which he established an academy for boys at Blue Springs, Kentucky, in 1825. The school was directed by the Baptists and supported enthusiastically for many years by the Choctaws. Twenty-five boys entered this Choctaw Academy in 1825, and the enrollment in some years ran to more than one hundred and fifty students. Other tribes, too, sent their boys

16. Report of Crawford, November 25, 1839, *House Executive Document* no. 2, 26th Cong., 1st sess., ser. 363, p. 344.
17. Report of Crawford, November 25, 1841, *House Executive Document* no. 2, 27th Cong., 2d sess., ser. 401, p. 241.

to the school.[18] But complaints arose about the school, and by 1841 the Choctaws had decided to educate their sons within the nation. Such a move was in accord with the Indian Department's views.

Crawford advised from the first against sending Indians away from home to distant schools, and in 1844 Secretary of War William Wilkins argued that education should be diffused as equally as possible through the whole tribe by establishing common schools within the Indian country. The education of a few individuals in a college or school away from their tribe did not promote the designs of the government, Wilkins argued, for he was afraid that men more highly educated than the mass of the tribe might employ their talents for selfish acquisition and oppression of their uneducated brothers.[19] By 1846 the Indian Department had clearly decided to adhere to the new policy.[20] "The practice so long pursued of selecting a few boys from the different tribes, and placing them at our colleges and high schools," Commissioner William Medill repeated in 1847, "has failed to produce the beneficial results anticipated; while the great mass of the tribe at home were suffered to remain in ignorance." The plan would be completely discontinued as soon as existing arrangements could be changed, and the resources of the Indian Office would be applied solely to the schools within the Indian country, where education could be extended to both sexes and generally spread throughout the tribe.[21]

To carry out the educational reform considerable money was expended in the Indian country. The civilization fund of $10,000 a year, which Congress had authorized in 1819, was apportioned among the various missionary societies in small amounts of a few hundred dollars each.[22] The effect of these small allowances in stimulating contributions by missionary groups is hard to evaluate, for other

18. Angie Debo, *The Rise and Fall of the Choctaw Republic* (Norman: University of Oklahoma Press, 1934), pp. 44–45; Carolyn T. Foreman, "The Choctaw Academy," *Chronicles of Oklahoma* 6 (December 1928): 453–80; 9 (December 1931): 382–411; 10 (March 1932): 77–114.

19. Report of Crawford, November 25, 1839, *House Executive Document* no. 2, 26th Cong., 1st sess., ser. 363, p. 344; Report of Wilkins, November 30, 1844, *Senate Document* no. 1, 28th Cong., 2d sess., ser. 449, p. 127.

20. Report of Marcy, December 5, 1846, *Senate Document* no. 1, 29th Cong., 2d sess., ser. 493, p. 60; Report of Medill, November 30, 1846, ibid., p. 227.

21. Report of Medill, November 30, 1847, *Senate Executive Document* no. 1, 30th Cong., 1st sess., ser. 503, p. 749. See also Report of Marcy, December 2, 1847, ibid., p. 70.

22. A year-by-year listing of expenditures from the fund for the period 1820–42 appears in *House Document* no. 203, 27th Cong., 3d sess., ser. 423. See also

federal funds also were poured into the mission schools. Chief among these were the funds specified for education in treaties made with the Indians or designated from annuity moneys by the tribes themselves for educational purposes. Thus the Choctaw treaty of 1830 stipulated that the government was to pay $2,000 annually for twenty years for the support of three school teachers, and the tribe itself in 1842 voted to apply $18,000 a year from its annuities to education.[23] A treaty with the Ottawas and Chippewas in 1836 specified that in addition to an annuity in specie of $30,000 for twenty years, $5,000 each year would be given for teachers, schoolhouses, and books in their own language, and $3,000 more for missions. These payments were to run for twenty years and as long thereafter as Congress would continue the appropriation.[24] In the year 1845, $68,195 was provided by treaties for Indian education, to which was added $12,367.50 from the civilization fund.[25] Subsequent treaties added to the school funds available. A treaty with the Kansas Indians in 1846, for example, provided for the investment of the sum paid for the cession of lands, and $1,000 a year from the interest was directed to schools within the Indian country. The treaty of 1846 with the Winnebagos provided that $10,000 of the cession payment was to be applied to the creation and maintenance of one or more manual labor schools.[26] To these government funds were added those supplied by the missionary societies themselves. The government also built schools and churches and supplied agricultural implements and domestic equipment, which could be used in the manual labor sort of education that the men of the 1840s advocated.

Although the number of students in the Indian schools was small, the optimism of the Indian Office and the missionaries was not without foundation. The Choctaws, although more interested in education than

George D. Harmon, *Sixty Years of Indian Affairs: Political, Economic, and Diplomatic, 1789-1850* (Chapel Hill: University of North Carolina Press, 1941), Appendix, table 5, pp. 378-79. Some information on the use of the fund usually appears in the annual reports of the Commissioner of Indian Affairs. For a discussion of the act, see Francis Paul Prucha, *American Indian Policy in the Formative Years: The Indian Trade and Intercourse Acts, 1790-1834* (Cambridge: Harvard University Press, 1962), pp. 221-24.

23. Charles J. Kappler, ed., *Indian Affairs: Laws and Treaties,* vol. 2, *Treaties* (Washington: Government Printing Office, 1904), p. 315; P. P. Pitchlynn to William Armstrong, December 12, 1842, *Senate Document* no. 1, 28th Cong., 1st sess., ser. 431, pp. 367-68.

24. Kappler, *Treaties,* pp. 451-52.

25. Harmon, *Sixty Years of Indian Affairs,* Appendix, table 7, p. 381.

26. Kappler, *Treaties,* pp. 553, 566.

many of the tribes, offered an example of what was possible. They began to build schools as soon as they arrived in the West. The missionaries of the American Board reported eleven schools with 228 Choctaw students in 1836, and in addition there were five schools supported by the Choctaw Nation and the three district schools provided by the 1830 treaty. In 1842 a comprehensive system of schools was begun. Spencer Academy and Fort Coffee Academy were opened in 1844; Armstrong and New Hope academies two years later. The national council also supplied support to four schools established earlier by the American Board. By 1848 the Choctaws had nine boarding schools supported by tribal funds, and neighborhood schools had been opened in many communities.[27] The Commissioner in that year reported exceptional progress as well among the Osages, Chickasaws, Quapaws, and Miamis.[28] The Cherokees also made remarkable progress, until they had a better common-school system than either Arkansas or Missouri.[29]

Comparative numbers give some indication of the progress, although reports were often incomplete. In 1842 forty-five schools (out of a total of fifty-two) reported 2,132 students enrolled. In 1848 there were sixteen manual labor schools with 809 students and eighty-seven boarding and other schools with 2,873 students; in 1849, although some reports were missing, a further increase in students was noted.[30]

These schools would have been impossible without the devoted work of Christian missionaries, and Indian education was a beneficiary of the missionary impulse of the Protestant churches that was an important element in the reform ferment of the age.[31] The Indian Office felt this influence strongly, for its goals and those of the missionary societies in the 1840s were identical: practical, moral, and religious education of the Indians, which would bring both Christianity and civilization to

27. Debo, *Choctaw Republic*, pp. 60–61; documents 69–72, attached to Report of Crawford, November 25, 1843, *Senate Document* no. 1, 28th Cong., 1st sess., ser. 431, pp. 367–72.

28. Report of Medill, November 30, 1847, *Senate Executive Document* no. 1, 30th Cong., 1st sess., ser. 503, p. 750.

29. Grant Foreman, *The Five Civilized Tribes* (Norman: University of Oklahoma Press, 1934), p. 410.

30. Document 83, attached to Report of Crawford, November 16, 1842, *Senate Document* no. 1, 27th Cong., 3d sess., ser. 413, pp. 520–22; Report of Orlando Brown, November 30, 1849, *House Executive Document* no. 5, 31st Cong., 1st sess., ser. 570, p. 956.

31. Tyler, *Freedom's Ferment*, pp. 31–32.

the aborigines.[32] Since the civilization fund that the federal government had at its disposal was small, the money had been used from the beginning as a stimulus to missionary societies to enter the work of Indian education. The government thus consciously and eagerly consummated a partnership with the churches by which federal funds and church funds were united to support the Christian missionaries—a union of church and state in which the participants seemed unaware of any Jeffersonian wall of separation.[33]

Reliance on the missionaries, indeed, was uppermost in the minds of the federal officials. Commissioner Crawford noted in his report of 1839: "No direction of these institutions [Indian schools] appears to me so judicious as that of religious and benevolent societies, and it is gratifying to observe the zeal with which all the leading sects lend themselves to this good work; discouragements do not seem to cool their ardor, nor small success to dissuade them from persevering efforts."[34] So successful was the Methodist school for the Shawnees that the War Department was eager to support similar establishments directed by other religious groups, "equally zealous, no doubt, in spreading the light of the Gospel among the Indians, and equally disposed to advance their moral culture."[35] The report of the Commissioner of Indian Affairs in 1847 indicates how enamored the Indian Office had become of its missionary auxiliaries:

> In every system which has been adopted for promoting the cause of education among the Indians, the Department has found its most efficient and faithful auxiliaries and laborers in the societies of the several Christian denominations, which have sent out missionaries, established schools, and maintained local teachers among the different tribes. Deriving their impulse from principles of philanthropy

32. There was a controversy at the time among the missionaries about which should come first, civilization or Christianity, but the Indian Office did not enter into the dispute since it was agreed that both were ultimately needed. See Robert F. Berkhofer, Jr., *Salvation and the Savage: An Analysis of Protestant Missions and American Indian Response, 1787-1862* (Lexington: University of Kentucky Press, 1965), pp. 3-9.

33. There is an excellent discussion of this cooperation in R. Pierce Beaver, *Church, State, and the American Indians: Two and a Half Centuries of Partnership in Missions between Protestant Churches and Government* (St. Louis: Concordia Publishing House, 1966).

34. Report of Crawford, November 25, 1839, *House Executive Document* no. 2, 26th Cong., 1st sess., ser. 363, p. 343.

35. Report of Poinsett, December 5, 1840, *Senate Document* no. 1, 26th Cong., 2d sess., ser. 375, p. 28.

and religion, and devoting a large amount of their own means to the education, moral elevation and improvement of the tribes, the Department has not hesitated to make them the instruments, to a considerable extent, of applying the funds appropriated by the government for like purposes. Their exertions have thus been encouraged, and a greater degree of economy at the same time secured in the expenditure of the public money.[36]

Agents in the field who were close to the missionaries and their work were strong in praise of the efforts of the churches. Thus Thomas H. Harvey, Superintendent of Indian Affairs at St. Louis, argued that the schools for the Indians should always be entrusted to missionaries. "I conceive that the missionary, or teacher of the Christian religion, is an indispensable agent in the civilization of the Indians," he said. "No one who is not steeled in prejudice can travel through the Indian country where they have missionaries without observing their beneficial influence." Harvey saw the schools of the missionaries as the centers of ever widening influence, for the educated Indians would soon give tone to the larger society.[37]

Much of the optimism of the officials in Washington regarding Indian improvement rested upon the reports of the missionaries. It was common for the church groups to describe the results of their efforts in highly favorable terms, and the Indian Office seemed ready to accept the reports uncritically. But this acceptance, unwarranted as it might have been at times, emphasizes the utopian, reform-minded views of the age.[38]

The visions of reform that the Indian Office and the missionaries had for the Indians, however, met serious obstacles. Removal of the Indians to lands west of the Mississippi had not in fact sequestered them

36. Report of Medill, November 30, 1847, *Senate Executive Document* no. 1, 30th Cong., 1st sess., ser. 503, p. 749. See also Report of Brown, November 30, 1849, *House Executive Document* no. 5, 31st Cong., 1st sess., ser. 570, p. 937.

37. Report of Harvey, October 8, 1844, *Senate Document* no. 1, 28th Cong., 2d sess., ser. 449, p. 436. See also his report of September 10, 1845, *Senate Document* no. 1, 29th Cong., 1st sess., ser. 470, p. 532, and his report of September 5, 1846, *Senate Document* no. 1, 29th Cong., 2d sess., ser. 493, pp. 282–83.

38. See Epilogue, "The Harvest Unreaped," in Berkhofer, *Salvation and the Savage,* pp. 152–60, for a critical appraisal of the missionaries' success up to 1860. Reports of the missionaries appear in such sources as the *Annual Report* of the American Board of Commissioners for Foreign Missions and in the Board's journal, the *Missionary Herald,* as well as in reports attached to the annual reports of the Commissioner of Indian Affairs.

from all contact with evil men. Traders under license were permitted in the Indian country according to the laws governing trade and intercourse with the Indians, and whereas traders had traditionally been drawn to the Indians in search of furs, they now came to the emigrant Indians principally to provide goods in return for annuity money. Concern for the Indians in the 1840s included a critical attack upon the system of annuity payments as it then existed and strenuous efforts to have the system changed.

Commissioner Crawford in his annual report of 1841 devoted a long section to the problems connected with annuity payments. The annuities did the Indians for whom they were intended little good, for the money was almost completely absorbed by traders, to whom the Indians had become indebted and who sat at the annuity-payment grounds ready to pounce upon the funds. "The recipients of money," Crawford complained, "are rarely more than conduit pipes to convey it into the pockets of their traders." He objected, too, to provisions in treaties for payment of debts owed to the traders by the Indians.[39] The annuities aggravated the very conditions that the Indian Office was trying to correct. As long as the Indians were assured of receiving their annual stipend, they did not exert themselves to earn a living, thus defeating the efforts of the reformers to turn them into hard-working farmers. Much of the annuity money was spent for worthless goods or trivial objects, so that the bounty of the government was misappropriated.[40] The annuity problem, furthermore, was closely tied to the problem of intemperance among the Indians, for the money was easily drained off into the pockets of the whiskey venders.[41]

The attack on the problem was made on several fronts, all aimed at directing the annuities toward the benefit of the Indians. A change was demanded, first, in the method of paying the annuities. The act of 1834 that reorganized the Indian Department provided for payment to the chiefs of the tribes.[42] The funds often did not reach the commonalty but were siphoned off by the chiefs and their special friends for purposes which might not benefit the tribe as a whole. To correct this deficiency, Congress, on March 3, 1847, granted discretion to the

39. Report of Crawford, November 25, 1841, *House Executive Document* no. 2, 27th Cong., 2d sess., ser. 401, pp. 238–39.

40. Report of James M. Porter, November 30, 1843, *Senate Document* no. 1, 28th Cong., 1st sess., ser. 431, pp. 58–59.

41. See for example the report of James Clarke, Iowa Superintendency, October 2, 1846, *Senate Document* no. 1, 29th Cong., 2d sess., ser. 493, p. 243.

42. *United States Statutes at Large*, 4:737.

President or the Secretary of War to direct that the annuities, instead of being paid to the chiefs, be divided and paid to the heads of families and other individuals entitled to participate or, with consent of the tribe, that they be applied to other means of promoting the happiness and prosperity of the Indians. The new law, in addition, struck boldly at the liquor problem. No annuities could be paid to the Indians while they were under the influence of intoxicating liquor nor while there was reason for the paying officers to believe that liquor was within convenient reach. The chiefs, too, were to pledge themselves to use all their influence to prevent the introduction and sale of liquor in their country. Finally, to protect the Indians from signing away their annuities ahead of time, the law provided that contracts made by Indians for the payment of money or goods were null and void.[43]

The War Department immediately took advantage of the discretionary authority provided by the act, and instructions were sent to the superintendents and agents to pay the annuities in all cases to the heads of families and other individuals entitled to them. The law, Commissioner Medill said in sending out instructions, "is probably one of the most salutary laws affecting our Indian relations that has ever been passed."[44] Although there were complaints from parties adversely affected by the new policy, the Indian Department was well pleased. Medill reported in 1848 that the per capita mode of paying annuities had been attended with "the happiest effects." It prevented extortion of the Indians through the means of national credits, and it gave to everyone a knowledge of his just rights. "In the whole course of our Indian policy," he said, "there has never been a measure productive of better moral effects."[45]

The profligacy of the Indians who squandered their annuities in quick order and then were destitute for the rest of the year was attacked by Medill at the same time. The annuities of many tribes were much larger than their wants required at the time of payment. In

43. Ibid., 9:203–4.
44. Medill to Harvey, August 30, 1847, *Senate Executive Document* no. 1, 30th Cong., 1st sess., ser. 503, p. 756.
45. Report of Medill, November 30, 1848, *House Executive Document* no. 1, 30th Cong., 2d sess., ser. 537, p. 400. For the reaction of Thomas H. Harvey to the new legislation, see his report of October 29, 1847, *Senate Executive Document* no. 1, 30th Cong., 1st sess., ser. 503, pp. 832–41. Commissioner Luke Lea in 1850, although conceding "the general wisdom and justice of the policy," argued that it tended to reduce the position of the chiefs, through whom the government dealt with the tribes. Report of Lea, November 27, 1850, *Senate Executive Document* no. 1, 31st Cong., 2d sess., ser. 587, pp. 44–45.

consequence, when immediate necessities had been provided for, the excess in funds enabled the Indians "to indulge in idleness and profligacy" or to buy items of no real value to them. Then when spring came they would be in a state of destitution and would resort to hunting for subsistence instead of turning their attention to farming. The Commissioner's solution was to divide the annuities when they were sufficiently large and to pay them semiannually. Benefits were sure to follow. "The spring payment will so far supply their necessities as to enable them to put in their crops, and, to some extent at least, await their maturing," he wrote; "where not sufficient for the latter purpose, a portion can resort to hunting, and the others remain to attend to the cultivation of the crops; and they will be encouraged to pursue this course. In this way much more attention may be paid to the peaceful and more profitable pursuits of agriculture, which will tend greatly to their advancement in civilization, and to increase the resources and comforts of civilized life among them."[46] The results of this policy, too, seemed satisfactory, and Medill, noting that opposition had been less than anticipated, recommended that the policy be continued.[47]

The stipulations of past treaties about payment and use of annuities were rigorously adhered to, but it was the sentiment of the Indian Office that efforts should be made to encourage the Indians to make use of their funds for worthwhile purposes that would lead toward the ultimate goal of civilization. Medill noted in 1848 the pernicious effects of large money annuities upon the welfare and prosperity of a tribe, and in all future negotiations with the Indians he wanted the government to have as much of the purchase money as possible set aside for purposes that would elevate and improve the condition of the tribes. He wanted, further, to induce tribes to whom large sums were already due to consent to the application of the funds to such purposes. The goal was always the same: "The less an Indian's expectations and resources from the chase, and from the government in the shape of money annuities," he said, "the more readily can he be induced to give up his idle, dissolute, and savage habits, and to resort to labor for a

46. Report of Medill, November 30, 1847, *Senate Executive Document* no. 1, 30th Cong., 1st sess., ser. 503, p. 746.

47. Report of Medill, November 30, 1848, *House Executive Document* no. 1, 30th Cong., 2d sess., ser. 537, p. 400. See, however, the remarks of D. D. Mitchell, Superintendent of Indian Affairs at St. Louis, October 13, 1849, in which he criticized the semiannual payment for small tribes, in *House Executive Document* no. 5, 31st Cong., 1st sess., ser. 570, p. 1068.

maintenance; and thus commence the transition from a state of barbarism and moral depression, to one of civilization and moral elevation."[48]

Another attempt to meliorate the condition of the Indians was a renewed attack upon the private traders. Secretary of War John C. Spencer declared in 1842 that the system in operation did not lead to the "improvement of the moral and intellectual condition of the Indians." Although Spencer acknowledged the presence of many honest and faithful traders, he noted the recklessness of the Indians, who purchased worthless goods or quantities of supplies far beyond their needs. These they wasted or bartered for liquor and soon were as destitute as before. He noted, too, the undue influence that the traders acquired over the Indians, which was greater than that of the government agents and sometimes used in opposition to government policy.[49]

The Secretary of War supported the plan put forth by Indian Commissioner Crawford for a new government "factory system," which Crawford first broached in his annual report of 1840. While emphatically asserting that he did not propose a return to the old factory system, which had been "rightly abolished," Crawford deemed its principle to be valuable. Because of the increased annual disbursements to the Indian tribes, the improved facilities for transportation, the greater need the Indians had for protection as they became surrounded by white population, and the growing dependency of the Indians upon their annuity payments, he urged an alternative to the existing system that would be more beneficial to the Indians. He outlined his plan in some detail:

> I would make a small establishment of goods, suitable to Indian wants, according to their location, at each agency. I would not allow these goods to be sold to any one except Indians entitled to a participation in the cash annuities, and I would limit the purchases to their proportion of the annuity; so that the Government would, instead of paying money to be laid out in whiskey and beads, or applied to the payment of goods at two prices bought from others, meet the Indians to settle their accounts, and satisfy them that they had received, in articles of comfort or necessity, the annuity due them for the

48. Report of Medill, November 30, *House Executive Document* no. 1, 30th Cong., 2d sess., ser. 537, pp. 393–94. See also Report of Brown, November 30, 1849, *House Executive Document* no. 5, 31st Cong., 1st sess., ser. 570, p. 958.

49. Report of Spencer, November 26, 1842, *Senate Document* no. 1, 27th Cong., 3d sess., ser. 413, p. 192.

year, at *cost*, including transportation. The Indians would be immensely benefited; and the expense would not be greater than that of the money-payments now almost uselessly made them.[50]

Under such a system Crawford believed that the government Indian agents would gain the position of weight with the Indians that they ought to have. The Indians would look to the government as its best friend, for from it would come the goods they needed. He was sure that the secret of the great attachment of the Indians in Canada to the British government was that the Indians received everything from the officers of the government. In contrast, the United States government paid the Indians what it owed them but then left them a prey to the traders, who absorbed all that the Indians had received. There was no intention, however, for the agents to enter into the fur trade as the old factors had done. Such business would be left to traders under license; but with competition from the government agents, the traders would be forced to furnish quality goods at fair prices or get out of the business.[51]

In subsequent years Crawford repeated and strengthened his original recommendations.[52] The House Committee on Indian Affairs took up the proposal in 1844 and reported a bill to authorize the furnishing of goods and provisions by the War Department, but the action died in the House.[53] Crawford did not give up. His plan, he asserted, would increase the comfort of the Indians; the comfort in turn would be a "leading string . . . to conduct them into the walks of civilization," and general improvement of the Indians would soon be seen everywhere.[54] But Crawford left office, and his scheme died. It was too much to ask in an age of private enterprise that the government go back into the Indian trade. Control of the evils of the Indian trade reverted to the old attempt to enforce the licensing system that was part of the traditional setup.

50. Report of Crawford, November 28, 1840, *Senate Document* no. 1, 26th Cong., 2d sess., ser. 375, p. 240.

51. Ibid., pp. 240–41.

52. Report of Crawford, November 16, 1842, *Senate Document* no. 1, 27th Cong., 3d sess., ser. 413, pp. 382–83. See also his report of November 25, 1841, *House Executive Document* no. 2, 27th Cong., 2d sess., ser. 401, pp. 239–40, and his report of November 25, 1843, *Senate Document* no. 1, 28th Cong., 1st sess., ser. 431, p. 266.

53. The bill (No. 430) was introduced on June 14, 1844, and was committed to the Committee of the Whole. *House Journal,* 28th Cong., 1st sess., p. 1112.

54. Report of Crawford, November 25, 1844, *Senate Document* no. 1, 28th Cong., 2d sess., ser. 449, pp. 312–13.

A strong movement in that direction came in 1847, under the direction of William Medill, Commissioner of Indian Affairs, and W. L. Marcy, Secretary of War. Although previous laws and regulations called for a careful surveillance of the traders and the elimination of those deemed unfit for dealing with the Indians, Medill found that lax enforcement had allowed licenses to be given to many persons who should never have been permitted to go into the Indian country. He insisted that licenses should be granted to "none but persons of proper character, who will deal fairly, and cooperate with the government in its measure for meliorating the condition of the Indians." He drew up new and tighter regulations, therefore, which were promulgated by the War Department.[55] The Secretary of War reported in 1848 that the new regulations and the rigid supervision over the conduct of the traders had put an end to many evils and abuses. How much real success this new drive had, nevertheless, is hard to judge, for at the end of the decade Orlando Brown, the new Commissioner of Indian Affairs, again urged circumventing the traders by paying the annuities in goods rather than in money.[56]

All problems or obstacles in improving the Indians' condition seemed to stem from or to be aggravated by intemperance. The cupidity of white men, who were eager to sell vile concoctions to Indians at exorbitant prices, could not be struck at directly, and restrictions on the sale of liquor to Indians were impossible to enforce. A primary justification for removing the Indians to the West had been to place them in a home free from temptations. In an age of reform, when many considered excessive drinking to be an important factor in the problems of delinquency and dependency among the general public, temperance was to be one of the agencies opening up "the fountains of hope" for the red man in the new lands.[57]

But removal alone did not prevent intemperance among the Indians. The whiskey venders were if anything more virulent on the western

55. *United States Statutes at Large,* 4:729–30; Report of Medill, November 30, 1847, *Senate Executive Document* no. 1, 30th Cong., 1st sess., ser. 503, pp. 750–51. The "Regulations concerning the Granting of Licenses to Trade with the Indians," dated November 9, 1847, and the forms of licenses and bonds to be used are printed in Appendix A, ibid., pp. 760–64.

56. Report of Marcy, December 1, 1848, *House Executive Document* no. 1, 30th Cong., 2d sess., ser. 537, pp. 83–84; Report of Brown, November 30, 1849, *House Executive Document* no. 5, 31st Cong., 1st sess., ser. 570, p. 958.

57. Report of Crawford, November 28, 1840, *Senate Document* no. 1, 26th Cong., 2d sess., ser. 375, pp. 233–34. The temperance crusade is discussed in Tyler, *Freedom's Ferment,* pp. 308–50.

frontier than in the settled regions of the East, and the means of stopping their nefarious commerce were less effective. Crawford began the decade almost with a cry of desperation:

> . . . [any] improvement, or attempt at benefiting the Indians, will meet the great obstruction to every effort of meliorating their condition—the inordinate use of ardent spirits. If you could civilize and christianize them, you might possibly correct the evil; but the misfortune is, that it must be eradicated before you can effect the former. To reason with them, experience has shown to be vain; to rely upon their own reflection and resolution for doing the good work, would be infatuation; . . . The remedy lies in keeping the poison beyond their reach.[58]

The Commissioner did not quite believe in the vicious circle he described, and as a man of his times, he pinned much of his hope for eradicating the vice upon education. "Whatever we can do to save them from self-immolation we are bound to do," he declared in 1841, "but, after all, the great security against this, as against every other vice, is education and civilization—for men have in all ages cast off the grosser vices, particularly, in the proportion in which they have advanced as social and intellectual beings." He believed that if the Indians themselves turned their attention earnestly to the subject, they could accomplish more than the United States and the states or territories combined.[59] In 1843 he reported that the exertions of the Indian Department had been strenuous and unremitting to prevent the use of ardent spirits by the Indians, and he described attempts on the part of the territories of Iowa and Wisconsin to prevent the trade. But his outlook was pessimistic that any final solution would come from legal enactments. His hope lay with the efforts of the tribes themselves, and he noted with pleasure that temperance societies had been organized in several of the tribes and that some tribes had passed laws to put down the sale and use of whiskey.[60]

Crawford professed to see signs of success. "The increase of temperance, and a contempt for the degradation of drunkenness, which has

58. Report of Crawford, November 28, 1840, *Senate Document* no. 1, 26th Cong., 2d sess., ser. 375, p. 241.

59. Report of Crawford, November 25, 1841, *House Executive Document* no. 2, 27th Cong., 2d sess., ser. 401, p. 243.

60. Report of Crawford, November 25, 1843, *Senate Document* no. 1, 28th Cong., 1st sess., ser. 431, pp. 270–71.

been most strikingly manifested in the Southwest," he wrote, "has been accompanied by a strong disposition to extend the means of Indian education." There were other indications, too, that there was some lessening in the evil. The Superintendent of Indian Affairs at St. Louis reported "a wonderful decrease in the quantity of spirituous liquors carried into the Indian country," which he attributed mainly to the increased vigilance of the officers of the Indian Department.[61]

While Crawford and others worked diligently to promote temperance through education, they did not neglect the frontal attack on the liquor trade in the Indian country that had long been a staple of American Indian policy. Laws in 1802, 1832, and 1834 had prohibited the introduction of whiskey into the Indian lands and had provided for fines for violations.[62] But the legislation had not been completely successful, and liquor continued to flow. Secretary of War James M. Porter in 1843 called for further legislation to prevent persons from introducing ardent spirits among the Indians, and his successor, W. L. Marcy, in 1845 called for a revision in the system of trade with the Indians by imposing more restrictions and severer penalties upon those who brought in liquor.[63]

Finally, on March 3, 1847, Congress acted. In addition to the fines provided by the act of 1834, the new law provided imprisonment up to two years for anyone who sold or disposed of liquor to an Indian in the Indian country and imprisonment up to one year for anyone who introduced liquor, excepting only such supplies as might be required for the officers and troops of the army. In all cases arising under the law, Indians were to be competent witnesses.[64] The Commissioner of Indian Affairs and the Secretary of War, however, were not satisfied to let the law serve by itself. New regulations, dated April 13, 1847, were promulgated by the War Department, which called attention to the provisions of the new law and the pertinent sections of the law of 1834

61. Ibid., p. 271; Report of D. D. Mitchell, September 29, 1843, ibid., p. 387. See also Report of Crawford, November 25, 1844, *Senate Document* no. 1, 28th Cong., 2d sess., ser. 449, pp. 311–12.

62. Prucha, *American Indian Policy in the Formative Years,* pp. 102–38, 267–68.

63. Report of J. M. Porter, November 30, 1843, *Senate Document* no. 1, 28th Cong., 1st sess., ser. 431, p. 59; Report of Marcy, November 29, 1845, *Senate Document* no. 1, 29th Cong., 1st sess., ser. 470, p. 205. A thorough discussion of the evils of the liquor traffic among the Indians is Otto F. Frederikson, *The Liquor Question among the Indian Tribes in Kansas, 1804–1881,* Bulletin of the University of Kansas, Humanistic Studies, vol. 4, no. 4 (Lawrence, 1932).

64. *United States Statutes at Large,* 9:203.

(copies of which were included with the regulations). The regulations then spelled out in detail just what duties were imposed by these laws upon the military officers and the Indian agents, who were enjoined to be vigilant in the execution of their duties and were threatened with removal from office if they did not succeed.[65]

Federal laws and regulations to control the liquor traffic had effect only within the Indian country and not in the adjoining states. In an attempt to prevent the Indians from moving across the line to obtain liquor, Secretary of War Marcy wrote a strong letter on July 14, 1847, to the governors of Missouri, Arkansas, and Iowa, invoking their aid. The stringent laws of Congress, he pointed out, failed to reach the most prolific source of the evil, which lay within the limits of the nearby states. He described the evils resulting from the trade and noted that the insecurity of the frontier whites often was the result of Indian retaliation for such injuries.[66]

The efforts to prevent whiskey from reaching the Indians met with considerable success. But all the laws of Congress and the strenuous efforts of the Indian agents and military officers on the frontier to enforce them did not end drunkenness. The frontier was too extensive and the profits to the whiskey dealers too large to make complete prohibition possible. More reliance was urged upon a system of rewards and punishments operating directly on the Indians themselves.[67]

The general reports of progress that came from the reformers as the decade neared its close were surely optimistic despite the lack of perfect success. The government officials held firm to their views of the perfectibility of the Indians, of the red man's ability to attain the civilization of the whites. Whatever evidence pointed in that direction they eagerly latched onto. They were convinced that the advances in education among some of the tribes proved conclusively that all Indians were amenable to such attainments, immediately or in the near future. They were sure that their efforts had contributed to the good result, and they spoke in justification of the faith they had had. Only a few

65. Regulations, April 13, 1847, *Senate Executive Document* no. 1, 30th Cong., 1st sess., ser. 503, pp. 764–66.

66. Marcy to governors of Missouri, Arkansas, and Iowa, July 14, 1847, ibid., pp. 767–69.

67. Report of Medill, November 30, 1848, *House Executive Document* no. 1, 30th Cong., 2d sess., ser. 537, p. 402; Report of Marcy, December 1, 1848, ibid., pp. 83–84; Report of Brown, November 30, 1849, *House Executive Document* no. 5, 31st Cong., 1st sess., ser. 570, p. 939. See also Frederikson, *Liquor Question,* pp. 55–64, on the Act of 1847 and its effect.

voices were raised in opposition, not to deny the possibilities nor even some of the accomplishments, but to point to the slowness of the progress.

Removal had caused tremendous disruptions in the Indian nations, yet many of the Indians made a rapid adjustment to their new homes. The Superintendent of the Western Territory wrote glowing reports of the progress and condition of the Choctaws, Chickasaws, Creeks, Seminoles, and Cherokees living under his jurisdiction. "Civilization is spreading through the Indian country," he reported as early as 1840, "and where but a few years past the forest was untouched, in many places good farms are to be seen; the whole face of the country evidently indicating a thrifty and prosperous people, possessing within themselves the means of raising fine stocks of horses, cattle, and hogs, and a country producing all the substantials of life with but a moderate portion of labor."[68] The Superintendent of Indian Affairs at St. Louis in 1846 reported rapid improvements among many of the tribes in agriculture and the general comforts of life. He listed the Shawnees, Wyandots, Delawares, Kickapoos, Munsees, Stockbridges, Ottawas, and Potawatomis as the tribes among whom the improvements were most visible, and he attributed the success to the influence of the missionaries and their schools.[69] The Choctaw chief Peter Pitchlynn, remonstrating in 1849 against a movement to establish a federated government for the tribes in the West, drew a pleasant picture of the advances of his nation:

Our constitution is purely republican, the gospel ministry is well sustained, and our schools are of a high order. Our people are increasing in numbers. Peace dwells within our limits, and plenteousness within our borders.

Schools, civilization upon Christian principles, agriculture, temperance and morality are the only politics we have among us; and adhering to these few primary and fundamental principles of human happiness, we have flourished and prospered: hence we want none other. We wish simply to be let alone, and permitted to pursue the even tenor of our way.[70]

68. Report of William Armstrong, October 1, 1840, *Senate Document* no. 1, 26th Cong., 2d sess., ser. 375, p. 310. See also his reports for the subsequent years attached to the annual reports of the Commissioner of Indian Affairs.

69. Report of Harvey, September 5, 1846, *Senate Document* no. 1, 29th Cong., 2d sess., ser. 493, p. 282.

70. Remonstrance of Col. Peter Pitchlynn, January 20, 1849, *House Miscellaneous Document* no. 35, 30th Cong., 2d sess., ser. 544, p. 3.

By the end of the decade success seemed assured and was in fact proclaimed from on high. Secretary of War Marcy in December 1848, reported: "No subject connected with our Indian affairs has so deeply interested the department and received so much of its anxious solicitude and attention, as that of education, and I am happy to be able to say that its efforts to advance this cause have been crowned with success. Among most of the tribes which have removed to and become settled in the Indian country, the blessings of education are beginning to be appreciated, and they generally manifest a willingness to cooperate with the government in diffusing these blessings." The schools, he concluded, afforded evidence that nearly all of the emigrated tribes were rapidly advancing in civilization and moral improvement, and he gave full credit to the Indian Department for the improved condition of the numerous tribes.[71] In the same year William Medill, then Commissioner of Indian Affairs, acknowledged the earlier decline and disappearance of the Indians. "Cannot this sad and depressing tendency of things be checked, and the past be at least measurably repaired by better results in the future?" he asked. His answer was cautious but reassuring. "It is believed they can," he wrote; "and, indeed, it has to some extent been done already, by the wise and beneficent system of policy put in operation some years since, and which, if steadily carried out, will soon give to our whole Indian system a very different and much more favorable aspect."[72]

The optimism of the next Commissioner of Indian Affairs, Orlando Brown, knew no bounds, but his report of 1849 differs only in degree and not in kind from the enthusiastic appraisals of his predecessors. "The dark clouds of ignorance and superstition in which these people have so long been enveloped seem at length in the case of many of them to be breaking away, and the light of Christianity and general knowledge to be dawning upon their moral and intellectual darkness," he wrote. Brown gave credit for the change to the government's policy of moving the Indians toward an agricultural existence, the introduction of the manual labor schools, and instruction by the missionaries in "the best of all knowledge, religious truth—their duty towards God and their fellow beings." The result was "a great moral and social revolution" among some of the tribes, which he predicted would be spread to others by adoption of the same measures. Within a few years he believed

71. Report of Marcy, December 1, 1848, *House Executive Document* no. 1, 30th Cong., 2d sess., ser. 537, p. 84.
72. Report of Medill, November 30, 1848, ibid., pp. 385–86.

that "in intelligence and resources, they would compare favorably with many portions of our white population, and instead of drooping and declining, as heretofore, they would be fully able to maintain themselves in prosperity and happiness under any circumstance of contact or connexion with our people." In the end he expected a large measure of success to "crown the philanthropic efforts of the government and of individuals to civilize and to christianize the Indian tribes." He no longer doubted that the Indians were capable of self-government. "They have proved their capacity for social happiness," he concluded, "by adopting written constitutions upon the model of our own, by establishing and sustaining schools, by successfully devoting themselves to agricultural pursuits, by respectable attainments in the learned professions and mechanic arts, and by adopting the manners and customs of our people, so far as they are applicable to their own condition."[73]

This was a bit too much, for we know that the Indians did not reach utopia. But it was quite in tune with the age, when zealous reformers saw no limit to the possibilities for ameliorating and perfecting the human condition, when the insane were to be cured, the slaves freed, the prisons cleansed, women's rights recognized, and Sunday Schools flourish. Certainly we can believe that they hoped for no less for the American Indian.

Why were not the hopes more fully realized? What darkened the visions of reform that seemed so bright to the officials of the 1840s?

Fundamentally, the work was a slower process than anyone at the time appreciated. Cultural transformation was not to be accomplished within a single generation, no matter how excellent the schools or how devoted the teachers.[74] The goals of the white society, which the missionaries and the men of the Indian Office accepted unquestioningly, did not seem so obviously good to many of the Indians. Perhaps if the isolation from white contacts behind the "permanent Indian frontier" had indeed been permanent, the happy beginnings depicted in the 1840s might have grown and blossomed in accordance with the visions. But this did not occur.

New problems came to absorb the interests and energies of the Indian Office, and new forces developed that cracked the fragile beginnings of effective Indian betterment. Manifest Destiny and the Mexican

73. Report of Brown, November 30, 1849, *House Executive Document* no. 5, 31st Cong., 1st sess., ser. 570, pp. 956–57.

74. See Berkhofer, *Salvation and the Savage*, pp. 156–60, on the lack of a realistic theory of culture among the reformers.

War renewed and reemphasized the expansion into Indian lands that the removal proponents had expected to be permanently closed. Emigrant whites moving to the Pacific Coast in unprecedented numbers brought a demand for an extinguishment of Indian titles to lands along their path and a greater concentration of the colonies of Indians in the West, which presaged the ultimate restriction of the Indians to small reservations. Wild tribes of the plains and Rockies, resisting the invasion of their lands by emigrants to Oregon and California, made the predominant concern of the Indian Office once again defense, not civilization, and the Indians of Oregon and Texas required administrative attention that severely strained the facilities of the Indian Office. These new developments had their roots in the 1840s and grew to such dimensions that the peaceful attempts to advance the Indians in white civilization received less emphasis, though they by no means completely disappeared.[75]

Although the attempts in the 1840s to improve the condition of the Indians did not fulfill all the hopes of the reformers, we cannot dismiss them as inconsequential. Although the goals were frequently unrealistic, we cannot accuse the Indian commissioners, the agents, and the missionaries of insincerity or worse still of hypocrisy. Other reform movements, too, petered out, only to reappear with new vigor at a later time. Much of the work of those who sought Indian betterment was substantial and enduring, and it was a foundation upon which future generations of reformers built.

75. See the discussion of the period as one of transition in James C. Malin, *Indian Policy and Westward Expansion,* Bulletin of the University of Kansas, Humanistic Studies, vol. 2, no. 3 (Lawrence, 1921).

12

Scientific Racism and Indian Policy

I have had a continuing dialogue with Reginald Horsman, even though the resulting publications may not indicate it clearly. Not convinced by the emphasis I placed on the belief in Indian reformability in my essay on the 1840s (an essay stimulated by Horsman's article on the origins of Manifest Destiny), Horsman in 1975 wrote an article in indirect rebuttal ("Scientific Racism and the American Indian in the Mid-Nineteenth Century," American Quarterly 27 [May 1975]: 152-68), which argued that Indian policy was dominated by a conviction, based on the science of the day, that Indians were innately inferior. My essay here is in response to that study. Horsman and I agree on many things, and no doubt the differences we exhibit in these writings will be resolved ultimately in some constructive way.

United States policy toward the Indians cannot be treated in a vacuum, set apart by the historian (consciously or unconsciously) from the main currents of American thought. Prominent ideas of the age had significant influence—or at least, to state the proposition negatively, Indian policy did not go counter to prevailing sentiments and attitudes. It is difficult, to be sure, to determine prevailing attitudes and ideas. Works like those of Perry Miller, Russel B. Nye, and Rush Welter, for example, are not completely satisfactory when used as background for Indian policy in the pre–Civil War period. And in fact, it probably is not a good idea to set up a paradigm against which Indian policy is then projected. A thorough study of Indian policy, in the light of the intellectual currents it reflected, may in the long run help us to test the completeness and accuracy of accepted analyses of the American mind, for intellectual historians sometimes jump to unwarranted conclusions about the effect on practice of the ideas they discover in the writings of a period.

Within this larger context, one can investigate the relationship between official Indian policy (as formulated by the federal government— President, Congress, and Indian Office) and philosophical and scientific views of race in the nineteenth century. Were there pervasive views of race upon which Indian policy was built? Did federal policy toward the Indians reflect changing scientific findings about inherent racial characteristics? Or did federal officials ignore or reject the work of the scientists and rely instead on other, more traditional views?

These questions have been discussed in a recent article by Reginald Horsman, "Scientific Racism and the American Indian in the Mid-Nineteenth Century."[1] Horsman notes the work of the "American School" of ethnology in the 1840s and 1850s, especially the writings of Samuel G. Morton, George R. Gliddon, Josiah C. Nott, and Ephraim G. Squier. He describes their theories of separate species for the different races, each separately created and innately superior or inferior to the others, and speaks of the "pervasive influence" of this new racism and "its success in the popular mind." Dismissing the arguments of the 1840s made by supporters of attempts to civilize the Indians as "the rhetoric and optimism of an older generation," he concludes:

> It seems that by the middle of the nineteenth century science itself had endorsed the earlier popular feeling that the Indians were not worth saving and envisaged a world bettered as the all-conquering Anglo-Saxon branch of the Caucasian race superseded inferior peoples. The American School of ethnologists in the eyes of many had made nonsense of the long-reiterated claim that given time the Indians were fully capable of absorbing American civilization and assimilable on an equal basis. The people of the United States now had scientific reasons to account for Indian failures and to explain and justify American expansion.[2]

Horsman is not alone in this kind of sweeping (and largely unsubstantiated) generalization. Most important are the similar statements in Thomas F. Gossett's widely used book *Race: The History of an Idea in*

---

1. *American Quarterly* 37 (May 1975): 152–68.
2. Ibid., p. 168. Horsman stated some of the same conclusions (without reference to the scientists) in his earlier article, "American Indian Policy and the Origins of Manifest Destiny," *University of Birmingham Historical Journal* 11, no. 2 (1968): 128–40.

America.[3] Gossett, like other writers on racism in the United States, is concerned primarily with attitudes and findings about blacks, and the Indians appear in many cases only incidently or lumped together with "other nonwhite races." But he does have a chapter on "The Indian in the Nineteenth Century" in which he makes a number of remarkable assertions, including the following:

> The nineteenth century was obsessed with the idea that it was race which explained the character of peoples. The notion that traits of temperament and intelligence are inborn in races and only superficially changed by environment or education was enough to blind the dominant whites. The Indians suffered more than any other ethnic minority from the cruel dicta of racism. The frontiersman, beset with the problem of conquering the wilderness, was in no mood to understand anything about the Indians except that they were at best a nuisance and at worst a terrible danger. The leading thinkers of the era were generally convinced that Indian traits were racially inherent and therefore could not be changed. The difference between the frontiersmen's view of the Indians and that of the intellectuals was more apparent than real. In general, the frontiersmen either looked forward with pleasure to the extinction of the Indians or at least were indifferent to it. The intellectuals were most often equally convinced with the frontiersmen that the Indians, because of their inherent nature, must ultimately disappear. They were frequently willing to sigh philosophically over the fate of the Indians, but this was an empty gesture.[4]

Similar statements appear in the writings of Russel B. Nye, woven into a rather loose discussion of views about the Indians:

> The anthropology of the times assumed that race was a determining factor in people's destiny; color, character, and intelligence went together; certain traits were inherent in certain races, nor could they be substantially altered by either education or environment. Some races were better than others, the Indian and Negro being lowest in the scale.

> The idea of the Indian as irremediably savage was the commonly accepted basis for thinking about him for the first half of the nineteenth century.

3. Thomas F. Gossett, *Race: The History of an Idea in America* (Dallas: Southern Methodist University Press, 1963).
4. Ibid., p. 244.

It was generally agreed that the Indian's racial inheritances made it impossible to civilize him.[5]

There is little doubt that whites in the nineteenth century, including the officials of the Indian Office and other policy makers, considered Indian *cultures* inferior to their own, for the cultural pluralism of today was not a viable idea at the time. The question, however, is not about the culture of the Indians but about their innate racial inferiority. Were the Indians judged to be biologically—as a race—inherently inferior, and if so, did this view affect Indian policy? The statements of Horsman, Gossett, and Nye jar strangely with fundamental documents on the formulation and underpinnings of Indian policy in the nineteenth century and with widespread patterns of belief.

We can look at the problem first in the Jeffersonian period.[6] The Enlightenment thought reflected by Thomas Jefferson and contemporary thinkers had no place for ideas of racial inferiority in regard to the Indians. Those men believed in the unity of mankind. "We shall probably find," Jefferson wrote of the Indians in his *Notes on the State of Virginia,* "that they are formed in mind as well as in body, in the same module with the 'Homo sapiens Europaeus.'"[7] They believed that mankind passed, inexorably, through stages of society, from savagism, through barbarism, to civilization. Jefferson expressed this view in a striking comparison of geographical states with temporal ones.

Let a philosophic observer commence a journey from the savages of the Rocky Mountains, eastwardly towards our seacoast. These [the savages] he would observe in the earliest stage of association living under no law but that of nature, subsisting and covering themselves with the flesh and skins of wild beasts. He would next find those on our frontiers in the pastoral state, raising domestic animals to supply the defects of hunting. Then succeed our own semi-barbarous citizens, the pioneers of the advance of civilization, and so in his progress he would meet the gradual shades of improving man until he would reach his, as yet, most improved state in our seaboard towns.

5. Russel B. Nye, *Society and Culture in America, 1830–1860* (New York: Harper and Row, 1974), pp. 214–15.

6. A valuable discussion of the problem is in Bernard W. Sheehan, *Seeds of Extinction: Jeffersonian Philanthropy and the American Indian* (Chapel Hill: University of North Carolina Press, 1973).

7. *Notes on the State of Virginia* (Richmond: J. W. Randolph, 1853), p. 67.

This, in fact, is equivalent to a survey, in time, of the progress of man from the infancy of creation to the present day.[8]

The Jeffersonians were environmentalists, holding that conditions and circumstances of life made men what they were and that by changing the environment man's culture would be changed. There was no room in this optimistic framework for innate, racial inferiority not amenable to perfecting influences. And in practice the men of the Enlightenment sought ways to bring about the transformation in Indian society which they believed possible and inevitable. Washington and Jefferson, and their secretaries of war, Knox and Dearborn, promoted the civilization of the tribes by the introduction of agriculture and domestic arts, and the trade and intercourse laws made provision for these measures. Success, they thought, was assured. Dearborn expressed his opinion to the Creek agent in 1803: "The progress made in the introduction of the arts of civilization among the Creeks must be highly pleasing to every benevolent mind, and in my opinion is conclusive evidence of the practicability of such improvements upon the state of society among the several Indian Nations as may ultimately destroy all distinctions between what are called Savages and civilized people."[9]

In the second, third, and fourth decades of the century, these philanthropic sentiments were still strong, but Enlightenment thought had in fact been mixed with, or perhaps it would be more accurate to say replaced by, another strain of thought, which for want of a better term can be called evangelical Christianity. The views about the nature of the Indians and the possibility of their transformation held by the rationalists and by the churchmen were much the same if not identical. But the basis was different. One built on the rationalism of the Enlightenment, on the laws of nature discovered in God's creation by rational men. The other was a product of a new surge of evangelical religion that came with the turn of the century, a new missionary spirit, a revivalism that was to be a dominant mark of Protestant Christian America for a full century or more. The faith of Christians was less easily dislodged by new scientific discoveries than was the rationalism of Jeffersonians.

Indicative of the new force as the establishment in 1810 of the

8. Jefferson to William Ludlow, September 6, 1824, *The Writings of Thomas Jefferson*, ed. Andrew A. Lipscomb, 20 vols. (Washington: Thomas Jefferson Memorial Association, 1903–1904), 16:74–75.

9. Dearborn to Benjamin Hawkins, May 24, 1803, Secretary of War, Letters Sent, Indian Affairs, vol. A, pp. 349–50, National Archives, Record Group 75.

American Board of Commissioners for Foreign Missions in Boston to evangelize the heathen—including the American Indians—and the Board's founding of a school for the Cherokees at Brainerd in 1816. It may be unfair to single out one missionary society, for Methodists and Baptists and Quakers and Episcopalians all at about the same time began or renewed their efforts to convert and civilize the Indians of the United States. However we mark the beginnings, official Indian policy and Indian missionary activities of these Protestant churches joined in a close partnership that lasted until the end of the century. So firmly entrenched was this religious missionary approach to Indian affairs that it could not be easily disrupted; it was the chief reason why Indian policy development was so frequently, if not universally, a reform movement.

There is evidence, from the first years of the new nation, of government-missionary cooperation, which harked back to colonial Christian enterprises among the Indians. Even Secretary of War Henry Knox, on whom depended much of the initial formulation of Indian policy, looked to missionaries to supply the aid the government wanted to provide the Indians in leading them to civilization. But the key man in developing missionary-government activity in Indian affairs in the early nineteenth century was Thomas L. McKenney, who, with his appointment as superintendent of Indian trade in 1816, began a lifetime of interest in and influence on Indian policy. McKenney, of Quaker background, can hardly be considered a man of the Enlightenment. He was a *Christian* humanitarian, for whom the civilization and Christianization of the Indians was of great moment. He was unequivocal in his stand on the equality of the red race and the reasons for his opinion. In a letter to Christopher Vandeventer in 1818, asking for a copy of a manuscript by Lewis Cass on Indian relations, McKenney said: "I will be gratified, I am sure, with a perusal of Gov. Cass's view of our Indian relations. I hope he has considered them as Human Beings,—because, if he has not, I shall believe the good book is profane to him, which says, 'of *one blood,* God made all the nations to dwell upon the face of the earth.' And were this not satisfactory an Anatomical examination would prove it—And it might be an affair of Mercy to let *skeptics* have a few Indians for dissection."[10]

10. McKenney to Christopher Vandeventer, June 21, 1818, Christopher Vandeventer Collection, Clements Library, University of Michigan, note supplied by Herman J. Viola. An excellent discussion of McKenney and his humanitarian views is Herman J. Viola, *Thomas L. McKenney: Architect of America's Early Indian Policy, 1816–1830* (Chicago: Swallow Press, 1974).

McKenney was a tireless instigator of missionary efforts for the Indians, and he made his Indian trade office a continuing center for planning and prodding. His big effort was persuading Congress to appropriate money for the education and civilization of the Indians. His success in getting the "civilization fund" established in 1819 was a great missionary and humanitarian victory. The use of the fund, determined by Secretary of War Calhoun, was dependent upon "benevolent societies," that is the missionaries, who were already at work in Indian education and for whom the federal funds were a tremendous inducement to expand their Christian enterprises.[11]

When McKenney was appointed by Calhoun in 1824 to head the Indian Office established in the War Department, he did not change his views about the inherent equality—and therefore capabilities—of the Indians, nor did he weaken his drive to provide them with the means to transcend their savage state and quickly assume the characteristics of the white Christian society of which McKenney and other humanitarians were so proud. In his first report he noted the laudatory reports from the superintendents of the Indian schools in operation and remarked:

They certainly demonstrate that no insuperable difficulty is in the way of a complete reformation of the principles and pursuits of the Indians. Judging from what has been accomplished since the adoption by the Government, in 1819 of the system upon which all Schools are now operating and making due allowance for the tardy advancements of the first 2 or 3 years, which are for the most part consumed in the work of preparation and in overcoming the prejudices and apprehensions of the Indians, there is good reason to believe, that an entire reformation may be effected, (I mean among the tribes bordering our settlements, and to whom those benefits have been extended,) in the course of the present generation.[12]

McKenney's immediate successors in the Indian Office were of the same mind. This is not surprising, for there were few questions in humane and rational men's minds about the fundamental equality of all men and the possibility, by proper education, of bringing the children of the forest up to the high cultural level of the whites.

11. The law is in *United States Statutes at Large,* 3:516–17. McKenney's promotion of the measure is treated in Viola, *McKenney,* pp. 39–46.

12. Report of the Commissioner of Indian Affairs, 1824, in *House Document* no. 2, 18th Cong., 2d sess., ser. 113, pp. 106–7.

The removal question, which dominated much of the public discussion of Indian affairs in the decade after 1825, did not upset the consensus. The question of the speed at which civilization was progressing, to be sure, was much argued, and the deleterious effects of proximity to the vices of white society much debated, but neither side doubted the innate capability of the Indian. The antiremoval crusade, led and dominated to a large degree by the evangelical humanitarians of the American Board of Commissioners for Foreign Missions, was, as might be assumed, the more vocal on the point of Indian capabilities. "I believe, sir," Senator Theodore Frelinghuysen declared in Senate debates in 1830, "it is not now seriously denied that the Indians are men, endowed with kindred faculties and powers with ourselves; that they have a place in human sympathy, and are justly entitled to a share in the common bounties of a benignant Providence. And, with this conceded, I ask in what code of the law of nations, or by what process of abstract deduction, their rights have been extinguished?" Senator Asher Robbins, of Rhode Island, declared with equal vehemence: "The Indian is a man, and has all the rights of man. The same God who made us made him and endowed him with the same rights; for 'of one blood hath he made all the men who dwell upon the earth.'"[13]

There was considerable argument in support of removal on the basis of unfavorable reports about the Indians' conditions and progress in civilization. But Wilson Lumpkin, of Georgia, the chief spokesman for removal, admitted: "I entertain no doubt that a remnant of these people may be entirely reclaimed from their native savage habits, and be brought to enter into the full enjoyment of all the blessings of civilized society. It appears to me, we have too many instances of individual improvement amongst the various native tribes of America, to hestiate any longer in determining whether the Indians are susceptible of civilization."[14]

Then, about 1840, the almost universal agreement about the nature of the Indians and their origin faced a dramatic challenge from the American School of ethnology. The cranial measurements of Morton, the somewhat flamboyant antics of Gliddon, and the propagandistic publications of Nott brought to the public an alternative view of the Indians, and one wrapped in the mantle of science.

Unable to reconcile accepted timetables of human history, based on a reading of the Bible, with the diversity of human races, the purveyors

13. *Register of Debates in Congress,* 6:311, 376.
14. Ibid., p. 1016.

of the new doctrine opted for polygenesis—the separate creation of the races as distinct species. Once it was admitted that the blacks and the Indians were different species from the Caucasians and that not all members of the human race were descended from Adam, it was easy to conclude that some races were inherently inferior to others. In the world of practical affairs, the new scientific doctrines could furnish support for the slave status of the blacks and the dispossession and extinction of the Indians.

The question, of course, is precisely this: Did the scientific findings in fact dominate the American mind, and did the formulators of public policy with regard to the nonwhite races accept and then act upon the theories?

In the case of the blacks we can rely upon the judgment of the most thorough and careful student of scientific racism before the Civil War, William R. Stanton. In his study, *The Leopard's Spots,* he concludes that in neither the North nor the South were the scientists' conclusions about the inferiority of blacks accepted as a basis for action. The scientists themselves were not tied together by any desire to support slavery but by an antireligious sentiment. "The conscious extrascientific bond which linked many of these men together," Stanton says, "was not sympathy for Southern institutions but anticlericalism and antibiblicism." He continues: "The doctrine [of diverse origins] was soothing to the cultural nationalism of the times, yet the response of the North might have been anticipated. The doctrine lent comfort to slavery and so could not be accepted as a guide to conduct. Northerners rejected in this context the Jeffersonian ideal that science should be the guide of political life and the arbiter of social problems."[15]

The South, presented with the opportunity to ground the defense of slavery on a scientific basis, turned away. "Southerners," says Stanton, "discerned in the doctrine of multiple origins an assault upon orthodox religion (a shrewd enough interpretation) and chose to hold fast to the latter. . . . The Bible did lend considerable support to slavery, but so did science. Opting for the Bible was the mark of the South's already profound commitment to religion. Heretofore this had not necessarily been an anti-intellectual position. But when the issue was clearly drawn, the South turned its back on the only intellectually respectable defense of slavery it could have taken up." The practical effect for slavery was negative; "the lasting significance of the American researches

---

15. William R. Stanton, *The Leopard's Spots: Scientific Attitudes toward Race in America, 1815-1859* (Chicago: University of Chicago Press, 1960), p. 193.

in ethnology before the Civil War must be sought in the history of science."[16]

A similar conclusion is reached by John S. Haller, Jr., who wrote: "The South was too fundamentalist and New England too moralistic to meet on scientific terms which were unbiblical and unemotional. . . . The stance of the North and South was basically Christian, biblical, and monogenist. The scientific argument of diverse origins, by reason of its generally more anti-biblical approach, moved more and more out of the public eye and back into the closed circle of a few scientific savants."[17]

So much for blacks. But did the doctrines of diverse origins and inferiority of races play a different role in Indian affairs? Can we conclude with Horsman that "the American School of ethnologists in the eyes of many had made nonsense of the long-reiterated claim that given time the Indians were fully capable of absorbing American civilization and assimilable on an equal basis"? Is Gossett correct in concluding that "the notion that traits of temperament and intelligence are inborn in races and only superficially changed by environment or education was enough to blind the dominant whites," that "the Indians suffered more than any other ethnic minority from the cruel dicta of racism"?

The answer is emphatically "no." If, for example, we take the commissioners of Indian affairs as representative of federal policy makers in the heyday of the American School, we find a uniform—and in some cases a very strong—adherence to traditional positions. There are few indications that they were aware of the new scientific theories. If the scientific racism is adverted to at all, it is rejected. The notion that the Indians were men, different from whites because of the conditioning factors of their savage or barbaric culture, but susceptible of reformation and complete civilization, was the fundamental basis of what the commissioners said and did. Although the exigencies of Indian removal in the 1830s disrupted the education and civilization programs, these humanitarian measures were picked up with new enthusiasm in the decades of the 1840s and 1850s. A few typical examples will make this clear.

T. Hartley Crawford, commissioner from 1838 to 1844, was not an easy enthusiast about Indian civilization. He was well aware of past failures, of the slow and tedious climb from savagery to civilization, and he felt that it was impossible without radically changing the ways of the

16. Ibid., pp. 194, 195.
17. *Outcasts from Evolution: Scientific Attitudes of Racial Inferiority, 1859–1900* (Urbana: University of Illinois Press, 1971), pp. 77–78.

Indians. Individual allotments of land, manual training schools (for girls as well as for boys), and persistence on the part of Christian teachers were all essential. At times he almost seemed to despair, but at the end of his term he spoke unequivocally. "Some of . . . [the] tribes," he wrote in 1843, "the most incredulous must admit, are fairly launched on the tide of civilization. The fact of Indian capability to become all that education and Christianity can make man is incontestably established." And the following year he reported: "The condition of the Indian race, as connected with the United States, is, in the general, one of improvement, and slow but sure approaches to civilization, very distinctly marked, in my judgment. It is proved, I think, conclusively, that it is in no respect inferior to our own race, except in being less fortunately circumstanced."[18]

William Medill, Crawford's successor, took a hard line on the necessity of teaching Indians to forsake the chase and take up agriculture: "Thus by slow but sure means may a whole nation be raised from the depths of barbarism to comparative civilization and happiness." Indians in the Pacific Northwest he reported on very favorably. "Through the benevolent policy of various Christian churches," he noted, "and the indefatigable exertion of the missionaries in their employ, they have prescribed and well adapted rules for their government, which are observed and respected to a degree worthy of the most intelligent whites. . . . Under these circumstances, so promising in their consequences, and grateful to the feelings of the philanthropist, it would seem to be the duty of the government of the United States to encourage their advancement, and still further aid their progress in the paths of civilization." He spoke of forcing the Indians to resort to labor, "and thus commence the transition from a state of barbarism and moral depression, to one of civilization and moral elevation."[19]

Orlando Brown, who served only a year as commissioner, declared in 1849: "A great moral and social revolution is . . . now in progress among a number of the tribes, which, by the adoption of similar measures in other cases, might be rapidly extended to most, if not all,

18. Report of the Commissioner of Indian Affairs, 1843, in *Senate Document* no. 1, 28th Cong., 1st sess., ser. 431, p. 273; Report of the Commissioner of Indian Affairs, 1844, in *Senate Document* no. 1, 28th Cong., 2d sess., ser. 449, p. 315.

19. Report of the Commissioner of Indian Affairs, 1845, in *House Document* no. 2, 29th Cong., 1st sess., ser. 480, pp. 454, 455; Report of the Commissioner of Indian Affairs, 1848, in *House Executive Document* no. 1, 30th Cong., 2d sess., ser. 537, p. 394.

of those located on our western borders; so that, in a few years, it is believed that in intelligence and resources they would compare favorably with many portions of our white population." He ended with high optimism: "There is encouraging ground for the belief that a large share of success will, in the end, crown the philanthropic efforts of the Government and of individuals to civilize and to christianize the Indians tribes. . . . [I]t is now no longer a problem whether [the Indians] are capable of self-government or not. They have proved their capacity for social happiness, by adopting written constitutions upon the model of our own, by establishing and sustaining schools, by successfully devoting themselves to agricultural pursuits, by respectable attainments in the learned professions and mechanic arts, and by adopting the manners and customs of our people so far as they are applicable to their own condition. To insure such gratifying results with tribes but recently brought within the jurisdiction of the United States, we have but to avail ourselves of the experience of the past."[20]

Commissioner Luke Lea spoke strongly in the same vein. "The history of the Indian furnishes abundant proof that he possesses all the elements essential to his elevation," he wrote in 1851; "all the powers, instincts, and sympathies which appertain to his white brother; and which only need the proper development and direction to enable him to tread with equal step and dignity the walks of civilized life. . . . That his inferiority is a necessity of his nature, is neither taught by philosophy, nor attested by experience." Lea admitted, however, that "prejudice against him originating in error of opinion on this subject" had been "a formidable obstacle in the way of his improvement."[21]

Another pre–Civil War example was George W. Manypenny. He was not overly sanguine, for he noted the slowness of the Indians' progress toward civilization, but there is nothing in his reports to indicate that he thought ultimate success was impossible. "Much has been effected," he said in 1853, "but far more remains to be done, to secure and accomplish the full and complete regeneration of this singular and interesting race within our borders; but the object is a noble one, and in all respects deserving of the attention and energies of the government of a great Christian people." Manypenny saw many drawbacks to Indian progress—including "erroneous opinions and prejudices in relation to the disposition, characteristics, capacity, and intellectual powers of the

20. Report of the Commissioner of Indian Affairs, 1849, in *House Executive Document* no. 5, 31st Cong., 1st sess., ser. 570, p. 957.

21. Report of the Commissioner of Indian Affairs, 1851, in *Senate Executive Document* no. 1, 32d Cong., 1st sess., ser. 613, p. 274.

race"—but he himself did not despair. "I believe," he said, "that the Indian may be domesticated, improved, and elevated; that he may be completely and thoroughly civilized, and made a useful element of our population."[22]

Crawford, Medill, Lea, Brown, and Manypenny clearly did not accept the view of the Indian proposed by Morton, Gliddon, Squier, and Nott. They did not subscribe to the racist positions of *DeBow's Review* and the *Democratic Review*. Their viewpoints and their actions (especially in regard to education for the Indians) continued to follow the pattern of evangelical Christianity of the first decades of the century.

Moreover, they consciously aligned themselves with the missionaries to the Indians, relying on the churches in large part for the program of education and civilization they espoused. This partnership was explicitly acknowledged by William Medill in 1847:

> In every system which has been adopted for promoting the cause of education among the Indians, the Department has found its most efficient and faithful auxiliaries and laborers in the societies of the several Christian denominations, which have sent out missionaries, established schools, and maintained local teachers among the different tribes. Deriving their impulse from principles of philanthropy and religion, and devoting a large amount of their own means to the education, moral elevation and improvement of the tribes, the Department has not hesitated to make them the instrument, to a considerable extent, of applying the funds appropriated by the government for like purposes. Their exertions have thus been encouraged, and a greater degree of economy at the same time secured in the expenditure of the public money.[23]

The commissioners, of course, were not alone in ignoring scientific racism nor in their understanding of the Indian and their hopes for his future. They no doubt felt reinforced by the opinions of men who knew the Indians from long contact and study.

Henry R. Schoolcraft, the longtime agent to the Chippewas and one of America's noted ethnologists, was disgusted with Nott and Gliddon's book, *Types of Mankind*. "Well," he remarked in 1854, "if this be all,

22. Report of the Commissioner of Indian Affairs, 1853, in *Senate Executive Document* no. 1, 33d Cong., 1st sess., ser. 690, p. 264; Report of the Commissioner of Indian Affairs, 1855, in *Senate Executive Document* no. 1, 34th Cong., 1st sess., ser. 810, pp. 338, 340.

23. Report of the Commissioner of Indian Affairs, 1847, in *Senate Executive Document* no. 1, 30th Cong., 1st sess., ser. 503, p. 749.

that America is to send back to Europe, after feasting on her rich stores of learning, science, philosophy & religion for three centuries, it were better that the Aborigines had maintained their dark empire of pow pows & jugglers undisturbed."[24]

Thomas L. McKenney, appearing on the lecture circuit in the 1840s with lectures on the "origin, history, character, and the wrongs and rights of the Indians," held firm to monogenesis.

> I am aware [he said] that opinions are entertained by some, embracing the theory of multiform creations; by such, the doctrine that the whole family of man sprang from one original and common stock, is denied. There is, however, but one source whence information can be derived on this subject—and that is the Bible; and, until those who base their convictions on Bible testimony, consent to throw aside that great land-mark of truth, they must continue in the belief that "the Lord God formed *man* of the dust of the ground, and breathed into his nostrils the breath of life, when he became a living soul." Being thus formed, and thus endowed, he was put by his Creator in *the* garden, which was eastward, in Eden, whence flowed the river which parted, and became into four heads; and that from his fruitfulness his species were propagated.[25]

The propagation of the entire human race from "an original pair," McKenney asserted, "is a truth so universally admitted, as to render any elaborate argument in its support superfluous." Since the Eden of Adam and Eve was not in America, the Indians could not have been indigenous to America. McKenney believed that the Indians were of Asiatic origin and had migrated to the New World by way of the Bering Strait.[26] He argued in his lectures against those who said that the Indian was irreclaimable.

The pioneer anthropologist Lewis Henry Morgan, too, seemed unaffected by the stir of scientific racism. Morgan's solution for the Indian problem was not destruction but assimilation. The Indians, he wrote in 1845, "must prepare to be incorporated into the great brotherhood of American nations as equal citizens; perhaps even be engrafted on our race. I sincerely hope this may be the result." His famous *League of the Iroquois* was intended, he wrote in the first sentence, "to

24. Quoted in Stanton, *Leopard's Spots*, p. 192.
25. Thomas L. McKenney, *Memoirs, Official and Personal; With Sketches of Travels among the Northern and Southern Indians*, 2 vols. in 1 (New York: Paine and Burgess, 1846), 2:14.
26. Ibid., p. 15.

encourage a kindlier feeling towards the Indian, founded upon a truer knowledge of his civil and domestic institutions, and of his capabilities for future elevation."[27] Morgan argued in 1852 that inequality among men was not innate, but rather social and artificial.

Horsman ends his study at 1859 and leaves the impression that by mid-century America had accepted the racist doctrines of the scientists, that the decades of the 1840s and 1850s were a watershed, which the men in the Office of Indian Affairs were a bit slow to cross ("repeating the old rhetoric") but which they would ultimately and inevitably reach. This might be a possible interpretation if one stops at mid-century (although it seems clear that the commissioners were not merely repeating old rhetoric), but it is not possible if one looks at the nineteenth century as a whole. In the first place, the polygenesis doctrines of the American School, on which they rested the diversity of human species and the inferiority of the nonwhite races, were rendered outmoded by the evolutionary theories of Charles Darwin. Morton and Nott and their friends turned out to be scientific oddities, their cranial measurements relegated to the attic like the phrenology with which they flirted. But, more significantly, the Indian policy of the post–Civil War decades continued the optimism and doctrines of Indian perfectibility with which we have been dealing.

The dominance of evangelical Protestant views in Indian policy after the Civil War was, if anything, stronger than it had been before. Three of the commissioners of Indian affairs—Nathaniel G. Taylor, E. P. Smith, and Thomas Jefferson Morgan—were ordained Protestant ministers, and others, like Hiram Price, were prominent laymen in their churches. The Board of Indian Commissioners, established in 1869, was almost a Protestant church body. The assignment of Indian agencies to missionary societies was an abdication by the government of fundamental Indian Office duties, which were thrust into the hands of churchmen and the agents they selected. And when, after 1880, the dominant influence on Indian policy reform came from new reform organizations like the Boston Indian Citizenship Committee, the Women's National Indian Association, the Indian Rights Association, and the Lake Mohonk Conference of the Friends of the Indian, professedly Christian philanthropists were in the saddle.

Scientific racism of the period from 1865 to 1900 was less clearly

27. Quoted in Carl Rezek, *Lewis Henry Morgan, American Scholar* (Chicago: University of Chicago Press, 1960), pp. 30–31, 43. It is interesting to note that this scholarly biography does not even mention any of the men of the American School.

marked toward the Indians than toward the blacks. For "colored races," it was argued, evolution had been slowed or stopped, leaving the Caucasian alone to continually progress. But this line of thought was not reflected in Indian policy formulation. Two examples will suffice.

Commissioner of Indian Affairs Nathaniel G. Taylor (1865–69) was the leader in the campaign to keep Indian affairs in civilian hands and out of the hands of the military. In his annual report of 1868 he presented a remarkable example of the doctrine of efficient causality in regard to civilizing the Indians. He asked the question, How can our Indian tribes be civilized? And he answered, in part:

> History and experience have laid the key to its solution in our hands, at the proper moment, and all we need to do is to use it, and we at once reach the desired answer. It so happens that under the silent and seemingly slow operation of efficient causes, certain tribes of our Indians have already emerged from a state of pagan barbarism, and are to-day clothed in the garments of civilization, and sitting under the vine and fig tree of an intelligent scriptural Christianity.

The example he pointed to was that of the Five Civilized Tribes, which only a short time before had been pagans and savages.

> But behold the contrast which greets the world to-day! The blanket and the bow are discarded; the spear is broken, and the hatchet and war-club lie buried; the skin lodge and primitive tepe have given place to the cottage and the mansion; the buckskin robe, the paint and beads have vanished, and are now replaced with the tasteful fabrics of civilization. Medicine lodges and their orgies, and heathen offerings, are mingling with the dust of a forgotten idolatry. School-houses abound, and the feet of many thousand little Indian children—children intelligent and thirsting after knowledge—are seen every day entering these vestibules of science; while churches dedicated to the Christian's God, and vocal with His praise from the lips of redeemed thousands, reflect from their domes and spires the earliest rays and latest beams of that sun whose daily light now blesses them as five Christian and enlightened nations so recently heathen savages.

"Thus the fact stands out clear, well-defined, and indisputable," Taylor declared, "that Indians, not only as individuals but as tribes, are capable of civilization and of christianization."[28]

28. Report of the Commissioner of Indian Affairs, 1868, in *House Executive Document* no. 1, 40th Cong., 3d sess., ser. 1366, pp. 476–77.

The commissioner then reached his point: "Now if like causes under similar circumstances always produce like effects—which no sensible person will deny—it is clear that the application of the same causes, that have resulted in civilizing these tribes, to other tribes under similar circumstances, must produce their civilization."[29] He pointed to localization of members of the tribe in limited areas, attention to agriculture and pastoral pursuits, and the teachings of Christian missionaries.

A second example is Thomas Jefferson Morgan, who was the epitome of the reforming spirit of the 1880s and 1890s. While he was commissioner of Indian affairs, he delivered an address in Albany on Indian education, which he entitled *A Plea for the Papoose*. It was a sort of fantasy, in which he spoke what he thought Indian infants would say if they could speak. It is a long statement of his belief in the unity of mankind and in the importance of environment. The Indian children had a "kinship with us," he said. "They, too, are human and endowed with all the faculties of human nature; made in the image of God, bearing the likeness of their Creator, and having the same possibilities of growth and development that are possessed by any other class of children."[30]

Morgan noted that many people had treated the Indians badly. "The term 'savage' is often applied to them as carrying with it a condemnation of them as inhuman beings," he wrote; "bloodthirsty, gloating in war, rejoicing in revenge, happy in creating havoc, and irreconcilably hostile to all that is noble, true and good. But if the Indian babies could speak for themselves, they would say that whatever of savagery or brutishness there has been in the history of their people has been due rather to unfortunate circumstances, for which they were not always responsible, than to any inherent defect of nature. Under proper conditions the Indian baby grows into the cultivated, refined Christian gentleman or lovely woman, and the plea for the papoose is that this humanity shall be recognized. Indian nature is human nature bound in red."[31]

He repeated this idea again and again. "All human babies inherit human natures," he insisted, "and the development of these inherent powers is a matter of culture, subject to the conditions of environment. The pretty, innocent papoose has in itself the potency of a painted savage, prowling like a beast of prey, or the possibilities of a sweet and

29. Ibid., p. 477.
30. *A Plea for the Papoose: An Address at Albany, N.Y., by Gen. T. J. Morgan* (n.p., n.d.), pp. 2–3.
31. Ibid., p. 3.

gentle womanhood or a noble and useful manhood. Undoubtedly," he admitted, "there is much in heredity. No amount of culture will grow oranges on a rose bush, or develop a corn-stalk into an oak tree. There is also, undoubtedly, much in the race differences between the Mongolian and the Caucasian, and between these and the African and the Indian, yet the essential elements of human nature are the same in all and in each, and the possibilities of development are limited only by the opportunities for growth and by culture forces. We are all creatures of culture."[32]

To be sure, Morgan and his friends in the reforming groups did not think that the Indians on their reservations should be allowed to stop the onward march of Anglo-Saxon civilization. But it seems clear that it was Indian culture that they condemned, not the innate qualities of the Indians, which they believed should be shaped by education and proper environment. There is just too much evidence, both before and after the Civil War, to permit the conclusion that "it was generally agreed that the Indian's racial inheritances made it impossible to civilize him."[33] The effect of scientific racism on the formulation of Indian policy in the nineteenth century was, indeed, practically nil.

32. Ibid., pp. 3–4.
33. Nye, Society and Culture in America, p. 215.

13

The Board of Indian Commissioners and the Delegates of the Five Tribes

This essay combines two of my interests related to Indian policy—the Board of Indian Commissioners, established in 1869 as a semiofficial body of philanthropists to promote the "peace policy" of President Grant, and the delegates (or agents) of the Five Civilized Tribes, who lobbied in Washington in the post–Civil War period for the welfare of the tribes. The two groups came together when the delegates sought the support of the Board for their special interests. The outcome, as the Board veered away from the position of the delegates, illustrates once again the power of the forces that were working for the dissolution of the tribes.

The goal of the United States government after the Civil War was to establish in the Indian Territory a new political arrangement, looking toward a confederation of the Indian nations into a single territorial government that would eventually become a state of the Union. The plan was explicitly proposed to the representatives of the tribes who met with United States commissioners at Fort Smith in September 1865 to reestablish the old relationships that had been severed by the Indians' adherence to the Confederacy. In addition to giving up western lands and emancipating their slaves, the Five Civilized Tribes were asked to agree to the formation of "one consolidated government."[1]

Printed source: *Chronicles of Oklahoma* 56 (Fall 1978): 247–64.

1. There are accounts of the Fort Smith conference in Roy Gittinger, *The Formation of the State of Oklahoma, 1803–1906* (Norman: University of Oklahoma Press, 1939), pp. 71–78, and Annie Heloise Abel, *The American Indian under Reconstruction* (Cleveland: Arthur H. Clark Company, 1925), pp. 173–218. The report of Dennis N. Cooley, president of the treaty commission, is printed in *House Executive Document* no. 1, 39th Cong., 1st sess., ser. 1248, pp. 482–83.

Although the Indian representatives rejected this proposal at Fort Smith, the treaties signed with the Seminoles, Choctaws and Chickasaws, Creeks, and Cherokees the next year all made elaborate provision for a general legislative council composed of representatives from the Indian nations in the Indian Territory.[2]

These provisions fell short of a full territorial organization, but they indicated the direction in which the federal government intended to move. These intentions were explicitly set forth in the statements of Ely S. Parker, one of the United States commissioners at Fort Smith, who was appointed Commissioner of Indian Affairs by President Ulysses S. Grant in 1869. Parker urged that action be taken to organize the general council spoken of in the treaties. "The accomplishment of this much-desired object," he said, "will give the Indians a feeling of security in the permanent possession of their homes, and tend greatly to advance them in all the respects that constitute the character of an enlightened and civilized people. The next progressive step would be a territorial form of government, followed by their admission into the Union as a State."[3] Bills to organize the Indian Territory as a regular territory of the United States were repeatedly introduced in Congress.[4]

The Indians, it is true, made feints in the direction of the general council indicated in the treaties of 1866. They met at Okmulgee in 1867 and in 1870 drew up a constitution, which provided for some confederated action. It seemed to the federal administration that this document signaled implementation of the government's policy, and President Grant sent it to the United States Congress with the remark: "This is the first indication of the aboriginees desiring to adopt our form of government, and it is highly desirable that they become self-sustaining, self-relying, Christianized, and civilized. If successful in this their first attempt at territorial government, we may hope for a gradual concentration of other Indians in the new Territory."[5] Grant, however, wanted some changes that would give the federal government more

2. Charles J. Kappler, *Indian Affairs: Laws and Treaties,* vol. 2, *Treaties* (Washington: Government Printing Office, 1904), pp. 913–14, 921–22, 935–36, 945–46.

3. Report of the Commissioner of Indian Affairs, 1869, *House Executive Document* no. 1, 41st Cong., 2d sess., ser. 1414, pp. 450–51.

4. A list of the principal bills introduced between 1865 and 1879 to organize the Indian Territory or otherwise to extend federal jurisdiction over the area appears in Gittinger, *Formation of the State of Oklahoma,* pp. 221–23.

5. Letter of Grant, January 30, 1871, *Senate Executive Document* no. 26, 41st Cong., 3d sess., ser. 1440, p. 1.

control over the territory, and the Indians themselves ultimately did not support the consolidation. The Okmulgee Council continued to meet, but it accomplished little, and the United States government continued its drive to provide a territorial government for the Indian Territory by congressional action.[6]

The autonomy of the Five Tribes was severely threatened by these moves, and the Indians fought valiantly and for some decades effectively against them. As an important means to this end, the Cherokees, Creeks, Chickasaws, Choctaws, and Seminoles, following a long-established custom, appointed important men as "delegates" to lobby in Washington for tribal interests. These men, astute and knowledgeable in the white man's world, made a significant impression on Washington officialdom. They missed no opportunity to present their position and argued it well on legal and moral grounds. They drew up and circulated memorials directed against specific territorial bills in Congress, appeared at committee hearings, and sought aid from Indian reform organizations.[7]

The delegates were encouraged at the beginning of Grant's administration by the inauguration of the new president's "peace policy"—an earnest attempt to bring integrity to the Indian service and, by removing fraud and corruption, to promote peaceful relations with the Indian tribes of the plains and mountains. One element of this new policy was the Board of Indian Commissioners, a semiofficial body of humanitarian and philanthropic men, created by Congress in April 1869 to serve without pay in supervising the expenditure of Indian appropriations and in general to share in the administration of Indian affairs. The men who made up the first Board of Indian Commissioners were wealthy businessmen, most of whom had served with the Christian Commission during the Civil War, and who were motivated, indeed driven by a sincere Christian philanthropic zeal. Chaired by Felix R. Brunot, who wrote their public reports, the Board vigorously condemned past

6. For a discussion of the Okmulgee Constitution and its failure, see Allen G. Applen, "An Attempted Indian State Government: The Okmulgee Constitution in Indian Territory, 1870–1876," *Kansas Quarterly* 3 (Fall 1971): 89–99.

7. The work of the delegates can be traced in the archives of the Five Civilized Tribes in the Oklahoma Historical Society and in the delegates' numerous printed memorials and statements, a great many of which are listed in Lester Hargrett, comp., *The Gilcrease-Hargrett Catalogue of Imprints* (Norman: University of Oklahoma Press, 1972). An informative study of the Cherokee delegates is Thomas M. Holm, "The Cherokee Delegates and the Opposition to the Allotment of Indian Lands" (M.A. thesis, University of Oklahoma, 1974).

injustices and promoted a program that it believed would lead to the civilization and Christianization of the Indians and their ultimate absorption into the body politic of the nation.[8]

It was to be expected that the delegates from the Five Tribes, ever alert to sources of aid for their cause, would not ignore the Board of Indian Commissioners. In fact, as early as January 17, 1870, Cherokee and Choctaw delegates appeared before a meeting of the Board. The Cherokee spokesman, William P. Adair, indicated their happiness in meeting the Board and their desire to invoke its aid in securing justice from the government. He discussed "with marked ability" pending treaties, proposed congressional actions, and the matter of territorial legislation. He was followed by Peter Pitchlynn, a Choctaw delegate, who asked for support for schools in his nation. Schools, he argued, "were the basis of civilization, and the gospel followed the path of the schools." The Indians were not an abandoned race, he insisted, for there were too many Christians among them to admit such an idea.[9]

More important to the delegates, however, than the formal business meetings of the Board were the conferences it sponsored each winter in Washington. One function of the Board was to act as liaison between the government and the missionary boards of the various churches who, at Grant's request, had agreed to provide agents and other personnel to manage the Indian reservations. In order to promote this cooperation and to provide a forum for discussion on Indian affairs, the Board held a meeting each January, to which it invited the secretaries of the mission boards to report on their work, and at which also the Commissioner of Indian Affairs and other government officials appeared. These annual meetings offered an important platform for the delegates of the Five Tribes.[10]

8. The composition and work of the Board is described in Francis Paul Prucha, *American Indian Policy in Crisis: Christian Reformers and the Indian, 1865-1900* (Norman: University of Oklahoma Press, 1976), pp. 30–46.

9. Minutes of the Board of Indian Commissioners, January 17, 1870, typed transcript in Newberry Library, Chicago, pp. 23–24. The original minutes are in Records of the Board of Indian Commissioners, National Archives, Record Group 75. A full discussion of Pitchlynn's activities as delegate is found in W. David Baird, *Peter Pitchlynn: Chief of the Choctaws* (Norman: University of Oklahoma Press, 1972).

10. The reports of the conferences, with the exception of the second one, are printed in the annual reports of the Board of Indian Commissioners. The report of the second conference was published separately as *Journal of the Second Annual Conference of the Board of Indian Commissioners with the Representatives of the Religious Societies Cooperating with the Government, and Reports of Their Work*

The Indians were right on hand for the first conference in January 1872 and addressed the assembled philanthropists and missionary leaders. William P. Ross, a Cherokee delegate, presented a brief history of the Cherokees, emphasizing their progress in education and in Christianization. Then he spoke about the attempts of designing whites and their railroad interests to open the Indian Territory and spoke against the changes made by Congress in the Okmulgee Constitution, which entirely changed its character, he said, and made it "simply a territorial government of the United States." He also pointed to the good work being done by the Five Tribes to promote peace and civilization among the "wild brethren of the plains." Ross was followed by Samuel Checote, principal chief of the Creek Nation, speaking through an interpreter, who told of the progress of the Creeks in civilization and Christianity and who condemned the attempts in Congress to organize a territorial government for his country. Such an action, he said, would let in a large class of bad white men with whom the Creeks could not cope, and a territorial government would be considered "as a great judgment sent to afflict his people." But he expressed his confidence in the religious men present. Finally, the meeting heard Peter Pitchlynn, who touched the hearts of his audience by a recital of the good work of missionaries among the Choctaws, with special emphasis on work for temperance. "It is the politicians who ruin us," he said. "I shall always remember with gratitude the 'American Board' and the 'Presbyterian Board'; they saved me."[11]

The Indian delegates were well received, in large part no doubt because most of them had been trained by missionaries of the churches represented at the conference. They spoke in favor of schools and other civilizing and Christianizing forces in terms that were understood and applauded by the assembled missionaries and public officials. At any rate, their plea was heard in 1872 by the Board of Indian Commissioners. In its official report to the President of the United States in November 1872, the Board declared: "The convictions of the Board that it is the imperative duty of the Government to adhere to its treaty stipulations with the civilized tribes of the Indian Territory, and to protect them against the attempts being made upon their country for the settlement of the whites, have undergone no change." The Board

---

among the Indians (Washington: Government Printing Office, 1873). These missionary conferences, held in January, were included in the annual report for the previous year; thus the January 1872 meeting was reported in the annual report for 1871.

11. *Report of the Board of Indian Commissioners,* 1871, pp. 170–72.

denied that "a barbarous, aboriginal race may shut out from the occupancy of civilization vast regions of country over which they may roam
simply because they were first on the soil," but it argued that this
principle did not apply to Indian reservations in general and especially
not to the Indian Territory, where the lands were not held by aboriginal
title but by a firm title conveyed by the United States by treaty. "If
national honor requires the observance of national obligations entered
into with the strong, how much more with the weak," the Board declared.

> To repudiate, either directly or by any indirection, our solemn treaty
> obligations with this feeble people, would be dishonor, meriting the
> scorn of the civilized world. The passage of any law for the organi-
> zation of a territorial government not acceptable to the civilized
> tribes, (which have long since ably demonstrated their capacity for
> self-government,) and which would indirectly open their country for
> the ingress of the whites, would, in the opinion of the Board, be such
> an infraction of our obligations.

The Board went out of its way to counter the arguments of proponents
of territorial organization that the Indians in the Indian Territory were
"a horde of savage nomads standing in the way of civilization" by
supplying detailed statistics comparing the Indian Territory, most
favorably, with other United States territories in population, schools,
crop production and the like.[12]

The Indian delegates knew that they could not relax their vigilance,
and they continued to attend the January meetings of the Board in
Washington. In 1873, when the secretary of the American Baptist
Home Missionary Association suggested that the Indians in the Indian
Territory had more land than they needed and that the territory should
be opened to whites, William P. Ross immediately arose to counter
those views with a well-reasoned and effective speech. Ross emphasized
the rights of the Cherokees to the land in fee simple and argued that
there could be no justification for limiting the amount of land any
individual Indian could hold. And he noted again that the nations had
been guaranteed the right of self-government when they were induced
to move west in the 1830s.[13]

As the agitation in Congress for territorial organization increased, the
Indian delegates became more outspoken. At the 1874 conference,

---

12. Ibid., 1872, pp. 11–13.
13. *Journal of the Second Annual Conference*, pp. 57–60.

Ross and Adair of the Cherokees and Pleasant Porter of the Creeks made explicit pleas for the support of the Board. They reiterated their descriptions of the civilized status of their people and insisted that they wanted to be left alone to develop along their own lines, according to the treaty stipulations for self-government under which they had left their homes east of the Mississippi. The extension of territorial government over the Indian Territory, Porter declared, was the most dangerous experiment that could be conceived. "You may think the Indians love their country," he said, "which they do; but they love self-government. Love to control themselves according to their own notions is far greater than anything else. They will give up their homes. They have done so since the first time the white man met the Indians—have gone westward, westward. Why? To govern themselves. That is the first idea of an Indian."[14]

Adair was even more forceful and plain-spoken, as he rose to support Porter's remarks:

> . . . the great question with us Indians is—as it is with everybody else under similar circumstances—that of existence; the question of our salvation. I feel a great deal like my friend Colonel Porter. These other questions are good to talk about; they are essential; but the great question with us is, whether we shall be permitted to exist, or whether we shall be rubbed from the face of existence. This question is now involved here, is pending before this Congress, and we would like to have the help of this commission.

He thanked the members for past help, for reporting in the previous year against territorial measures and for their praise of Indian education and improvement. The Indians' situation had improved still more, he noted, and he wanted the Board again to support their position.[15]

Adair praised the peace policy and its success. "It is based upon philanthropic ideas," he said, "upon ideas of justice. I know it has been assailed, but its assailants have been those opposed to the principles which lie at the foundation of the policy. A great many would like to see the policy abandoned, because they would like to see the Indians destroyed." After reciting the facts of their removal from the East and the guarantees given of protection of their rights, he indicated clearly what territorial organization would mean. "You all know, gentlemen, that the very moment that country is made a Territory of the United

14. *Report of the Board of Indian Commissioners*, 1873, pp. 211–12.
15. Ibid., pp. 213–14.

States instead of being, as now, a confederation of Indian tribes, at that very moment Congress will turn its inhabitants into citizens of the United States. That would be the logical result. I do not see how it could be any other way." Because the Constitution declared that citizens of any state or territory had equal rights in all, he argued, as a regular territory the Indian Territory would necessarily be open to all. He ridiculed the provisions inserted into some of the bills in Congress which purported to protect the Indians' rights. "It is a bait, a deception, a myth," he said; "it means nothing in view of the Constitution."[16]

The Indian delegates won again in this assembly. The conference voted to reaffirm its former action in support of the "sacredness of the rights of the Indians to the territory they enjoy." The formal report of the Board of Indian Commissioners, dated January 20, 1874, strongly reconfirmed the position taken a year earlier.[17]

It was the delegates' last victory with the Board of Indian Commissioners, for the year 1874 brought a striking change in the composition of the Board and with it a reversal of the Board's official position on the question of territorial government for the Indian Territory. The first members of the Board of Indian Commissioners had begun their work with great enthusiasm and an optimism that looked for a rapid and successful elimination of fraud and corruption. They expected to have—and to a large extent at first did have—a strong voice in the spending of money for the purchase of Indian goods and the supplying of the agencies and in the general management of Indian affairs. But their goodness and their Christian outlook proved in the long run to be no match for unscrupulous politicians and spoilsmen in the Indian service. Little by little their recommendations and prescriptions were ignored, until in 1874 they gave up in disgust and resigned en masse. The Board was not destroyed, for new members, with Clinton B. Fisk as chairman, were appointed to fill the posts vacated, but the new Board seemed to lack the purpose and the strength of the old. Although ostensibly the replacements were similar men of Christian motivation and philanthropic spirit, they lacked the willingness or the ability to stand up to the currents of Indian policy that dominated much of the executive branch and the Congress. The new Board was a more pliant group, considerably less heedful of the views of the Indian delegates from the Five Tribes, and willing to accept the arguments of the Commissioner

16. Ibid., pp. 214–15.
17. Ibid., pp. 4–5, 215.

of Indian Affairs and the Secretary of the Interior that the Indian Territory was badly governed by the Indians.

At its meeting in November 1874, the Board appointed a committee of its members to travel to the Indian Territory in order to confer with the leaders of the Five Tribes and to investigate firsthand the conditions in the territory about which the advocates of territorial government and their Indian opponents were so much at odds. Assembling at St. Louis, Missouri, on December 9, 1874, the committee, led by Fisk, journeyed as a body to Muskogee, Indian Territory, to confer with the delegates from the Indian nations "touching the condition of the Territory, and such legislation in behalf thereof as might be deemed necessary to give better security to persons and property therein."[18] The committee members did not go as neutral observers, however, for they had already endorsed the views of the Commissioner of Indian Affairs and the Secretary of the Interior in their recent annual reports, which stressed the state of lawlessness in the Indian Territory. "The efforts of the Indians to organize a government which will enforce law and give security to persons and property," Secretary Delano had declared, "have thus far totally failed, and the lawlessness and violence that prevail in that Territory call for immediate legislation." He recommended a territorial government or, if that was impossible, federal courts within the territory. It was a view, the committee noted, endorsed by President Grant in his annual message of December 7, 1874.[19]

After discussion and deliberation, the Indian delegations of the Cherokees, Creeks, Chickasaws, and Seminoles who were present issued a joint response to the committee. They expressed their thanks and appreciation to the members of the Board of Indian Commissioners and to President Grant "for his benign Indian policy, and their admiration for his views on the Indian question, and their gratitude for his steady adherence to the same." But with these polite conventions out of the way, they flatly rejected the recommendations that had been presented to them. They reaffirmed "their adherence to the stipulations of their treaties with the United States," and asked that they "be fully carried out in good faith." They declared their unwillingness "to take the initiative or to participate in any movement that may lead to a change in their national condition or of their relations with the United States."

18. *Report of the Board of Indian Commissioners,* 1874, p. 97.
19. Secretary Delano's report is in *House Executive Document* no. 1, pt. 5, 43d Cong., 2d sess., ser. 1639, pp. xiv–xv; Grant's endorsement is in *House Executive Document* no. 1, pt. 1, 43d Cong., 2d sess., ser. 1634, p. xviii.

Then they listed a series of grievances for which they sought redress "without endangering any rights now guaranteed to them, either in soil or self-government." Among the grievances were delays in paying moneys due to tribes, contingent grants of lands in the Indian Territory made to railroads by Congress, failure of the government to protect the Indians from intrusion and trespass on their lands, and the "injury done the people of this Territory by the constant agitation of measures in Congress, including bills to organize the Indian country into a Territory of the United States, which threaten the infraction of rights guaranteed to them, and which thus keep them unsettled as to their future, and which entail upon them large and ruinous expense in the defense of their interests."[20]

This was an uncompromising stand, reaffirming the position taken by the official delegates of the tribes from the beginning of the agitation for territorial organization, but it was seriously weakened in the eyes of Fisk and his committee by the presentation at the conference of a minority report by a group of Cherokees, led by Elias Cornelius Boudinot. Boudinot, member of a distinguished Cherokee family, had opted for the territorial organization of the Indian Territory, for opening surplus lands there to whites, for United States citizenship for the Indians and in general for the incorporation of the territory and its inhabitants into the United States. He took it upon himself to publicly counter the arguments proposed by the official representatives of the nations. In a forceful statement Boudinot supported land in severalty, a territorial government, establishment of United States courts in the Indian Territory and a delegate from the territory in Congress. And he said, "We are so well satisfied that a majority of our people would indorse the propositions herein made, that we challenge those who oppose our views to consent that they shall be submitted to a fair vote of the people, under the authority and direction of the United States Government."[21]

The committee of the Board of Indian Commissioners came down firmly on the side of Boudinot. They recommended legislation that would provide a territorial government with an executive appointed by the President and a legislature elected by the people, establishment of United States courts in the territory, and a delegate in Congress.

20. *Report of the Board of Indian Commissioners,* 1874, pp. 97–98.
21. Ibid., pp. 98–99. Boudinot thus continued a sharp division within the Cherokee Nation between the Ross and Ridge-Watie-Boudinot factions, which had its origin in removal from Georgia and was renewed and exacerbated during the Civil War.

Such action by Congress, they asserted, "would receive the hearty in-
dorsement of a great majority of the inhabitants of the Territory, and
the applause of their constituency, who desire that these remnants of a
once powerful people shall be accorded all the protection and benefits
of a Christian civilization." The full Board accepted the report of the
committee and made the three-fold recommendation its own. It added
the words "not inconsistent with existing treaties" to their proposal
for a territorial government.[22]

The question of existing treaty obligations, of course, was the crux
of the matter. The Indian delegates stressed the guarantees of self-
government and exclusion from any state or territory, as well as the fee
simple patent to the land provided by the removal treaties of the 1830s.
The territorial advocates emphasized the protection that the federal
government had promised and the indication of a move toward territorial organization in the treaties of 1866. But it is hard to see how the
recommendation of the Board of Indian Commissioners for establishment of a territorial government consistent with existing treaty rights
was anything but internally inconsistent.

The Chickasaw and Creek delegates responded quickly to the Board's
report with memorials to Congress refuting the assertion that a majority
of the inhabitants of the Indian Territory were in favor of the advocated changes.[23] And delegates continued to attend the conferences
of the Board to fight for support of their rights. At the meeting of
January 13-14, 1875, Cherokee, Creek, and Choctaw spokesmen
renewed their opposition to territorial government, but Boudinot was
also on hand to speak in favor of the move.[24] The Board relented a
little in the stand it had taken in its official report, for it instructed its
acting chairman to write to the House Committee on Indian Affairs,
"explaining the intention of the Board in the views expressed in their
annual report relative to the Indian Territory, as opposed to the establishment of any government for said territory which does not fully
protect the Indians against the introduction of white persons and
alienation of the lands; also expressing the wish of the Board that

22. *Report of the Board of Indian Commissioners,* 1874, pp. 13, 100.

23. Chickasaw memorial, January 15, 1875, *Senate Miscellaneous Document*
no. 34, 43d Cong., 2d sess., ser. 1630; Creek memorial, January 26, 1875, *Senate
Miscellaneous Document* no. 71, 43d Cong., 2d sess., ser. 1630.

24. Minutes of the Board of Indian Commissioners, January 13-14, 1875,
typed transcript, pp. 103-5; *Report of the Board of Indian Commissioners,* 1874,
p. 122.

legislation for the establishment of courts be not endangered by connection with any other measure."[25]

The Board of Indian Commissioners had been well briefed by both sides, and in its 1875 report it included an admirable summary of the two positions. "In this radical conflict of views among the civilized Indians," it noted, "the path of duty may not seem entirely plain; but looking to the greatest good of the greatest number, this board would recommend the establishment of a territorial government *not inconsistent with existing treaties,* and that the lands be surveyed and allotted in severalty . . . , provided, however, that Congress repeal all railroad grants of land within said Territory, and forever annul such rights." In the following year it restated this recommendation in substantially the same terms.[26]

The question of territorial government faded somewhat in the face of the growing interest of the Board of Indian Commissioners and other reformers in the allotment of land in severalty to the Indians as a civilizing panacea.[27] Although there had been severalty provisions in particular laws and treaties for many years, the year 1879 marked the beginning of a drive for a general allotment law that could be applied to all Indians, and the allotment of lands among the Five Tribes became a new crusade. Although the humanitarian reformers promoted allotment on the basis of principle—they saw no possibility of universal civilization of the Indians without individual ownership of land—it was also clear that allotment of limited parcels of land to individuals would open up considerable "surplus" land for whites. Allotment in the Indian Territory, furthermore, would break up land monopolies that the reformers saw developing there.

The Indian delegates were as quick to condemn allotment in severalty as they were to fight territorial organization, realizing the effect it would have on the traditional arrangements in the Indian Territory, and

25. Minutes of the Board of Indian Commissioners, January 15, 1875, typed transcript, p. 108.

26. *Report of the Board of Indian Commissioners,* 1875, p. 14 (italics in original); minutes of the Board of Indian Commissioners, January 20, 1876, typed transcript, p. 128.

27. For a brief history of the movement for allotment, see Prucha, *American Indian Policy in Crisis,* pp. 227–57. There is a detailed account of the Board's agitation for severalty in Henry E. Fritz, "The Board of Indian Commissioners and Ethnocentric Reform, 1878–1893," in Jane F. Smith and Robert V. Kvasnicka, eds., *Indian-White Relations: A Persistent Paradox* (Washington: Howard University Press, 1976), pp. 57–78.

they continued to use the meetings of the Board of Indian Commissioners as one forum in which to advance their cause and to protect their interests.

At the January 1879 meeting of the missionary boards with the Board of Indian Commissioners, the committee of missionary leaders appointed to draw up the platform of resolutions for the conference presented a comprehensive statement reaffirming their "common convictions on several points deemed by them important to the progress of . . . [the] civilization [of the Indians]." These included opposition to transfer of the Indian Bureau to the War Department, extension of a system of law over the Indians, and the establishment by the federal government of an adequate common-school system for Indian children. The second in the list of points called for allotment of land in severalty, with a title in fee and with temporary safeguards against alienation, as "indispensable to the progress of civilization." The Cherokee delegate, William P. Adair, immediately objected. The manner of alloting lands, he told the meeting, was left to the Indians in their treaties. He was willing to accept the rest of the resolutions. "But if the second proposition is to apply to our people," he insisted, "we shall interpose an objection and ask that our treaties be carried out." The resolutions committee weakly replied that their report was not intended to apply to cases where provision was made by treaty.[28]

Indian attendance at the January meetings dropped off in the early 1880s, as the Board of Indian Commissioners continued its strong advocacy of territorial government and allotment of lands in severalty. The secretary of the Board, Eliphalet Whittlesey, made a special investigating tour of the Indian Territory in December 1882, and returned with a report that strengthened the views of the Board.[29] The Board once again reaffirmed its belief in the necessity of more effective government for the territory. It repeated its recommendations of 1874 and added: "Such a measure [for territorial government] would contemplate the ultimate abolition of present tribal relations, the giving of lands in severalty to Indian citizens, and the sale for their benefit of the lands which they will never need and can never use. Under wise legislation the Indian Territory may soon become prosperous, and be admitted a strong and wealthy State into the American Union."[30]

28. *Report of the Board of Indian Commissioners,* 1878, pp. 127–28.
29. Ibid., 1882, pp. 26–36.
30. Ibid., pp. 8–9.

The Board of Indian Commissioners, together with the voluntary organizations devoted to Indian reform that sprang up about 1880, was a firm supporter of the Dawes bill, legislation introduced by Senator Henry L. Dawes of Massachusetts as the last in a series of bills that authorized the President to survey reservations and allot the land in severalty to the Indians. The Senate bill, after long delay, was finally passed by the House of Representatives on December 16, 1886, and sent to the conference committee to iron out amendments.[31] The Board at its meeting of January 6, 1887, made the Dawes bill one of its important pieces of business. The key resolution proposed by the business committee of the conference was this:

> *Resolved,* That we hail with much hope and pleasure the passage by the House of Representatives of the Senate bill providing for the allotment of lands in severalty under wise restrictions, the extension of the laws of the States and Territories over the Indians, giving the protection, rights, and immunities of citizens. That this conference memorialize the President with reference to the importance of making this bill a law by signing it after it has been amended so as to secure in the best way possible these ends. . . .[32]

The severalty legislation was opposed by a small but articulate group at the conference. These were members of the National Indian Defence Association, founded in 1885 by Dr. Thomas A. Bland, editor of the *Council Fire.* Bland and members of his group were on hand to put forth their views, and they were accorded a place on the committee that drew up the resolutions. The Indian Defence Association relied heavily on the Indians from the Indian Territory for membership and for financial support, and the minority report of the resolutions committee was presented by the Creek delegate, Pleasant Porter. While accepting the other resolutions, Porter disagreed with the one on severalty. "I regard this last resolution as relating to the material question," he said. "Whether or not the Indian is to be preserved, depends upon what you do with his land; what laws you establish for his government." He gave a long and eloquent speech against imposing severalty upon the Indians, noting that where it had been tried, it had uniformly failed, and he submitted to the conference an alternate resolution, which read as follows:

31. See the *Report of the Board of Indian Commissioners,* 1884, pp. 10–11; ibid., 1886, p. 9; ibid., 1889, p. 9.

32. *Report of the Board of Indian Commissioners,* 1886, p. 134.

Resolved, That the first thing necessary in the solution of the Indian question is to secure their confidence by fulfilling our treaty stipulations with them; second, to educate them mainly on their reservations in our literature and industrial arts; third, to respect their rights to hold their lands in their own way until we can teach them that our plan is better than theirs, and that full citizenship in the United States is better than membership in a tribe; fourth, to recommend that all bills to open Indian lands to white settlement be laid aside until a commission shall have visited the various tribes, and reported to the Government what reservations can be reduced with safety to the Indians and with their consent.[33]

In the discussion and vote that followed, Porter and his friends lost out. His resolution was overwhelmingly defeated by a vote of forty-seven to thirteen. Then the committee's resolutions were agreed to "by a large majority."[34]

The Board of Indian Commissioners in the next decade moved completely away from the position of the Indian delegates, and the missionary conference in 1895 listened complacently as Charles H. Mansur, former Congressman from Missouri, castigated the delegates from the Five Tribes as "white Indians" and asserted that "the whiter the Indian the more intolerant he was in his argument" and that "the thinner and more diluted the Indian blood, the more capable they become of deceit."[35] The Board accepted the evidence and arguments presented by the Commission to the Five Civilized Tribes (Dawes Commission), which was authorized by Congress in 1893 to negotiate with the tribes for allotment of land and establishment of a territorial government, that the Territory was lawless and that the United States government had an obligation to step in.[36] The proviso of the Board's 1874 proposal, "consistent with existing treaties," had disappeared, and the treaties on which the Indian delegates had rested their case were no longer a bulwark. The Board expressed its views without reservation in early 1896:

33. Ibid.
34. Ibid., p. 136.
35. Ibid., 1894, p. 65.
36. See the *Annual Report of the Commission to the Five Civilized Tribes,* 1894. Similar criticisms of the conditions in the Indian Territory were contained in the report of a Senate Committee headed by Henry M. Teller, in *Senate Report* no. 377, 53d Cong., 2d sess., ser. 3183, and in Charles F. Meserve, *The Dawes Commission and the Five Civilized Tribes of Indian Territory* (Philadelphia: Indian Rights Association, 1896).

The time has come when the United States must see to it that law, education, and possibilities of justice for white men, as well as black men and red men, shall be firmly established and maintained in that Territory. The Indians of the Five Civilized Tribes, under the influence of a few shrewd and selfish leading men, seem to oppose any change in their condition, and claim the right, under treaties with the United States, to be let alone and to manage their own affairs. But our clear conviction is that they have not faithfully observed the purpose and intent of those treaties. The language in which the original grant of the Indian Territory was made to the Five Civilized Tribes, as well as that by which they made subgrants to other tribes, provides plainly and emphatically that the lands "shall be secured to the whole people for their common use and benefit." That this has not been done is well known. A few enterprising and wealthy Indians have managed to occupy and use large tracts of fertile land, while the poor and ignorant have been pushed away into rough and almost barren corners. We believe it to be the duty of the United States Government to maintain its supreme sovereignty over every foot of land within the boundaries of our country, and that no treaties can rightfully alienate its legislative authority, and that it is under a sacred obligation to exercise its sovereignty by extending over all the inhabitants of the Indian Territory the same protection and restraints of government which other parts of our country enjoy.[37]

When the Five Tribes, seeing that further resistance was futile, signed agreements with the Dawes Commission and when Congress in 1897 provided for courts and in 1898 destroyed the tribal governments by the Curtis Act, the Board rejoiced. These actions, it said, "must work a complete revolution in the affairs of the Territory and place it practically under the Government of the United States."[38] And so it was. The "drift of civilization," accepted and encouraged by the Board of Indian Commissioners, proved too strong for the Indian nations and their leaders.[39]

37. *Report of the Board of Indian Commissioners,* 1895, p. 6.
38. Ibid., 1898, pp. 5–6.
39. The quoted phrase is from the *Report of the Board of Indian Commissioners,* 1897, p. 6.

14

A "Friend of the Indian" in Milwaukee: Mrs. O. J. Hiles and the Wisconsin Indian Association

The rise of voluntary associations devoted to Indian rights and Indian welfare included the Women's National Indian Association, founded in Philadelphia in 1879. Its initial purpose was to agitate for protection of treaty rights of the Indians, but it soon adopted the reform measures popular in the day—allotment of lands to individual Indians, education for the Indians, and Indian citizenship. The national association augmented its own work by affiliating with it state and local organizations, which could promote the same ends in their areas. An excellent example of such a local association, I discovered, was the Wisconsin Indian Association, organized in Milwaukee in 1888 and dominated by a powerful leader, Mrs. O. J. Hiles. Much can be learned about the whole movement from this case study.

The last two decades of the nineteenth century were remarkable for tremendous humanitarian concern for the American Indians. As white population multiplied and exerted ever increasing pressure on the Indians and their lands, a crisis developed in Indian affairs that struck the conscience of many Americans. New organizations appeared which devoted themselves to Indian rights and Indian welfare in an effort to solve, at last, the "Indian problem."[1]

Printed source: *Historical Messenger of the Milwaukee County Historical Society* 29 (Autumn 1973): 78–95.

1. For a general discussion of the Indian reform movement in the latter part of the nineteenth century, see Loring B. Priest, *Uncle Sam's Stepchildren: The Reformation of United States Indian Policy, 1865–1887* (New Brunswick: Rutgers University Press, 1942). [A more recent work is Francis Paul Prucha, *American Indian Policy in Crisis: Christian Reformers and the Indian, 1865–1900* (Norman: University of Oklahoma Press, 1976).]

In 1879 a group of dedicated women in Philadelphia, distressed by the disregard for Indian rights in Indian Territory, organized an association to arouse the nation's interest, to lobby in Washington for the Indians, and to aid directly in assuaging the misery of the Indians by home missionary activities. The group adopted the name Women's National Indian Association, and it soon developed a network of state and local auxiliary organizations to further its cause. In 1882 a comparable group of philanthropic men, also in Philadelphia, established the Indian Rights Association, which, under the leadership of Herbert Welsh, served as a watchdog for Indian rights and promoted legal defense of them. These groups worked closely with the semiofficial Board of Indian Commissioners, a body of religious-minded, humanitarian businessmen and intellectual leaders appointed by the President to advise the Indian Office and to help in the formulation of Indian policy.

Beginning in 1883 these groups and other like-minded men and women met annually at a resort hotel at Lake Mohonk, New York. They were guests of the Quaker owner of the resort, Albert K. Smiley, a member of the Board of Indian Commissioners, who invited them to spend three days each autumn in the beautiful surroundings of his resort to discuss Indian affairs and to draw up resolutions on Indian policy, for which they sought public and governmental support. The members unabashedly called themselves the Lake Mohonk Conference of Friends of the Indian, and for two decades and more they were the most influential group in the nation in reforming Indian policy.[2]

One notable characteristic of the Lake Mohonk Conference and of the associations whose members participated in it was their heavily eastern composition. Such centers of humanitarian activity as Boston and Philadelphia dominated the group, and New England and the Middle Atlantic states were strongly represented.

It is striking, then, and of unusual interest that a prominent national figure in the first decade of the movement for Indian reform was a woman from Milwaukee, Mrs. Osia J. Hiles.

Osia Jane Joslyn was born near Batavia, New York, in 1832, but when nineteen years old she migrated to Illinois. There, two years later, she married John Hiles, and the young couple moved to Milwaukee in 1854, where John Hiles and his partner, Truman H. Judd, built up a thriving business in the manufacture of doors, sashes, and blinds.

2. The origin and work of the Lake Mohonk Conference is treated in Larry E. Burgess, "'We'll Discuss It at Mohonk,'" *Quaker History* 40 (Spring 1971): 14–28.

When her husband died in the sinking of the lake steamer *Ironsides* near Grand Haven, Michigan, in 1873, Mrs. Hiles managed her husband's business interests with great skill and then increasingly devoted her talents and energy to philanthropic causes. She was a charter member of the Women's Club of Wisconsin, founded in 1876, and with her special business acumen was an instigator in the formation of a stock company for the erection of the Athenaeum, a stately building at the corner of Kilbourn and Cass, which still serves as the headquarters of the Woman's Club of Wisconsin.

There were few good causes that she did not have a hand in. She was a founder and director of the Nurses' Training School and a director of the Wisconsin Humane Society, and in 1890 Governor William D. Hoard appointed her one of the Wisconsin delegates to the National Conference of Charities and Corrections. She was, in addition, a person of literary ambition, frequently reading original papers before literary and other societies and contributing poetry to the local press. She was described as "a woman of wealth, of stately presence and great personal magnetism, and of a thorough literary understanding." At her death a friend recalled: "She was a woman of remarkable thought and persua- sive eloquence. . . . She was a clear, forceful speaker, and her logic was strong and convincing, while she was at all times gracious and fair to opponents who did not possess equal literary and natural ability."[3]

She was also a firm believer in the ability of women to affect the course of public events. At the Lake Mohonk Conference in 1887, in the midst of discussion about the campaign for Indian rights, she commented: "Now I suppose the subject to be taken up is: What women can do in this work. I think it would be better to tell what they cannot do. I do not believe there is anything that a woman can't do if she undertakes to do it."[4] The talents of this remarkable woman came to be directed primarily to the cause of the American Indians.

Mrs. Hiles's interest in the Indians seems to have been stirred up at first by the writings of Helen Hunt Jackson, a minor literary figure who had become interested in the government's treatment of the Indians.

3. Howard Louis Conard, ed., *History of Milwaukee County from Its First Settlement to the Year 1895,* 3 vols. (Chicago: American Biographical Publishing Company, n.d.), 2:128, 318–20; Fred L. Holmes, ed., *Wisconsin,* 5 vols. (Chicago: Lewis Publishing Company, 1946), 2:517; *Milwaukee Sentinel,* November 3 and 27, 1889, May 3, 1890, February 27, 1902; *Evening Wisconsin* (Milwaukee), February 26, 1902. In most of her articles and public correspondence Mrs. Hiles signed herself "Mrs. O. J. Hiles" and frequently simply "O. J. Hiles."

4. *Lake Mohonk Conference Proceedings,* 1887, p. 52.

In 1881 Mrs. Jackson had published an emotional indictment of United States policy, a book called *A Century of Dishonor,* and followed it three years later with a novel, *Ramona,* which concerned the plight of the Mission Indians of California. It was the latter story which struck Osia Hiles's heart. In a long letter to the Milwaukee *Sentinel,* published on August 9, 1885, Mrs. Hiles made her initial public appeal for the Indians, with a laudatory reference to *Ramona*: "Within the past year a book has been published, which, advocating justice for the Indians, is not only one of the most comprehensive, but also one of the tenderest pleas that has ever been made for an oppressed race. . . . 'Ramona' is an impassioned prayer to the American people, imploring that the Indians shall not be disturbed in the possession of lands upon which they are settled." Mrs. Hiles condemned plans afoot to destroy all the Indian reservations and distribute the Indians throughout the country. "It would," she wrote, "be the modern story of civilization at the point of the bayonet." Should Indian rights to the land be protected, she asked, or "shall these people be 'scattered as fast and as far as possible,' heartbroken, hopeless, a mute reproach to a nation that has been, toward them, faithless from the beginning?"[5]

Mrs. Hiles swung her energy and her financial resources against such an eventuality, taking as her first project immediate action to preserve the Mission Indians on their remnants of land. She made a trip to California in 1886 to investigate conditions first hand, and in October of that year she appeared at the Lake Mohonk Conference to report to the national meeting upon her findings. She reviewed the history of the California Indians and of their land grants, and she described the miserable condition to which they had fallen. "The case of these Indians is exceedingly pitiful; they are so down-trodden," she said. "I never knew before the meaning of the word down-trodden." She urged that an able attorney be employed to contest the encroachment on the Indian lands, a lawyer who could build up a solid case in the lower courts and then carry it successfully to the Supreme Court. Her report started considerable discussion among the participants of the Conference, and her offer to contribute to a fund to pay for a lawyer to

5. *Milwaukee Sentinel,* August 9, 1885. Mrs. Hiles sent a clipping of this article to President Grover Cleveland, excusing her boldness on the ground that "in the contest between Right and Wrong every stroke of the hammer counts, no matter how feebly it is administered." Mrs. John Hiles to President Cleveland, August 12, 1885, in Records of the Office of Indian Affairs, Letters Received, 1885 #19236, National Archives, Record Group 75.

represent the Mission Indians was indicative of her sincerity and made a deep impression on those present.[6]

For two years Mrs. Hiles concentrated her efforts on the cause of the Mission Indians, returning to Lake Mohonk in 1887 to report again on the matter, and she soon was acknowledged as a national leader. The Women's National Indian Association appointed her chairman of its Committee on Mission Indians, and with that backing she moved aggressively on behalf of the suffering Indians. In May 1887 she met with Secretary of the Interior L. Q. C. Lamar and with Commissioner of Indian Affairs J. D. C. Atkins, who encouraged her to report directly to them, and in January 1888 she began an extensive survey of the situation in California.[7]

She boldly reported what she found to Atkins and to the new Secretary of the Interior, William F. Vilas, who replaced Lamar in January 1888. "I arrived here in January last," she wrote to Vilas from Beaumont, California, on April 2, 1888, "and have visited fourteen Reservations and Mexican grants, and from the general conditions found in these, I can deduce fair conclusions regarding those unvisited, more especially as the ones visited are the largest and numerically the most important in this section of the state." She pointed out how useless the existing survey of the Indians' lands had been and how the reservations were being invaded. "On every one the whites are crowding the Indians from their cultivated fields," she wrote, "and causing great disturbance. Taking a little piece of land that has been redeemed from desert barrenness is bad enough, but that is of little moment when compared with its direct results. For instance, water is turned from its natural channels; roads are fenced with wire fences, cattle and horses are turned loose; and, worst of all, personal violence is threatened until the Indians, from being helpless become hopeless. They are unsettled; what they had supposed to be theirs is not theirs; what is left they believe, and rightly, may at any time be taken. It would be useless to say that they should stand for their rights; they are the wards of the Government, not American citizens." She urged that agents be sent to California to protect the Indians and to make sure that when individual allotments of land were made to the Indians that they would get suitable parcels.[8]

Not content to appeal to the Secretary of the Interior, Mrs. Hiles

6. *Lake Mohonk Conference Proceedings*, 1886, pp. 37–38.

7. Ibid., 1887, pp. 93–94.

8. Mrs. O. J. Hiles to William F. Vilas, April 2, 1888, in Records of the Office of Indian Affairs, Letters Received, 1888 #9592.

the following day wrote a long and impassioned letter to the Commissioner of Indian Affairs, in which she reiterated and amplified her complaints. "The Indians never had been shown the boundaries of their reservations," she wrote, "and consequently have no intelligent comprehension of what is actually included within their limits. Hence, when white men take their cultivated lands, which they had fully believed within reservation limits, and tell them they have filed on it, the poor Indians are absolutely and pitably helpless. And they are so much afraid of personal violence,—if a white man kills an Indian, you know he always does it in self-defence;—they stand in such fear of having their few horses and sheep taken should they resist, that they give no sign—unless indeed, their faces take on an added sadness."[9]

Vilas referred Mrs. Hiles's letter to the Commissioner, who did not deign to answer either it or the one he himself had received. But the rebuff did not stop Mrs. Hiles. When she returned to Milwaukee, she wrote again to Vilas, begging for an interview so that she could repeat her plea for the Indians in person. "I will gladly make the journey to Washington," she wrote, "provided you will give me two hours (and I beg to assure you I will ask no more) either in the day or in the evening, at any time most convenient for yourself."[10]

Although the Washington officials took no immediate notice of her reports, she continued her campaign. She was again at Lake Mohonk in October 1888, where her efforts received favorable attention, and in November the Women's National Indian Association published her report of the Committee on the Mission Indians. Then her agitation for the Mission Indians slackened, for ill health prevented her making a trip to California in 1889 as she had planned.[11]

The influence that this one dedicated woman had on the Mission Indian question cannot be accurately assessed, of course, for other reformers repeated her petitions. The Indian Rights Association, in fact, made the Mission Indians a point of special attention until Congress in 1891 finally made provision for the rights of these neglected people. But Mrs. Hiles's reports in public forums, if not her personal appeal to high officials in the government, were an important element in the pressure for reform that brought an eventual solution.

The Mission Indians were but the first of Mrs. Hiles's Indian causes.

9. Mrs. O. J. Hiles to J. D. C. Atkins, April 3, 1888, ibid., 1888 #95720.
10. Mrs. O. J. Hiles to the Secretary of the Interior, May 4, 1888, ibid., 1888 #12912.
11. *Lake Mohonk Conference Proceedings*, 1888, pp. 67, 83, 96; *The Indian's Friend* 1 (November 1888): 4.

Not satisfied with helping to solve that distant problem, she turned also to the Indians of her home state. And in this she enlisted the support of the Woman's Club of Wisconsin. That she was the guiding force amidst a group of benign but relatively unknowledgeable ladies can be seen from the report of a meeting of the Woman's Club in December 1887. It was the last meeting of the club before entering its new rooms in the Athenaeum and was held in the large drawing rooms of Mrs. H. H. Button. A report sent to the Women's National Indian Association described the event:

Mrs. O. J. Hiles read an instructive and original paper upon the Indian question of to-day. It was a strong paper, for the reader remarked that she felt very much in earnest. She certainly seemed imbued with all the fire and enthusiasm of Helen Hunt Jackson in her subject. It was a surprise to her audience, for very few of the ladies had given much if any thought to that which should be a just and Christian dealing with the red race. It bristled with facts and showed a woman's view of the dealings of the United States with the Indians from an Indian standpoint. It is true the whites have dealt unjustly and the red man has retaliated with fiendish and inhuman acts, but the paper taught that when the whites are first humane and just and then Christians that no more broken treaties will exist and that the Indian, as has been proved, is ready to accept a God of love in place of his religion, after which, civilization followed easily. Mrs. Hiles said, that it will belong to the people of our country and to missionaries to hurry on this most necessary work and atone for our sins as a nation.

The hundred or more ladies present listened with silent attention, sometimes with tears, to convincing facts.[12]

Out of this meeting grew the Wisconsin Indian Association, which was formally organized in January 1888 and began its active work in May. It functioned as an auxiliary of the Women's National Indian Association and 1889 already had sixty-five members. Mrs. S. S. Merrill, whose husband was for many years general manager of the Milwaukee Road, was elected president of the Association. Mrs. Hiles was chosen secretary, from which position she was the moving spirit of the organization. She not only kept up the interest of the Milwaukee club women in Indian affairs, but she seems almost singlehandedly to have carried on the public activities of the Association.[13]

12. Ibid., 1 (December 1888): 3.
13. The activities of the Wisconsin Indian Association can be traced year by year in the *Annual Reports* of the Women's National Indian Association. See also *The Indian's Friend* 1 (June 1889): 1; 2 (January 1890): 3.

The members of the Wisconsin Indian Association decided that their first interest would be the Indians of Wisconsin, and they soon had a cause to engage their energies. In February 1888 Congressman Thomas R. Hudd, of Wisconsin, introduced a bill in Congress providing for the allotment of lands on the Oneida reservation in Wisconsin. Unlike the provisions of the general allotment law of 1887 (the Dawes Act), which declared allotted lands inalienable for twenty-five years in order to protect the new individual owners from white sharpers until the Indians had adjusted well to their new roles, the Hudd bill permitted the sale of the Oneida allotments after only five years.[14] When Mrs. Hiles and her associates discovered that white men near the reservation were strong supporters of the bill in the hope of quickly acquiring the Indians' lands and that purported approval of the allotment measure by an Oneida council had come only from "thriftless members of the tribe," the women began a campaign against the Hudd bill. We can let Mrs. Hiles tell the story herself:

We at once wrote to each member and Senator from Wisconsin, asking their opposition. We even wrote to the framer of the bill. We secured the names of the sober, industrious members of the tribe, appended to a statement that the "council" had been held and signatures obtained without their knowledge or consent, and forwarded the same to Washington. We wrote to Senator Dawes and to General Whittlesey [Secretary of the Board of Indian Commissioners] and Herbert Welsh, Esq., asking co-operation. We wrote newspaper articles for our own papers, that the people of Wisconsin might know of the danger to right and truth within their borders. We sent a petition to the President asking that, should the bill succeed in reaching him, he would consider our representations before signing; and we appealed to him, should our representations show sufficient strength, not to sign the bill. We afterwards wrote a second set of letters to the Wisconsin delegation.[15]

Although Hudd's bill passed the House, it was adversely reported in the Senate by Senator Dawes's Committee on Indian Affairs and thereby failed. It was an effective victory for the Milwaukee women.[16]

14. *House Journal,* 50th Cong., 1st sess., ser. 2529, pp. 678, 1861; *House Report* no. 2079, 50th Cong., 1st sess., ser. 2603.

15. *The Indian's Friend* 2 (January 1890): 3. See also *Milwaukee Sentinel,* August 1, 1888; Mrs. S. S. Merrill to the President of the United States, June 8, 1888, in Records of the Office of Indian Affairs, Letters Received, 1888 #15943.

16. *House Journal,* 50th Cong., 2d sess., ser. 2625, p. 415; *Senate Journal,* 50th Cong., 2d sess., ser. 2609, p. 316.

Mrs. Hiles discussed the matter of the Oneida allotments thoroughly at the Lake Mohonk Conference in 1889 and 1890. Although rejoicing that the Hudd bill with its short trust period for allotments had been defeated, she was in favor of applying the Dawes Act to the Oneidas as a means of protecting their landownership. She told of her visit to the Oneidas during the summer of 1889 and how she had urged them to accept allotments. "I think," she said, "that, under the advisement of their friends, aided by the advice of the missionaries, they will submit to the allotment, hoping and trusting that the watchfulness of their friends will prevent any legislation unfriendly to their interests in the future." Her description of the Oneidas for her Lake Mohonk friends clearly indicated her desire to see the Indians all assimilated into the white man's culture:

> I wish you could see them. I have sat here to-day thinking about them as I saw them, while this question of civilizing the Indian had been discussed. Without knowing it, the Oneidas have settled the question. It was a large gathering which I met in July; and it was characterized by perfect order and decorum. Except for their faces and their unusually grave and dignified bearing, I should not have known them from a similar assemblage of whites. Every woman was well dressed; every little child was dressed as neatly as a white child would be dressed at such a gathering; every infant was clothed in a long white dress, trimmed and embroidered, and spotlessly white. Men and women alike listened to the words that were said to them with evident comprehension. I was greatly impressed with the perfect atmosphere among them of the white man's manner.[17]

The success of Mrs. Hiles and her Association in the Oneida case encouraged them soon to undertake another task, this time concerned with the sale of pine from the Indian lands in Wisconsin. As pine was cut and sold on the Indian reservations, large sums of money passed into the hands of the Indians. The result was not material progress but demoralization, for the Indians used the money to buy liquor, with great detriment to missionary and educational endeavors among the tribes. Such a condition understandably distressed Mrs. Hiles and her friends, and they set about to apply a remedy. The Wisconsin Indian Association sent a delegate to the annual meeting of the Wisconsin

17. *Lake Mohonk Conference Proceedings, 1889*, pp. 42–43. Mrs. Hiles's remarks at Lake Mohonk in 1890 were about the threats to Oneida lands from whites in the region. Ibid., 1890, pp. 146–47.

W.C.T.U. in June 1889, to ask that organization to work for better enforcement of the liquor laws of the state. But the Association turned also to what it considered more effective means: to strike at the source of money flowing into Indian hands that made possible the purchase of debilitating liquor. It urged that the timber be sold at auction and that the total receipts be funded or held in trust by the government, with only the interest therefrom (plus some small part of the principal, if necessary) paid to the Indians from time to time to meet their essential needs.[18]

Mrs. Hiles drew bold pictures of the existing condition of the Indians and of the wonderful contrast that would occur if the plan of the women were enacted. "Under the present method," she wrote in an article for the *Sentinel,* "setting aside the question of worse than thriftless habits which will work their ruin, the future of these Indians is being slowly hauled away with the timber; and when the last money shall have been received and paid out for liquor freely furnished, their future will be suddenly shut out—nothing will lie ahead. They will be stranded on sandy, almost worthless pine lands, where white man's thrift would scarcely save from starvation. An Indian, unaccustomed to farming, with no money, and with 160 acres of stumps set in sand, must feel hedged in from any thought of the morrow."[19]

To the Secretary of the Interior, John W. Noble, she pictured the moneys from the pine sales making "a rapid circuit, either through saloons or through contract stores, back into the hands of the whites"; of the ten million dollars paid for pine on the reservations within the past ten years, little remained, she asserted, "excepting results—drunkenness, disoluteness, and general demoralization."[20]

Her plan would change all that. "If the money should be funded, the cutting of the timber would be a positive benefit for the Indians," she asserted; "it would furnish them a steady income and help clear the land for whatever of agricultural power it may hold. It would likewise encourage them into a manly self-support. When every Indian, not alone in Wisconsin but in the whole country, shall know that, beyond a certain annual income for whose expenditure he himself is responsible, nothing but work lies between him and starvation, with 160 acres either of good or poor land belonging to himself on which he must cast his

18. *The Indian's Friend* 3 (January 1891): 3.
19. *Milwaukee Sentinel,* February 1, 1889.
20. Mrs. O. J. Hiles to John W. Noble, July 24, 1889, in Records of the Office of Indian Affairs, Letters Received, 1889 #21212.

venture, that part of the Interior department now presided over by the commissioner of Indian affairs at such expense to the people of the United States, can virtually be done away with."[21] The Indians, she told Noble, "would be saved to themselves; the whites would lose nothing really belonging to them unless in individual instances lumbermen should be obliged to pay more nearly the value of the timber;— supposing the timber to be sold at auction;—and Wisconsin would have eight thousand working people instead of eight thousand paupers, as must inevitably result under the present management."[22]

With such convictions, Mrs. Hiles and her associates began an active campaign. The Wisconsin Indian Association presented its views to the Secretary of the Interior, the Commissioner of Indian Affairs, and Wisconsin Congressmen and Senators, and it carried its appeal to the public in the newspapers.[23] A passionate plea to the people of Wisconsin, written by Mrs. Hiles, appeared in the Milwaukee *Sentinel,* January 31, 1890:

> In the sadness and desolation of this sad year, not many in our civilized communities are sick and dying without beds, without warmth or food, without medical aid, without Christian help and Christian consolation. But in our own state, not far from these civilized communities, hundreds are sick and dying with almost nothing but pain, cold, starvation and God's pity. Had the money for their pine been funded they would now, every one of them, the poor, infirm and the tender little children, be in comparative comfort. More than this; they would have souls not so badly burned with drink, bodies not so disfigured with its devastating influence. Will the people and their representative, the press of Wisconsin, advocate with words too earnest to be lightly considered the passage of the bills now before congress which ask—one bill unconditionally, one with the president's sanction—that all moneys hereafter paid for pine on the Menominee reservation shall be funded and the Indians receive the interest, and a small percentage of the principal should such disposition of a portion of the principal be so determined.[24]

21. *Milwaukee Sentinel,* February 1, 1889.

22. Mrs. Hiles to Noble, July 24, 1889.

23. See Mrs. O. J. Hiles to T. J. Morgan, November 7, 1889, in Records of the Office of Indian Affairs, Letters Received, 1889 #33173; letters from the officers of the Wisconsin Indian Association to Myron H. McCord, December 12, 1889, and to T. J. Morgan, January 7, 1890, ibid., 1890 #692 and #1132; *Milwaukee Sentinel,* January 17 and 31, March 19, 1890.

24. *Milwaukee Sentinel,* January 31, 1890.

On January 13, 1890, Congressman Myron H. McCord had introduced a bill in the House with the provisions that the women wanted. At the insistence of the Indian Bureau, however, changes were made which authorized the Indians to do the lumbering themselves rather than auction off the standing timber, and a comparable bill was introduced in the Senate by Senator Philetus Sawyer.[25] Although the amendments did not please Mrs. Hiles, she considered them nonessential to the purposes the Association had in mind; and when the Senate version of the measure became law on June 12, 1890, the women chalked up another victory. "We feel," Mrs. Hiles reported, "well pleased with our work."[26]

The Milwaukee women also strongly supported Indian education, which in 1888 and 1889 became a major concern of the reformers at Lake Mohonk. The new Commissioner of Indian Affairs, Thomas J. Morgan, presented to the Lake Mohonk Conference in 1889 a detailed scheme for a national government school system for the Indians, which won immediate support.[27] It had become clear that the allotment of individual homesteads to the Indians, provided by the Dawes Act of 1887, would be useless unless the Indians were properly educated for them. Mrs. Hiles was so dismayed by reports of opposition to Morgan's plan as "entirely chimerical and impracticable" that she wrote a forceful defense of Commissioner Morgan:

> The friends of the Indians—and who are not—consider the present issue as most vital and serious and they are looking to the country for the endorsement of this, the first systematic effort that the government has ever made to provide a secular education for all the Indian children of the United States. We do not believe it is chimerical; we do not believe it is impracticable; on the contrary, we believe it is indicative of sound policy, of a humane, just and wise administration of affairs.[28]

Although action to influence national legislation was the principal work of the Wisconsin Indian Association—and in this it followed the

25. *House Journal*, 51st Cong., 1st sess., ser. 2713, pp. 112, 424, 695; *Senate Journal*, 51st Cong., 1st sess., ser. 2677, pp. 250, 261, 306; *House Report* no. 1206, 51st Cong., 1st sess., ser. 2810; *United States Statutes at Large*, 26:146–47.

26. *The Indian's Friend* 3 (January 1891): 3. See also Report of Thomas J. Morgan, September 5, 1890, *House Executive Document* no. 1, pt. 5, 51st Cong., 2d sess., ser. 2841, p. cxl.

27. *Lake Mohonk Conference Proceedings*, 1889, pp. 16–34. This report was repeated in Commissioner Morgan's annual report for 1889.

28. *Milwaukee Sentinel*, January 15, 1890.

pattern of the national Indian organizations—it considered also a practical project for aiding Wisconsin Indians. In the fall of 1889 the Association became interested in establishing a small "Home School," or boarding school, for Indians. Someone placed at its disposal a country residence on a lake twenty miles west of Milwaukee, with forty acres of good farm land and excellent buildings, which could accommodate fifteen Indian pupils. The plan was to hire a man and wife "competent to both teach and practice high morality." The rest of the operation would be handled by "one strong woman servant" and an additional teacher, with occasional day help from a man. "Our plan," Mrs. Hiles wrote to Commissioner Morgan, "would be to make our school tributary to one of your grammar schools, and to do this we should endeavor to get children at about the ages of ten and twelve years, or younger if you thought preferable, and carry them in books to the points necessary to give them admission into the grammar schools."[29]

Although Mrs. Hiles carried on correspondence with Morgan for several months about the projected school, there was one basic obstacle to the plan. The women expected the government to supply per capita support for the Indian pupils, as it was doing at the time by contracts with schools of missionary societies. In the end, on March 21, 1890, Morgan wrote to Mrs. Hiles, declaring that, although he would be "pleased to assist your noble enterprise," there was no possibility of extending the contract school system to accommodate her plan.[30] The best the Wisconsin Indian Association could do was gather shoes, hose, shawls, mittens, jackets, coats, vests, and trousers for the twenty-five pupils in the Oneida school and to aid in sending children to the government school opened at Tomah, Wisconsin.[31]

Mrs. Hiles and the Association took an interest in many aspects of the movement for reform in Indian policy that agitated the eastern reformers, publishing in Wisconsin papers articles dealing with payments to the Sioux, Civil Service reform in the Indian Bureau, the

29. Mrs. O. J. Hiles to Thomas J. Morgan, December 9, 1890, in Records of the Office of Indian Affairs, Letters Received, 1889 #35396. See also Mrs. Hiles to Morgan, November 16, 1889, and March 15, 1890, ibid., 1889 #33350 and 1890 #8435; Morgan to Mrs. Hiles, November 23 and December 30, 1889, in Records of the Office of Indian Affairs, Letters Sent, vol. 20 Education, p. 370, and vol. 21 Education, p. 30.

30. T. J. Morgan to Mrs. O. J. Hiles, March 21, 1890, ibid., vol. 22 Education, p. 151 (second pagination).

31. *The Indian's Friend* 3 (December 1890): 3; *Milwaukee Sentinel,* November 9, 1890; *Annual Report of the Women's National Indian Association,* 1891.

proposed removal of the Utes from Colorado, and the troubles at Wounded Knee.[32] In 1891 the Association petitioned the President of the United States not to allow "Buffalo Bill" Cody to enroll Indians in his exhibition because "such manifestation of uncivilized life, for no high aim or end, would be prejudicial to the interests of the Indians generally."[33] But in these matters, which did not directly touch the Indians of Wisconsin, the Wisconsin Indian Association was merely parroting the views of the national reform organizations.

One indication of the Association's promoting the Indian work of the national group to which it was tied was its subscriptions to *The Indian's Friend,* a monthly publication begun in 1887 by the Women's National Indian Association as a means of communicating with its auxiliaries and advancing the Indian cause. In their first blush of enthusiasm for the Indians the Milwaukee women eagerly subscribed to the paper, some of them ordering multiple copies for distribution or for Sunday school use. The national headquarters was much pleased.[34] But this action, too, depended largely on the drive of Mrs. Hiles.

The Wisconsin Indian Association, in fact, was little more than the lengthened shadow of Osia J. Hiles. When ill health curtailed her activities and then stopped them altogether, the work of the Milwaukee women for the Indians weakened and died. At the end of 1888 Mrs. Hiles complained of "a somewhat arduous struggle with a congested brain," and illness forced her to cancel the trip to California she had planned for early 1889.[35] Her last participation in the Lake Mohonk Conference was in October 1890. The Wisconsin Indian Association's report for 1891 noted that "the work done by this Auxiliary during the past year has been less than that of preceding years" because of "the long continued illness of the Secretary." After 1891 Mrs. Hiles was able to do very little, and the Milwaukee group ceased to send a delegate to the annual meeting of the Women's National Indian Association. In 1894 no report was sent to national headquarters, "owing to the protracted illness of the Secretary," and by 1895 even subscriptions to *The Indian's Friend* had died out.[36] For the

32. Ibid.; *Milwaukee Sentinel,* January 4 and 12, 1891.

33. Mrs. S. S. Merrill and Mrs. O. J. Hiles to President Benjamin Harrison, May 27, 1891, in Records of the Office of Indian Affairs, Letters Received, 1891 #20749; Report of Thomas J. Morgan, October 1, 1891, *House Executive Document* no. 1, pt. 5, 52d Cong., 1st sess., ser. 2934, pp. 78–79.

34. *The Indian's Friend* 2 (June 1890): 3.

35. Ibid. 1 (January 1889): 4.

36. *Annual Report of the Women's National Indian Association,* 1894, p. 23.

last five years of her life, Mrs. Hiles was confined to her room in her residence at 1 Waverly Place, and there she died on February 25, 1902, at the age of seventy.

Mrs. Hiles and her Milwaukee friends were representative of the national movement for reform in Indian policy. Mrs. Hiles at least—it is difficult to make the same assertion about the others—had a deep and sincere interest in the Indians as an oppressed minority and a zealous willingness to work for protection of their rights and improvement of their condition. At great expense of energy and through periods of declining health Mrs. Hiles devoted herself to the cause. Nor was she niggardly with her financial resources. At her death it was reported, "Mrs. Hiles, being a woman of wealth, has been able to put money as well as zeal into her philanthropic work."[37] Her trips to California to investigate the Mission Indians are evidence of her attempts to gain firsthand knowledge of the people she sought to aid, and she did not hesitate to appeal directly to the highest officials of the government.

But she was indistinguishable from the other "Friends of the Indian," whose primary mission was to transform the Indians into exact replicas of white American citizens, completely eradicating Indian culture in the process. Representative of the evangelical Protestants who wanted the United States to remain a "Christian nation" dominated by their principles, they hoped to "civilize" and "Christianize" the Indians, to imbue them with the virtues of hard work, sobriety, and thrift, and to individualize them as self-supporting farmers on their own homesteads. Their plea to the nation was for atonement for the evils perpetrated upon the Indians in the past by sweeping them up into one glorious homogeneous mass of Christian American citizenry. That the Indians may not have wanted to discard their Indianness seems not to have occurred to them. But Mrs. Hiles should not be condemned for failing to see beyond the horizons of her age. She had noble intentions and accomplished much good, for which she was duly praised by those who knew her and her work. It is to be regretted that her efforts did not fundamentally help to solve the "Indian problem" as she so eagerly hoped and confidently believed they would.

37. *Evening Wisconsin* (Milwaukee), February 26, 1902.

15

Indian Policy Reform
and American Protestantism, 1880–1900

In 1971 Ray Allen Billington undertook the task of editing a Festschrift for Everett Dick. Since Dick, a long-time teacher at Union College, did not have doctoral students who might have contributed to such a volume, Billington invited a number of historians of western America to participate. My essay, growing out of a larger work upon which I was engaged at the time, traces the influence of evangelical Protestantism on the formulation of Indian policy in the late nineteenth century. It illustrates my growing conviction about the importance of reform sentiment in Indian policy and the predominance of Protestant thought within the reform movements. The broader context of the essay can be seen in my American Indian Policy in Crisis: Christian Reformers and the Indian, 1865–1900 *(Norman: University of Oklahoma Press, 1976), in which the essay appears in different form as parts of chapters 5 and 10.*

The Trans-Mississippi West in the years after the Civil War was marked by scattered Indian reservations, the remnants of vast areas once claimed exclusively by the native Americans. With the aggressive expansion of the whites in the post-war years these reservations and their Indian inhabitants came under severe pressure. The Indians were considered a barrier to the advance of civilization and to the exploitation of the resources of the Great West. Their resistance to the invasion of their homelands by miners and settlers and to the devastating inroads into their cultural patterns that came with the wanton destruction of

Printed source: Ray Allen Billington, ed., *People of the Plains and Mountains: Essays in the History of the West Dedicated to Everett Dick* (Westport, Conn.: Greenwood Press, 1973), pp. 120–45.

the buffalo led to wars that dominated the dozen years after Appomattox and dragged on for a dozen more. An abortive "Peace Policy" during President Grant's administration proved the existence of widespread sentiment in favor of just and peaceful dealings with the Indians, but only after military subjugation of the tribes did humanitarians have a free hand to develop a solution for the abiding "Indian problem."

Indian policy reform in the last two decades of the nineteenth century was led by a tight little group of dedicated men and women, who were convinced that at last they had discovered a proper answer to the question of what to do about the Indians. By insistent propaganda to awaken and inform the national conscience and thereby bend Congress and federal officials to their will, the reformers successfully shaped government policy and gave new drive and a new orientation to Indian-white relations in the United States.[1]

They were able to achieve so much because they were united and well organized. Organizations, indeed, sprang up spontaneously in several places at once as Indian affairs received public attention. In Boston a group of leading citizens, disturbed by the forced removal of the Ponca Indians from their lands in Dakota to Indian Territory, formed the Boston Indian Citizenship Committee in 1879 to fight for Indian rights and for the recognition of the Indian as a person and a citizen. At the same time a similar organization was getting under way in Philadelphia, led by a group of women who were aroused by injustices to the Indians and who hoped to stir up the people of the United States to demand reform in Indian affairs. Their organization began informally in 1879 but quickly acquired formal structure as the Women's National Indian Association, with branches throughout the nation. In 1882 a number of Philadelphia men, led by Herbert Welsh, founded the Indian Rights Association, which became the most important of the reform groups. Closely associated with these organizations was the official Board of Indian Commissioners. Originally established

---

1. The Indian policy of the United States in the period after the Civil War has been studied in Loring Benson Priest, *Uncle Sam's Stepchildren: The Reformation of United States Indian Policy, 1865–1887* (New Brunswick: Rutgers University Press, 1942); Henry E. Fritz, *The Movement for Indian Assimilation, 1860–1890* (Philadelphia: University of Pennsylvania Press, 1963); Robert Winston Mardock, *The Reformers and the American Indian* (Columbia: University of Missouri Press, 1971); [and Francis Paul Prucha, *American Indian Policy in Crisis: Christian Reformers and the Indian, 1865–1900* (Norman: University of Oklahoma Press, 1976)]. These books provide a general background for the reform movement in Indian affairs from 1880 to 1900.

in 1869, it was made up of a group of humanitarian businessmen appointed to bring rectitude into Indian affairs by supervising the financial operations of the Indian Office. The Board eventually gave up direct participation in governing Indian relations and turned its efforts toward influencing public opinion.[2]

The work of these separate organizations was coordinated at an annual conference held each year at a resort hotel on Lake Mohonk, near New Paltz, New York. Here in a sylvan setting the self-denominated "Friends of the Indian" met to discuss Indian reform, to hear speakers on matters of concern, and to formulate resolutions that could be broadcast to the public and used to lobby for specific goals with Congress and government officials. The instigator of the Lake Mohonk Conferences and a continuing presence behind them was the owner of the resort, the Quaker Albert K. Smiley, who in 1879 had been appointed a member of the Board of Indian Commissioners. Dissatisfied with the brief meetings of the Board in Washington, he decided to invite its members and other interested persons to spend three days each year as his guests at Lake Mohonk. The first group assembled in 1883, and soon the meetings became the chief forum for the reformers. Their aim, as Smiley saw it, was "to unite the best minds interested in Indian affairs, so that all should act together and be in harmony, and so that the prominent persons connected with Indian affairs should act as one body and create a public sentiment in favor of the Indians."[3]

Their harmony was based on a common philanthropic and humanitarian outlook expressed in Christian terms, for the reform organizations had a strong religious orientation. The Women's National Indian Association was established under Baptist auspices, and although assuming a nondenominational posture, it consciously drew on church

2. General information on these organizations can be found in the books by Priest, Fritz, Mardock, [and Prucha] cited above. For details about the programs and activities of the Women's National Indian Association, see the annual reports of the Association, the numerous pamphlets published by the group, and its periodical, *The Indian's Friend*, begun in 1888. The Indian Rights Association reported its activities in its annual reports and published a great many informational and hortatory items in pamphlet form. The Board of Indian Commissioners also issued substantial annual reports.

3. *Lake Mohonk Conference Proceedings*, 1885, p. 1. The *Proceedings* of the Lake Mohonk Conferences appeared under varying titles. Ultimately the standard form was, for example, *Proceedings of the Fifth Annual Meeting of the Lake Mohonk Conference of Friends of the Indian*. Throughout this chapter a simplified citation, with the year, will be used. The *Proceedings* were also printed in the annual reports of the Board of Indian Commissioners.

support. Its executive board in 1884 listed members from eight Protestant denominations—Baptist, Presbyterian, Episcopal, Congregational,
Methodist, Quaker, Reformed, and Unitarian—and in the previous year
had included Lutherans also. In 1883, moreover, the women specifically added missionary and school work to their efforts, and the Association took on many of the characteristics of a home missionary society.
The leaders quoted with approbation in their publications a remark
made by the Reverend Joseph Cook in 1885: "The first motto of all
Indian reformers should be Indian evangelization. . . . Let us not depend on politicians to reform the Indian. We cannot safely depend even
on the Government schools to solve the Indian problem. The longest
root of hope for the Indians is to be found in the self-sacrifice of the
Christian Church."[4] The Indian Rights Association, too, acknowledged
the Christian motivation of its work. Herbert Welsh asserted that the
Indian needed "to be taught to labor, to live in civilized ways, and to
serve God." "The best Christian sentiment of the country," he said,
"is needed to redeem the Indian, to stimulate and guide the constantly
changing functionaries of the government who are charged with the
task of his civilization."[5]

The atmosphere of deep religiosity in which the reformers worked
was most notable at the Lake Mohonk Conferences. Each began with an
invocation, and the discussions were redolent with religious spirit
terminology. Part of this was due, no doubt, to the influence of the
Quaker host; part, also, to the participation of many religious leaders.
Of the names listed in the membership rosters, 1883–1900, more than a
fourth were ministers, their wives, and representatives of religious
groups, and a great many others were prominent lay leaders in their
churches. The editors of the leading religious journals and papers, too,
were regularly on hand. Presiding over the meetings in the 1890s was
Merrill E. Gates, president of Rutgers and then of Amherst, a fervent
promoter of the Christian spirit. His remarks at the opening of the
conference in 1899 were not unrepresentative of the mood. He noted
the beauty of the natural surroundings at Lake Mohonk and then
continued:

4. The missionary work is reported in the annual reports and in special pamphlets published by the Association. See *Missionary Work of the Women's National
Indian Association, and Letters of Missionaries* (Philadelphia, 1885), and *Sketches
of Delightful Work* (Philadelphia, 1893). The statement of Cook appears on the
title page of *Missionary Work*.

5. Herbert Welsh, *The Indian Question Past and Present* (Philadelphia: Indian
Rights Association, 1890), pp. 15, 18.

We believe in the government of a God whose will is at once beauty in the material world, and moral order in the world of will and action. We believe in the moral government of the universe; and we rejoice in the beauty of the physical earth as part of God's ordained order. We assemble as those who have faith in Him; and believing in the reign of His holy will we delight in the beauty with which He surrounds us. But we come with earnest purpose, too. We recognize that we are not here for pleasure alone. We believe that we have a duty to the less-favored races; and in considering together the problems connected with these people we are touching almost every question of social reform and governmental administration.[6]

The conviction that they were engaged in Christian work was repeatedly expressed and universally assumed. "It may be taken for granted," the Reverend Lyman Abbott observed at Lake Mohonk in 1885, "that we are Christian men and women; that we believe in justice, good-will, and charity, and the brotherhood of the human race." And President Gates declared in 1891:

This is essentially a philanthropic and Christian reform. Whatever may be our views, our slight differences of view or differences that may seem to us profound, we all gather here believing that the Lord of the world is the Lord Jesus Christ; believing that, ever since God himself became incarnate, for a man to see God truly, he must learn to see something of God in his fellow-man, and to work for his fellow-men. We come in the spirit of service.[7]

The word *Christian* dropped unselfconsciously from the lips of the reformers as they set about to do God's will, to guide the Indian "from the night of barbarism into the fair dawn of Christian civilization," as Herbert Welsh expressed it in 1886. The only hope for a solution to the Indian problem, Gates declared at the end of nearly two decades of organized humanitarian effort, was to bring the Indians "under the sway of Christian thought and Christian life, and into touch with the people of this Christian nation under the laws and institutions which govern the life of our States and Territories." As he welcomed the members of the Lake Mohonk Conference in 1900, he recalled again the Christian foundation of their work for Indian reform. "Nothing less than decades of years of persistent effort," he said, "years of effort

6. *Lake Mohonk Conference Proceedings*, 1899, p. 9.
7. Ibid., 1885, p. 50; 1891, p. 11.

prompted by that love of one's fellow-men which has its perennial root in the love of Christ for us, can do the work which here we contemplate and discuss." He welcomed especially the devoted missionaries who labored so diligently for their charges, but he gave a clue to the pervasive Christianity of the age when he turned to welcome, too, representatives of the Indian Bureau, whom he described as "Christian men of high purpose, whose aim in the issuing of regulations and the administration of Indian affairs is identical with the aims of the Christian workers in the field, and the Christian friends of the Indian who gather here."[8]

Sentiments such as these gave the tone to their public meetings, but the unity of the reformers was of a more fundamental nature than these pious expressions of Christian good will. Although there were debates and differences of opinion among the prominent men and women working for reform in Indian affairs in the 1880s and 1890s, there was strong underlying agreement in outlook and in goals. If we seek the foundation of this agreement, we find it principally in American evangelical Protestantism, which defined what the term "Christian" meant to these Friends of the Indian.

This was not surprising, for the history of the United States throughout the nineteenth century was marked by a strong evangelical movement.[9] So dominant was this force that one historian of American religion has asserted that the story of American evangelicalism is "the story of America itself in the years 1800 to 1900, for it was Evangelical religion which made Americans the most religious people in the world, molded them into a unified, pietistic-perfectionist nation, and spurred them on to those heights of social reform, missionary endeavor, and imperialistic expansionism which constitute the moving forces of our history in that century."[10] The evangelicals, in fact, sought to create

8. Herbert Welsh, "The Needs of the Time," *Lake Mohonk Conference Proceedings,* 1886, p. 13; ibid., 1900, pp. 13, 21.

9. I have learned much about evangelical Protestantism from Robert T. Handy, "The Protestant Quest for a Christian America," *Church History* 22 (March 1953): 8–20; Robert T. Handy, *A Christian America: Protestant Hopes and Historical Realities* (New York: Oxford University Press, 1971); Martin E. Marty, *Righteous Empire: The Protestant Experience in America* (New York: Dial Press, 1970); William G. McLoughlin, ed., *The American Evangelicals, 1800–1900: An Anthology* (New York: Harper and Row, 1968); and Sidney E. Mead, *The Lively Experiment: The Shaping of Christianity in America* (New York: Harper and Row, 1963).

10. McLoughlin, *American Evangelicals,* p. 1. He concludes: "The history of American Evangelicanism is then more than the history of a religious movement. To understand it is to understand the whole temper of American life in the nineteenth century." Ibid., p. 26.

what has been called a "righteous empire" in America. They set out with considerable success "to attract the allegiance of all the people, to develop a spiritual kingdom, and to shape the nation's ethos, mores, manners, and often its laws."[11]

This religious motivation had important consequences for the nation's dealings with the Indians from 1800 to 1900; witness the continuing efforts, beginning early in the century, to educate, civilize, and Christianize the Indians and thus bring them into the national fold.[12] What marked the last decades of the century, however, was an intensification of the desire for unity, a new energy in the "quest for a Christian America," and an increasing emphasis on a secularized, as opposed to a theological, formulation of goals and activities. And it was exactly at this time that the "Indian problem" demanded a long overdue solution. The coincidence of an ultimate crisis in Indian affairs, brought about by the overwhelming pressure of aggressively expanding white civilization and the intensified religious drive for a unified American society, led to a new program of Indian policy reform. The consequences for the Indians and for the United States were as significant as the dramatic military encounters with the plains tribes that electrified the nation after the Civil War.

The distinguishing mark of American evangelicalism was its insistence on individual salvation; the conversion and reformation of individuals would, evangelists believed, correct the evils of society. The Indian reformers eventually realized the fundamental conflict between this principle and the communal life and customs of the Indians. Their solution was to ignore the wishes of the Indians, and insist on their individualization and acculturation freed from bondage to the tribe. "The Indian as a savage member of a tribal organization cannot survive, ought not to survive, the aggressions of civilization," the Indian Rights

11. Marcy, *Righteous Empire,* Foreword.

12. For examples of these efforts, see Robert F. Berkhofer, Jr., *Salvation and the Savage: An Analysis of Protestant Missions and American Indian Response, 1787–1862* (Lexington: University of Kentucky Press, 1965); Francis Paul Prucha, "American Indian Policy in the 1840s: Visions of Reform," in John G. Clark, ed., *The Frontier Challenge: Responses to the Trans-Mississippi West* (Lawrence: University Press of Kansas, 1971), pp. 81–110; and the accounts of Grant's Peace Policy in Priest, *Uncle Sam's Stepchildren;* Fritz, *Movement for Indian Assimilation;* [and Prucha, *American Indian Policy in Crisis*]. The religious aspects of the Peace Policy are fully treated in Robert H. Keller, Jr., "The Protestant Churches and Grant's Peace Policy: A Study in Church-State Relations, 1869–1882" (Ph.D. diss., University of Chicago, 1967).

Association declared in a typical statement in 1884, "but his *individual redemption* from heathenism and ignorance, his transformation from the condition of a savage nomad to that of an industrious American citizen, is abundantly possible."[13]

"The philosophy of the present [Indian] policy," Senator Henry L. Dawes, chairman of the Senate Committee on Indian Affairs, said in 1884, "is to treat him as an individual, and not as an insoluble substance that the civilization of this country has been unable, hitherto, to digest, but to take him as an individual, a human being, and treat him as you find him." Thomas Jefferson Morgan, a former Baptist minister and public school educator who was appointed Commissioner of Indian Affairs in 1889, urged that the tribal relation be broken up, socialism destroyed, and "the family and the autonomy of the individual substituted." Merrill Gates saw in individualism "the keynote of our socio-political political ideas of this century" and thought he could find sympathetic vibrations of it even among the Indians.[14] He epitomized the sentiments of the reformers as he summed up their two decades of work in 1900:

> We have learned that education and example, and pre-eminently, the force of Christian life and Christian faith in the heart, can do in one generation most of that which evolution takes centuries to do.
>
> But if civilization, education and Christianity are to do their work, they must get at the individual. They must lay hold of men and women and children, one by one. The deadening sway of tribal custom must be interfered with. The sad uniformity of savage tribal life must be broken up! Individuality must be cultivated. Personality must be developed. And personality is strengthened only by the direction of one's own life through voluntary obedience to recognized moral law. At last, as a nation, we are coming to recognize the great truth that if we would do justice to the Indians, we must get at them, one by one, with American ideals, American schools, American laws, the privileges and the pressures of American rights and duties.[15]

13. *Report of the Indian Rights Association,* 1884, p. 5. Emphasis added.

14. *Report of the Board of Indian Commissioners,* 1883, p. 69; Report of Morgan, October 1, 1889, *House Executive Document* no. 1, 51st Cong., 1st sess., ser. 2725, p. 4; Merrill E. Gates, "Land and Law as Agents in Educating Indians," *Report of the Board of Indian Commissioners,* 1885, p. 26.

15. *Lake Mohonk Conference Proceedings,* 1900, p. 14.

The fight for individualization was carried on on many fronts by the evangelical reformers. Most important was the movement to break up tribal ownership and substitute the allotment of land in severalty.[16] Communal landholding was considered to be the substructure upon which tribal power rested. If it could be destroyed, the way would be clear for treating the Indian as an individual and absorbing him into American culture.

Allotments of land in severalty had been advocated from the days of Thomas Jefferson, and piecemeal legislation had authorized allotments for a number of tribes. Now such a process was too slow and uncertain to satisfy the new reformers. The panacea they sought was a general allotment law that would turn all Indians into individual land owners and break up traditional tribal relations. Allotment, said the Commissioner of Indian Affairs in 1881, would have the effect "of creating individuality, responsibility, and a desire to accumulate property" and would teach the Indians "habits of industry and frugality." It would be "the entering-wedge by which tribal organization is to be rent asunder," the Indian Rights Association declared in 1884.[17]

By concerted effort the reformers persuaded Congress to enact the Dawes Severalty Act of February 8, 1887, authorizing the President to allot portions of reservations to individual Indians, with the provision that the allotments be inalienable for twenty-five years. The Indians were to be made citizens when they received their allotments, and the surplus lands of the reservations were to be opened to white settlement.[18] Humanitarians hailed the Dawes Act as the "Indian Emancipation Act" and spoke of the beginning of a new epoch in Indian affairs. The importance attached to the principle embodied in the measure can be seen in Merrill Gates's paean to it in 1900:

16. The movement for land in severalty that culminated in the Dawes Act of 1887 is carefully traced in Priest, *Uncle Sam's Stepchildren,* section IV. See also D. S. Otis, "History of the Allotment Policy," in *Adjustment of Indian Affairs,* Hearings before the Committee on Indian Affairs, House of Representatives, 73rd Cong., 2d sess., on H.R. 7092 (Washington, 1934), pt. 9, pp. 428–89 [published as D. S. Otis, *The Dawes Act and the Allotment of Indian Lands,* ed. Francis Paul Prucha (Norman: University of Oklahoma Press, 1973)]; and J. P. Kinney, *A Continent Lost—A Civilization Won: Indian Land Tenure in America* (Baltimore: Johns Hopkins Press, 1937).

17. Report of Hiram Price, October 24, 1881, *House Executive Document* no. 1, 47th Cong., 1st sess., ser. 2018, p. 17; *Report of the Indian Rights Association,* 1884, p. 6.

18. *United States Statutes at Large,* 24:388–90. A good contemporary account of the Dawes Act is James B. Thayer, "The Dawes Bill and the Indians," *Atlantic Monthly* 61 (March 1888): 315–22.

The supreme significance of the law in marking a new era in dealing with the Indian problem, lies in the fact that this law is a mighty pulverizing engine for breaking up the tribal mass. It has nothing to say to the tribe, nothing to do with the tribe. It breaks up that vast "bulk of things" which the tribal life sought to keep unchanged. It finds its way straight to the family and to the individual. It recognizes and seeks to develop personality in the man and in the woman.[19]

The principle was further extended by a drive to treat the Indians as individual citizens before the law. Tribal jurisdiction, which hindered absorption into American life, was an abomination, and every effort to destroy it carried its own justification. "Acknowledge that the Indian is a man," said Henry S. Pancoast of the Indian Rights Association, "and as such give him that standing in our courts which is freely given as a right and a necessity to every other man." Professor James B. Thayer of Harvard Law School, the most vigorous of the reformers seeking to incorporate the Indians into the legal system of the United States, declared in 1886 that it was high time to put an end to "the monstrous situation of having people in our country who are not entitled to the full protection of our national constitution, who are native here and yet not citizens." He cared little about whether or not the Indians wanted to abandon their tribal relations; the United States could simply ignore the tribes and deal directly with individuals. "There is little harm in men associating together," Thayer said, "whether in tribes of Shakers or Oneida communities, or Odd Fellows, or Masons, or Germans, or colored men, or Indians, if they like; but as we do not carry on a separate commerce with the tribes of Shakers we had better stop doing it with the Indians."[20]

The individualism of the evangelical Protestants was tied closely to the Puritan work ethic. Hard work and thrift were virtues that seemed to be at the very basis of salvation. The reformers could conceive of no transformation for the Indians that did not include self-support. Annuities to the tribes and rations to subsist the Indians were blocks that prevented realization of the ideal. Until these were abolished and the Indians made to labor to support themselves and their families, there would be no solution to the Indian problem. Allotment of land in severalty was insisted upon because the reformers believed that without

19. *Lake Mohonk Conference Proceedings*, 1900, p. 16.
20. Henry S. Pancoast, *Impressions of the Sioux Tribes in 1882, with Some First Principles in the Indian Question* (Philadelphia: Franklin Printing House, 1883), p. 22; James B. Thayer, *Remarks Made at a Meeting in Cambridge, Mass., Called by the Women's Indian Association of That City, May 3, 1886* (n.p., n.d.).

the labor needed to maintain the private homestead the virtue of hard work could never be inculcated.

Reformers commonly saw in labor a fulfillment of an essential command of God, as Merrill Gates did in 1885, when he criticized past efforts to aid the Indians. "Above all else we have utterly neglected to teach them the value of honest labor," he said. "Nay, by rations dealt out whether needed or not, we have interfered to suspend the efficient teaching by which God leads men to love and honor labor. We have taken from them the compelling inspiration that grows out of His law, 'if a man will not work, neither shall he eat!'"[21] The precepts of work and thrift reechoed again and again in Gates's addresses to the Lake Mohonk gatherings. In 1896 he explained once more the common goal and spoke of wakening in the Indian broader desires and ampler wants:

> To bring him out of savagery into citizenship we must make the Indian more intelligently selfish before we can make him unselfishly intelligent. We need to *awaken in him wants.* In his dull savagery he must be touched by the wings of the divine angel of discontent. Then he begins to look forward, to reach out. The desire for property of his own may become an intense educating force. The wish for a home of his own awakens him to new efforts. Discontent with the teepee and the starving rations of the Indian camp in winter is needed to get the Indian out of the blanket and into trousers,—and trousers with a pocket in them, and with a *pocket that aches to be filled with dollars!*[22]

Without personal property, Gates argued, there would be no strong development of personality, and he noted that the Savior's teaching was full of illustrations of the right use of property.

Individual development and the stimulation of honest labor, in the evangelical Protestant worldview, were possible only in the perspective of the family. Glorification of hearth and home was an essential element in their program for Christian living, for the Christian purity and virtues that they extolled could take root and be nurtured to full maturity only within the Christian family.[23] What the reformers saw

21. "Land and Law as Agents in Educating Indians," *Report of the Board of Indian Commissioners,* 1885, p. 18.

22. *Lake Mohonk Conference Proceedings,* 1896, p. 11.

23. McLoughlin, speaking of the middle third of the century, notes: "It is difficult to find a collection of Evangelical sermons in this period which does not devote at least one sermon to 'The Christian Home' and another to 'Motherhood.' It was the Evangelicals who made home and hearth the central features of American sentimentalism." *American Evangelicals,* p. 17.

of Indian life, therefore, seriously offended their sensibilities. Not understanding a culture that differed so markedly from their own, humanitarians saw only heathen practices, which they were obliged to stamp out as quickly and as thoroughly as possible. Polygamy was a special abomination, and the whole tribal arrangement was thought to create and perpetuate un-Christian modes of life. Gates's lengthy attack upon tribalism in 1885 was premised on the belief that it destroyed the family. "The family is God's unit of society," he declared. "On the integrity of the family depends that of the State. There is no civilization deserving of the name where the family is not the unit in civil government." But the tribal system, he believed, paralyzed both "the desire for property and the family life that ennobles that desire." As allegiance to the tribe and its chiefs grew less, its place would be taken "by the sanctities of family life and an allegiance to the laws which grow naturally out of the family."[24]

The goals envisaged for the Indians were deemed possible because the humanitarians believed in the unity of mankind. If the Indians were basically no different from other human beings—except for the conditioning coming from their environment—then there could be no real obstacle to their assimilation. "Let us forget once and forever the word 'Indian' and all that it has signified in the past," Charles C. Painter, lobbyist for the Indian Rights Association in Washington, told the Lake Mohonk Conference in 1889, "and remember only that we are dealing with so many children of a common Father." The doctrine of the brotherhood of man was a cardinal principle of the reformers, who wanted to erase all lines of distinction that separated the Indians from the rest of the nation. In the process traditional Indian customs were to be simply pushed aside as unimportant. In speaking of the proposal for severalty legislation, Philip C. Garrett said in 1886:

If an act of emancipation will buy them life, manhood, civilization, and Christianity, at the sacrifice of a few chieftain's feathers, a few worthless bits of parchment, the cohesion of the tribal relation, and the traditions of their race; then, in the name of all that is really worth having, let us shed the few tears necessary to embalm these relics of the past, and have done with them; and, with fraternal cordiality, let us welcome to the bosom of the nation this brother whom we have wronged long enough.

24. "Land and Law as Agents in Educating Indians," *Report of the Board of Indian Commissioners,* 1885, pp. 27–29.

Commissioner of Indian Affairs Morgan, in speaking of Indian children, stressed first of all "their kinship with us." "They, too, are human and endowed with all the faculties of human nature," he observed; "made in the image of God, bearing the likeness of their Creator, and having the same possibilities of growth and development that are possessed by any other class of children."[25]

What especially marked the development of evangelical Protestantism and gave it its peculiar flavor during the last decades of the nineteenth century, however, was the subtle transformation that brought about an almost complete identification of Protestantism with Americanism. This shift culminated a movement extending through the century. During the early 1800s the coordination of the two elements, indeed, had been very close; Americanism and Protestantism protected each other. "So close was the bond, so deep the union," says one scholar, "that a basic attack on American institutions would have meant an attack on Protestant Christianity itself. Positively, defense of America meant a defense of the evangelical empire."[26] This "ideological amalgamation of Protestant denominationalism and Americanism" was not simply an acceptance of evangelical religion by the officials of the state. It came increasingly to be a complacent defense of the social and economic status quo by the churches. "Protestants, in effect," notes one writer, "looked at the new world they had created, were proud of its creator, and like Jehovah before them, pronounced it very good." Ironically, despite warnings of the necessity of separation of church and state, the churches gave a religious endorsement to the American way of life. Thus, under a system of official separation, Protestants eventually became "as completely identified with nationalism and their country's political and economic system as had ever been known in Christendom."[27] The perceptive English observer Lord Bryce noted in 1885: "Christianity is in fact understood to be, though not the legally established religion, yet the national religion."[28]

As the nineteenth century drew to a close, two forces intensified the

25. Charles C. Painter, "The Indian and His Property," *Lake Mohonk Conference Proceedings,* 1889, p. 88; Philip C. Garrett, "Indian Citizenship," *Lake Mohonk Conference Proceedings,* 1886, p. 11; Thomas J. Morgan, *A Plea for the Papoose: An Address At Albany, N.Y., by Gen. T. J. Morgan* (n.p., n.d.), pp. 2-3.

26. Marty, *Righteous Empire,* p. 89.

27. Mead, *Lively Experiment,* pp. 142, 156-57.

28. Quote in McLoughlin, *American Evangelicals,* p. 26. See also John Edwin Smylie, "National Ethos and the Church," *Theology Today* 20 (October 1963): 313-21.

union between Protestantism and Americanism. One was the weakening of traditional theological interest, so that the principles of Americanism became in large part the religious creed. The other was the growing threat to the dominance of the "righteous empire" by new forces in the United States, principally the influx of millions of European immigrants who did not fit the Anglo-Saxon Protestant pattern of America, and the growing industrialization and urbanization of the nation, which upset the foundations of the traditional rural Protestant outlook.

Afraid that the unity of America was being weakened, the churches promoted new measures to strengthen union and conformity. None of these was more important than a universal public school system, which, while reflecting and continuing evangelical Protestant virtues (under a cloak of "nonsectarianism") would instill the Americanism that had become a basic religious goal.[29] Typical was the stand taken by Thomas J. Morgan in his *Studies in Pedagogy,* published in the same year that he assumed direction of government Indian affairs. The "free schools of America," he wrote, would create a universal Americanism. The goal of teachers should be to bring about a common life among the various peoples who made up the nation. He considered the public schools to be "safeguards of liberty," the "nurseries of a genuine democracy," and "training schools of character." "They are American," Morgan declared. "Nothing, perhaps, is so distinctly a product of the soil as is the American school system. In these schools all speak a common language; race distinctions give way to national characteristics. . . ."[30]

The Indians were engulfed in this flood of Americanism. Their Americanization, indeed, became the all-embracing goal of reformers in the last two decades of the century. "The logic of events," Commissioner Morgan declared in his first annual report, "demands the absorption of the Indians into our national life, not as Indians, but as American citizens."[31] Nor were the Indians to be allowed to stand in the way of American progress. The reformers were convinced of the divine approbation of the spread of American culture, and the development of

29. Robert T. Handy notes: "The cultural dominance of Protestantism was illustrated in the transition to a public tax-supported school system; this transition was palatable to Protestants because the schools were rather clearly Protestant in orientation, though 'non-sectarian.'" "The Protestant Quest for a Christian America," p. 11. See also Handy, *A Christian America,* pp. 101–5.

30. Thomas J. Morgan, *Studies in Pedagogy* (Boston: Silver, Burdett and Company, 1889), pp. 327–28, 348–50.

31. Report of Morgan, October 1, 1889, *House Executive Document* no. 1, 51st Cong., 1st sess., ser. 2725, p. 3.

the West as an indication of that progress was part of the Protestant American mission. Tribal rights that would obstruct the fruitful exploitation of the nation's domain had to be sacrificed. The reform-minded Secretary of the Interior, Carl Schurz, saw that the advance of an enterprising people could not be checked, and he hoped to persuade the Indians to accept individual allotments of land that could be protected. "This done," he said, "the Indians will occupy no more ground than so many white people; the large reservations will gradually be opened to general settlement and enterprise, and the Indians, with their possessions, will cease to stand in the way of the 'development of the country.'" He hoped to maintain peace and to protect the Indians "by harmonizing the habits, occupations, and interests of the Indians" with those of the nation.[32]

Whereas Schurz lamented the inability of the government to protect the Indians against the march of progress, more radical reformers advocated absorbing the Indians as a matter of principle. "Three hundred thousand people have no right to hold a continent and keep at bay a race able to people it and provide the happy homes of civilization," Lyman Abbott told his colleagues at Lake Mohonk. "We do owe the Indians sacred rights and obligations, but one of those duties is not the right to let them hold forever the land they did not occupy, and which they were not making fruitful for themselves or others." The Indian reservations should be abolished, letting the full blast of civilization rush in upon the Indians. "Christianity is not merely a thing of churches and school-houses," Abbott insisted. "The post-office is a Christianizing institution; the railroad, with all its corruptions, is a Christianizing power, and will do more to teach the people punctuality than school-master or preacher can." Morgan put it just as bluntly: "The Indians must conform to 'the white man's ways,' peaceably if they will, forcibly if they must. They must adjust themselves to their environment, and conform their mode of living substantially to our civilization. This civilization may not be the best possible, but it is the best the Indians can get."[33]

The reformers acknowledged their obligations to educate the Indians and to provide them, as much as possible, with the tools of civilization. But then individualism was to take its course. Once the doors were

32. Carl Schurz, "Present Aspects of the Indian Problem," *North American Review* 133 (July 1881): 17, 23.

33. *Lake Mohonk Conference Proceedings*, 1885, pp. 51–52; Report of Morgan, October 1, 1889, *House Executive Document* no. 1, 51st Cong., 1st sess., ser. 2725, p. 3.

opened and the new light shown to the Indians, it would be up to them as individuals to make their own way; the law of the "survival of the fittest" would take over.

The means for their Americanization seemed to be at hand. Building on the foundation of individualism supplied by the land-in-severalty legislation and the provisions for granting American citizenship, reformers envisaged a universal national school system, which would do for the Indians what the public school system of the states was doing to assimilate other alien groups into the republic. The government and the humanitarian reformers joined hands to educate the Indians as individual Christian patriotic American citizens.

As early as 1880 the Board of Indian Commissioners remarked: "If the common school is the glory and boast of our American civilization, why not extend its blessings to the 50,000 benighted children of the red men of our country, that they too may share its benefits and speedily emerge from the ignorance of centuries?"[34] After the enactment of the Dawes Act, Indian education loomed as ever more important, for reformers realized at last that neither the individual homestead nor the citizenship that went with it would transform the Indians into real Americans unless they had education that would fit them to meet the responsibilities of their new status.

The Lake Mohonk Conference of 1888 devoted most of its time to a discussion of Indian education. The conference began with a formal paper read by Lyman Abbott, who in his usual forthright manner called for a plan "for solving the educational problem of the Indian race,—for converting them from groups of tramps, beggars, thieves, and sometimes robbers and murderers, into communities of intelligent, industrious, and self-supporting citizens." He insisted that this was the responsibility of the national government and could not be relegated to voluntary associations (that is, in the main, to missionary groups). The conference, following his lead, adopted a platform that condemned the "ill-organized and unsystematic educational methods of the Government" and called for a "well-organized system of popular education, framed in accordance with the principles of our American institutions, and competent to provide the entire Indian race with adequate education." It noted that the cost of education was only a fraction of the cost of war, that the expense of educating the Indian for self-support was less than one-tenth the cost of keeping him in pauperism, and it pledged its cordial cooperation in efforts "to remove at once the

---

34. *Report of the Board of Indian Commissioners,* 1880, p. 9.

National dishonor of supporting ignorant and barbaric peoples in the heart of a Christian civilization."[35]

A blueprint for a systematized universal school system for the Indians was soon provided. Only three months after Thomas J. Morgan entered upon his duties as Commissioner of Indian Affairs he presented the Lake Mohonk Conference with a ready-made plan. Morgan began with a stance of humility, seeking the counsel of those present. "When President Harrison tendered me the Indian Bureau," Morgan related, "he said, I wish you to administer it in such a way as will satisfy the Christian philanthropic sentiment of the country. That was the only charge that I received from him. I come here, where the Christian philanthropic sentiment of the country focuses itself, to ask you what will satisfy you." He had but one motive, he told the conference: "to embody in administrative work the highest thought which you elaborate in regard to the treatment of the Indians."[36]

Morgan outlined a school system modeled upon the public schools, with special provisions for high schools, grammar schools, and primary schools. The education was intended for all Indian children and was to be compulsory, and although special stress was placed on industrial training that would fit the Indians to earn an honest living, Morgan asked also for "that general literary culture which the experience of the white race has shown to be the very essence of education," for which command of English was indispensable. Elements in his proposal strikingly reflected the goals of the Christian America he and the Lake Mohonk philanthropists idealized.

"The chief thing in all education," he asserted, "is the development of character, the formation of manhood and womanhood. To this end the whole course of training should be fairly saturated with moral ideas, fear of God, and respect for the rights of others; love of truth and fidelity to duty; personal purity, philanthropy, and patriotism. Self-respect and independence are cardinal virtues, and are indispensable for the enjoyment of the privileges of freedom and the discharge of the duties of American citizenship." The Protestant emphasis on the virtues of hard work and regularity was evident. "Labor should cease to be repulsive, and come to be regarded as honorable and attractive," Morgan insisted. And the students were to learn the virtue of economy

35. *Lake Mohonk Conference Proceedings,* 1888, pp. 11, 94-95.
36. Ibid., 1889, p. 16. Morgan's address at Lake Mohonk was submitted on December 1, 1889, to the Secretary of the Interior as a "Supplemental Report on Indian Education," and printed in *House Executive Document* no. 1, 51st Cong., 1st sess., ser. 2725, pp. 93-114.

and to understand that waste was wicked. The grammar schools were to be organized and conducted so that they would accustom the pupils to systematic habits. "The periods of rising and retiring, the hours for meals, times for study, recitation, work and play," he directed, "should all be fixed and adhered to with great punctiliousness." His goal was to replace the "irregularities of camp life" with "the methodical regularity of daily routine." Such routine would develop "habits of self-directed toil," and teach the students "the marvelous secret of diligence." "When the Indian children shall have acquired a taste for study and a love for work," he proclaimed, "the day of their redemption will be at hand."[37]

Morgan's proposed educational system would strengthen home and family life, as the reformers understood it. "Owing to the peculiar surroundings of the mass of Indian children," he declared, "they are homeless and are ignorant of those simplest arts that make home possible." So the schools he proposed were to be boarding schools wherever possible, schools that would draw the Indian children away from "the heathenish life of the camp." The grammar school years, especially, were looked upon as a period in which it would be possible "to inculcate in the minds of pupils of both sexes that mutual respect that lies at the base of a happy home life, and of social purity." And it was Morgan's aim for the children to be taken into the schools "at as early an age as possible, before camp life has made an indelible stamp upon them."[38]

To all these goals of Indian education was to be added inculcation of American patriotism. Indian children were to be "instructed in the rights, duties, and privileges of American citizens, taught to love the American flag, . . . imbued with a genuine patriotism, and made to feel that the United States and not some paltry reservation, is their home." They were to be educated, not as Indians, but as Americans. "In short," Morgan noted, "the public school should do for them what it is so successfully doing for all the other races in this country,—assimilate them."[39]

The exclusively Protestant character of the Americanism represented by the Indian reformers was demonstrated by the growing attack upon Roman Catholicism in the 1880s and 1890s. The increased immigration of Catholics from southern and central Europe, the unfortunate emphasis and interpretation given to the declaration of papal infallibility,

37. "Supplemental Report on Indian Education," pp. 98–101.
38. Ibid., pp. 99–101, 103.
39. Ibid., p. 96.

and the impolitic appointment of Monsignor Satolli as Apostolic Delegate gave great concern to Protestants, whose domination of American society appeared to be threatened. "Patriotic" organizations, which preached a "pure" Americanism, began to thrive and eventually coalesced into the nativistic American Protective Association at the very time that Indian reform reached a climax. The school question was the center of much of the bitterness, as Catholics, objecting to the Protestant Christianity that pervaded the "nonsectarian" public schools, established parochial schools and then sought to win support from public funds.[40]

The Indians were to be victims of this conflict. A system of mission schools supported in part by government funds had emerged in the 1870s and 1880s. These so-called contract schools fit well into the traditional cooperation between the federal government and missionary societies for the education of Indian youth. Churches supplied the school buildings and the teachers, and the government paid an annual amount to the school for each child enrolled. By the end of the 1880s, however, Protestants discovered with alarm that the great bulk of the contract school funds were going to Roman Catholics. In 1889, $347,672 out of a total of $530,905 was distributed to Catholic schools; the Presbyterians with $41,825 ran a poor second.[41] Thomas J. Morgan, who had lashed out at Catholics when he was principal of a school in Rhode Island, did not shed his views about the sanctity of the public school system when he became Commissioner of Indian Affairs in 1889. Catholic fears were increased when Daniel Dorchester, who had previously condemned the Catholic school system in Boston, was appointed Superintendent of Indian Schools in Morgan's department. Catholics worked zealously to prevent Senate confirmation of the two appointments, but without success. The two men, it is true, maintained a careful objectivity in their public acts, but the dominant atmosphere of Indian

40. The best account of anti-Catholicism in the late nineteenth century is Donald L. Kinzer, *An Episode in Anti-Catholicism: The American Protective Association* (Seattle: University of Washington Press, 1964). See also John Higham, *Strangers in the Land: Patterns of American Nativism, 1860–1925* (New Brunswick: Rutgers University Press, 1955), chapters 3 and 4.

41. The figures are given in the Report of Morgan, September 5, 1890, *House Executive Document* no. 1, 51st Cong., 2d sess., ser. 2841, p. xvii. An excellent history of church-state cooperation in Indian schools is R. Pierce Beaver, *Church, State, and the American Indians: Two and a Half Centuries of Partnership in Missions between Protestant Churches and Government* (St. Louis: Concordia Publishing House, 1966).

reform was hostile to government support of the Catholic contract schools.[42]

Foremost among the critics of the Catholic mission schools was the Reverend James M. King, secretary of the National League for the Protection of American Institutions, who spoke at Lake Mohonk in 1890 on "The Churches: Their Relation to the General Government in the Education of the Indian Races."[43] Over the next years his attack gained intensity. In 1892, he referred to an "unscrupulous" attack made by a Catholic missionary on the government schools "because they have the Protestant Bible and gospel hymns in them." Then he went on to make his point: "In this Columbian year it becomes us to remember that our civilization is not Latin, because God did not permit North America to be settled and controlled by that civilization. The Huguenot, the Hollander, and the Puritan created our civilization. Let us not put a premium by national grants on a rejected civilization in the education of a race who were here when Columbus came." King concluded that "much Roman Catholic teaching among the Indians does not prepare them for intelligent and loyal citizenship. The solution of the Indian problem consists in educating them for citizenship as we educate all other races."[44]

Although Catholic action against Morgan's administration of Indian affairs helped to defeat President Benjamin Harrison in 1892, and Morgan and Dorchester left office, the pressure against the contract schools was too widespread to overcome. The Protestant denominations quietly withdrew from the program, preferring to lose their own meager benefits rather than to see the Catholics profit. And little by little Congress wore away the contract school system. In 1896 the funds were reduced to 80 percent of the previous year's, and by 1900 the government support of church-run schools for the Indians was cut off altogether. The Catholics won a favorable decision in regard to money that came from the Indians through treaty rights, rather than by direct appropriation,

42. Information on the conflict over contract schools is in Harry J. Sievers, "The Catholic Indian School Issue and the Presidential Election of 1892," *Catholic Historical Review* 38 (July 1952): 129–55. [See also Francis Paul Prucha, *The Churches and the Indian Schools, 1888–1912* (Lincoln: University of Nebraska Press, 1979).]

43. *Lake Mohonk Conference Proceedings*, 1890, pp. 51–58.

44. Ibid., 1892, pp. 63–64. A strong Catholic attack upon the sectarian nature of the government Indian schools was made by the Reverend J. A. Stephan, Director of the Bureau of Catholic Indian Missions, in 1893. The attack brought sharp reaction from the Protestants. See the *Report of the Board of Indian Commissioners*, 1893, pp. 112–13.

but the position of the Protestant reformers won the day.[45] The Indians were to be educated in government schools, in order to become exemplary American citizens in the Protestant tradition of the nation.

The opposition to contract schools did not mean that Christian influences upon the Indians were eliminated. Great emphasis continued to be placed on Christian endeavor outside the formal school system. When President Edward H. Magill of Swarthmore College had addressed the Lake Mohonk gathering in 1887, he had noted that the Dawes Act opened the way to the civilization of the Indians but had added, "For the realization of all our highest hopes for the Indian, for his education and training, for his introduction as an equal among a civilized people, and for his preparation for the high and responsible duties of American citizenship, we must look largely, if not chiefly, to the religious organizations of our country." Commissioner Morgan, while fighting government appropriations for missionary schools, had admitted the need for "the influence of the home, the Sabbath-school, the church, and religious institutions of learning" and for "consecrated missionary work."[46] In 1893 Merrill Gates turned again to his oft-repeated theme. He told the people at Lake Mohonk:

> Only as men and women who are full of the light of education and of the life of Christ go in and out among these savage brothers and sisters of ours, only as the living thought and the feeling heart touch their hearts one by one, can the Indians be lifted from savagery and made into useful citizens. . . . As we get at them one by one, as we break up these iniquitous masses of savagery, as we draw them out from their old associations and immerse them in the strong currents of Christian life and Christian citizenship, as we send the sanctifying stream of Christian life and Christian work among them, they feel the pulsing life-tide of Christ's life.[47]

45. The official actions of the Presbyterians, Baptists, Episcopalians, Congregationalists, and Methodists are appended to the Report of Morgan, August 27, 1892, *House Executive Document* no. 1, 52d Cong., 2d sess., ser. 3088, pp. 177–82. See also Beaver, *Church, State, and the American Indians,* p. 167, and Laurence F. Schmeckebier, *The Office of Indian Affairs: Its History, Activities, and Organization* (Baltimore: Johns Hopkins Press, 1927), pp. 212–13.

46. *Lake Mohonk Conference Proceedings,* 1887, p. 60; Morgan, "Supplemental Report on Indian Education," p. 97.

47. *Lake Mohonk Conference Proceedings,* 1893, p. 12. This personal and persuasive approach, which marked Protestant missionary effort, contrasted with the more sacramental approach of the Roman Catholics. For an excellent comparison of the two groups of missionaries on a single reservation, see Howard L. Harrod, *Mission among the Blackfeet* (Norman: University of Oklahoma Press, 1971).

This "pulsing life-tide" found eager transmitters in the committed Christians working as teachers within the government Indian schools, for it was understood that these schools would reflect the Protestant Americanism that had been the goal of their founders. Lyman Abbott outlined the pattern when he spoke against the contract schools in 1888: "Religion is, after all, a matter of personal influence more than of catechetical instruction. If the Government will come to the churches for Christian teachers, the churches may well agree to leave the catechisms out of the schools in which these Christian teachers do their work."[48]

Clearly the Indian reformers of the late nineteenth century were not, as they have sometimes been depicted, a small, peripheral group of men and women, who by clever machinations and unjustified propaganda foisted a program of reform upon Congress and the Indian service.[49] Neither the men nor their impact can be understood in that narrow perspective. Rather, they represented or reflected a powerful and predominant segment of Protestant church membership, and thereby of late nineteenth century American society. When they spoke, they spoke for a large majority of the nation, expressing views that were widely held, consciously or unconsciously. They were the chief channel through which this Americanism came to bear upon the Indians.

It was the fate of the Indians that the "solution" of the "Indian problem" that had troubled the national conscience throughout the nineteenth century should have been formulated when such a group was in command. The Friends of the Indian set out with good intentions to stamp out Indianness altogether and to substitute a uniform Americanness; to destroy all remnants of corporate existence or tribalism and to replace them with an absolute rugged individualism that was foreign to the traditions and hearts of the Indian peoples. Through landownership, citizenship, uniform legal status, and above all through education, the Indians were to be turned into patriotic Americans. If the reformers were wrong in both goals and methods (as subsequent events demonstrated that they were), they erred because the America they represented was so satisfied with its vision of the world that everyone was expected to accept and conform. The humanitarians who

48. *Lake Mohonk Conference Proceedings,* 1888, p. 15.
49. This view is taken, for example, by George E. Hyde in *A Sioux Chronicle* (Norman: University of Oklahoma Press, 1956). In a chapter entitled "The Brethren" he ridicules the work of the humanitarian reformers.

so confidently devoted their energy and good will to solving the Indian problem simply mirrored the tenets of American civilization and gave them the added force of religious endorsement.

16

The Decline of the Christian Reformers

The first two decades of the twentieth century were a transition period in Indian policy, between the religiously dominated reform program that produced the Dawes Act and a national Indian school system and the more secularly oriented reform of John Collier in the 1920s and 1930s. Historians of Indian affairs have not yet come to an agreement about the forces at work from 1900 to 1920 nor about the broad patterns of change and what caused them. One thing seems clear to me, however: the dominance of the "Christian reformers" was badly eroded if not completely destroyed. This essay, presented in a session called "Indian Policy during the Progressive Era" at the 1978 meeting of the Organization of American Historians in New York, is a brief beginning attempt to look at that phenomenon. It grew out of a more detailed study of Protestant-Catholic controversy in Indian affairs at the turn of the century, which has been published as The Churches and the Indian Schools, 1888–1912 *(Lincoln: University of Nebraska Press, 1979).*

The history of Indian affairs in the Progressive Era is a complex and confusing subject. Recently scholars have begun to investigate the first two decades of the twentieth century to see what was happening to Indians as the policies enacted at the end of the nineteenth century began to be worked out in practice, but it is too early yet to announce any indisputable patterns for the period as a whole. To promote our knowledge and understanding it will help to look at one element or

252

aspect of the problem: the place of the old humanitarian reformers and their reform principles in the new era—for new it was (I think everyone will agree to that).

Before considering the "decline of the Christian reformers," it will be necessary to identify briefly "the Christian reformers" and to describe the position from which they "declined." Development and substantiation of this background material cannot be done here, although I have done so in another place.[1] It is possible, however, to begin with the following four propositions:

1. American Indian policy reform in the last two decades of the nineteenth century was dominated by a group of humanitarian men and women, who organized themselves into reform organizations, of which we may note the Board of Indian Commissioners, the Indian Rights Association, and the Lake Mohonk Conference of Friends of the Indian.

2. These reformers were evangelical Protestants, thoroughly convinced of and eagerly promoting principles of individualism and Americanism.

3. Following their principles, they agitated for—and won—a legislative program for the Indians that called for allotment of the Indian lands in severalty (the Dawes Act), a legal status for the Indians that would give them American citizenship, and an educational program that would transform the rising generation of Indian youth into citizens indistinguishable from their white neighbors. In this they had the support of the executive branch—the President, the Secretary of the Interior, and the Commissioner of Indian Affairs—and of Congress as well.

4. Imbued as they were with Protestantism and Americanism, they fought, again successfully, what they considered the threatening growth of Roman Catholic influence in Indian affairs. Their main target was the system of mission schools supported in part by federal moneys, the so-called contract schools, which had grown to such an extent that they competed effectively with the government school system, newly established to civilize and Americanize the Indians. The success of this anti-Catholicism was a mark of Protestant dominance.

---

1. See Francis Paul Prucha, *American Indian Policy in Crisis: Christian Reformers and the Indian, 1865-1900* (Norman: University of Oklahoma Press, 1976).

By 1900, these men and women could look down from a high plateau of success. They had established their legislative programs. They looked upon themselves as the guardians of the Indians and the watchdogs and arbiters of national Indian policy. They saw themselves as the effective force in moving the Indians into an individualized, Americanized society (which meant to them a Protestant Christian nation).

In the dozen years after the turn of the century their position was severely shaken, if not indeed shattered. I would like to point out a number of instances of this debilitation and decline.

In the first place, the Christian reformers—still operating in the reform organizations that had been so strong before 1900—were no longer able to control legislative formulation of Indian policy. The two laws of this period comparable to the Dawes Act illustrate the changed situation. The first of these was the Burke Act of 1906, which amended the Dawes Act by making discretionary the period in which the allotted lands were held in trust for the Indians and providing for the granting of United States citizenship at the end of the trust period instead of at the beginning.[2] The Burke Act reversed—or at least it slowed down—the individualizing, Americanizing process of the Dawes Act, and it was severely criticized and strongly opposed by the reformers' groups.[3]

The second law was the so-called Lacey Act of 1907.[4] (It, too, might have been called a "Burke Act," for the measure introduced by Congressman Lacey was in fact replaced by provisions introduced by Congressman Burke.) The act dealt with the allotment of the money held in trust for the Indians in the United States Treasury. It was intended, in the minds of the reformers who initiated it, to break up the Indian trust funds (held in common by each tribe) in exactly the way that the Dawes Act had broken up the reservation lands. Such a measure was considered to be a second and necessary step on the Indians' road to civilization.[5]

But when the act finally passed the House and the Senate, it had been emasculated. Instead of being a directive authorizing the President to allot the trust funds when he considered a tribe ready, the law was merely permissive, and it required an Indian to apply for his allotment before any action could be taken. Spokesmen for the Indian Rights

2. *United States Statutes at Large,* 34:182-83.

3. *Report of the Board of Indian Commissioners,* 1906, p. 8; *Report of the Indian Rights Association,* 1906, pp. 45-48.

4. *United States Statutes at Large,* 34:1221-22.

5. See, for example, *Lake Mohonk Conference Proceedings,* 1900, pp. 18-20; ibid., 1901, pp. 5-8; *Report of the Board of Indian Commissioners,* 1902, p. 22.

Association strongly objected. The Association's Washington agent wrote that the tribal relation "defeats the effort for individual advancement and responsibility, a weakness so apparent in all systems of communal ownership of property." The revised bill, he said, would not remedy that evil, for it would affect only those Indians who applied for their pro rata share of the money, and precisely those who needed the law most would be least likely to take advantage of it. But Congress did not listen now as it had in the 1880s. The Lacey Act was, to the reformers, no more than a "makeshift substitute."[6] In basic legislation, then, the old Christian reformers lost the battle.

Second, the Christian reformers lost their decisive influence with the Commissioner of Indian Affairs and the executive branch in general. At the end of the nineteenth century, the reform organizations worked hand in glove with the Commissioners of Indian Affairs. Perhaps, after the Indian Rights Association and the Lake Mohonk Conference got well under way, it would be more accurate to say that the Commissioners worked hand in glove with the reformers. The reform groups, with their investigating trips, their yearly conferences at Lake Mohonk where they formulated policies and programs, and their effective lobbying, were a force to be reckoned with. They spoke out fearlessly, and they were listened to. They were convinced that they were the special guardians of Indian rights and could not be turned aside in their righteous campaigns.

Then they ran into Commissioner Francis E. Leupp. Leupp had at one time in the 1890s been the Washington agent of the Indian Rights Association. When he was appointed Commissioner of Indian Affairs in 1904 by his good friend Theodore Roosevelt, the reformers rejoiced. To their dismay, they learned that Leupp had a mind of his own and that he intended to run his office without their advice, and in fact sometimes in sharp opposition to them. Two instances will suffice to show the change.

One of these concerned the Crow Agency in Montana, where the Indian Rights Association sought an investigation into alleged violations of Indian rights by the stockmen and the Indian agent. The Washington representative of the Association was turned away when he went out to Montana to investigate, and the Secretary of the Association was actually arrested by the Indian agent when he appeared for the same purpose.

---

6. S. M. Brosius to James S. Sherman, March 27, 1906, Indian Rights Association Papers, Historical Society of Pennsylvania (microfilm reel 18); *Report of the Indian Rights Association,* 1911, pp. 28–29.

The Indian Rights Association fought unsuccessfully to defeat the Senate confirmation of a special inspector sent out to look into the charges.[7] "I have been twenty-six years a student of Indian affairs...," Herbert Welsh, the long-time head of the Indian Rights Association, wrote to a friend, "and it is my deliberate opinion that this Crow agency affair is the worst piece of business on the part of the government that has come within my knowledge. Heretofore our endeavors to correct wrongs in the Indian Service have on the whole been sympathetically received by the Indian Department and our cooperation accepted. Mr. Leupp, in my opinion, clearly intended to drive the Indian Rights Association from the field."[8]

The second case involved eight Navajo Indian outlaws, arrested and confined without specific charges and without trial. The Indian Rights Association insisted that the Indians be released; Leupp countered that he would do what he thought necessary to protect the peaceful Indians, "law or no law."[9]

The Indian Rights Association was delighted when Leupp resigned. "It is a cause of congratulation," the president of the Association wrote, "that a commissioner whose egotism had made it impossible for him to catch other people's point of view, should give place to one of a more open mind and a less assured infallibility."[10]

It might be argued that Leupp had been forced out by his critics among the reformers. But their disenchantment with Leupp was only one tile in a larger mosaic of diminishing influence. And Leupp had the last word in his book, *The Indian and His Problem* (1910), in which he lectured the philanthropists for their unrealistic positions.[11]

The Board of Indian Commissioners fared little better. It had a running battle with the Secretary of the Interior, who was intent on cutting off its funds. Though it survived (to be finally eliminated by FDR), its position in relation to the administration was not strong. The

7. See the discussion in *Report of the Indian Rights Association,* 1908, pp. 4–20.

8. Herbert Welsh to Richard H. Dana, January 25, 1909, Indian Rights Association Papers (microfilm reel 78).

9. *Report of the Indian Rights Association,* 1908, pp. 32–35; letter of Carl E. Grammer and Matthew K. Sniffen, March 6, 1909, Indian Rights Association Papers (microfilm reel 78); Francis E. Leupp, "'Law or No Law' in Indian Administration," *Outlook* 91 (January 30, 1909): 261–63.

10. Statement of Carl E. Grammer, published in *The North American* (Philadelphia), June 16, 1909.

11. Francis E. Leupp, *The Indian and His Problem* (New York: Charles Scribner's Sons, 1910), chap. 15, "Philanthropy and Criticism."

Lake Mohonk Conference, with which the Board of Indian Commissioners was informally linked, also declined in its influence in Indian affairs. To begin with, after 1900 it broadened its activities to include the peoples in the territories acquired after the Spanish-American War. It in fact changed its title to Friends of the Indian and Other Dependent Peoples. Then its founder and guiding light, Albert K. Smiley, grew old, moved to California, and died in 1912. The year 1916 marked the last of the historic Lake Mohonk Conferences.

In the third place, the courts were no more sympathetic to the programs and policies of the reformers than Congress and the executive branch. The Indian Rights Association undertook two legal cases that went to the Supreme Court, in which it supported Indian litigants against the federal government.

In *Lone Wolf* v. *Hitchcock,* Lone Wolf, a Kiowa Indian, sought an injunction against the government's carrying out an agreement of 1892 disposing of reservation lands, on the ground that the consent of two-thirds of the adult male Indians called for by the Treaty of Medicine Lodge had not been obtained. The case was taken to the Supreme Court, and in January 1903 the Court ruled against the Indians.[12]

In *Quick Bear* v. *Leupp,* the Indian Rights Association, in the name of certain Rosebud Sioux, sought an injunction against the use of Indian trust and treaty funds for support of Catholic Indian mission schools, on the ground that Congress had prohibited such use. The Supreme Court ruled in 1908 that the Congressional prohibition did not apply to such funds.[13]

The Quick Bear case was only one skirmish in the losing battle the evangelical Christian reformers fought with the Roman Catholics. In most of the nineteenth century it was taken for granted that the United States was a Protestant nation. Catholics, who came in large numbers at the end of the century as part of the "new immigration," were considered alien to the traditions of the nation, outsiders who were suspect in their understanding of or loyalty to "American" principles. The decade of the 1890s, with the growth of the American Protective Association, was a high-water mark of anti-Catholicism, and it was exactly at that time that the Protestant reformers (supported

12. 187 U.S. Reports, 553. The case is discussed in *Report of the Indian Rights Association,* 1903, pp. 20–24.

13. 210 U.S. Reports, 50; see also *Report of the Indian Rights Association,* 1908, pp. 22–25, [and Francis Paul Prucha, *The Churches and the Indian Schools, 1888–1912* (Lincoln: University of Nebraska Press, 1979), pp. 149–60.]

by the Indian Office and Congress) were successful in eliminating direct appropriations to support the Catholic mission schools.

The Catholics, however, did not accept defeat, and they did not quietly withdraw from the schools they had laboriously established and developed since 1880. They determined to keep the schools going and to find what support they could for them. When Congress ended direct appropriations from public moneys, they hit upon the scheme of drawing upon the trust and treaty funds held for the Indians in the United States Treasury and administered by the Interior Department. These funds, they argued, were not public money, but Indian money due to the Indians according to treaty stipulations and in payment for land cessions. If some Indians requested the use of their shares of the tribal funds for support of Catholic schools for their children, the money should be so used.[14]

When, at the end of 1904, the Indian Rights Association and its allies discovered that indeed Indian trust moneys were being paid by the government to the Indian schools of the Catholics, a violent campaign against the practice began. Charging that such use of funds for sectarian schools violated the sacred American principle of separation of church and state, the Protestants attacked the President, the Secretary of the Interior, and the Commissioner of Indian Affairs with a barrage of protests. They had friendly Congressmen and Senators introduce in Congress a series of bills and amendments to bills that would have explicitly prohibited the use of the Indian trust and treaty funds. And ultimately they sought the injunction in the courts.[15] In all of this they were rebuffed.

The Christian reformers charged a politico-ecclesiastical conspiracy on the part of the Catholic hierarchy, but they failed to realize that Catholics with their substantial numbers were winning a place in the political life of the nation. And this was reflected in Indian affairs. The Board of Indian Commissioners, which had been a Protestant preserve from the time of its founding in 1869, got two Catholic members in

14. As an example of the Catholic arguments, see *Report of the Director of the Bureau of Catholic Indian Missions for 1904–'05,* pp. 23–46. See also the argument for appellees in *Quick Bear* v. *Leupp,* 210 U.S. Reports, 50. I have also relied heavily on the Papers of the Bureau of Catholic Indian Missions, Marquette University Library, Milwaukee, Wisconsin.

15. The history of Protestant opposition to the use of tribal funds for Catholic Indian schools can be traced in the *Report of the Indian Rights Association,* 1904–1908, and in the Indian Rights Association Papers for the same period. [See also Prucha, *The Churches and the Indian Schools.*]

1902, and from that time on included, as a matter of policy, Catholic members (including Archbishop Ryan of Philadelphia, Cardinal Gibbons, and ultimately the Reverend William H. Ketcham, Director of the Bureau of Catholic Indian Missions). Catholic leaders were invited to the sacrosanct conference halls at Lake Mohonk and spoke out forcefully.[16]

Even the activities of the government Indian schools—which were strongholds of Protestantism, with their Protestant religious services, gospel hymns, Sunday school lessons, and auxiliary organizations like the YMCA—were successfully attacked by Catholics. Despite the cries of Protestant missionary groups, who had been willing to curtail their own Indian schools because the government schools served them so well, the Indian Office prescribed equal religious rights for the Catholic Indian students in government schools and eliminated many of the positive Protestant elements of the schools.[17]

It is relatively easy to describe *what* happened during the Progressive Era to the Christian humanitarians and their particular approach to Indian policy. It is much more difficult to determine with any certainty *why* the changes occurred and the relationship, if any, between Indian policy and the movement that historians called "Progressivism."

A number of answers have been suggested to describe and to some extent explain the change. Did it come from new scientific doctrines about the inferiority of non-Anglo-Saxon peoples, which clouded the Christian reformers' vision of complete Americanization and assimilation? (I am hesitant to allot to the scientific thought of anthropologists much influence on public policy and even less on the Christian reformers themselves.)

Did it come from a new grouping of the Indians with blacks and Asiatics as "backward" peoples to be admitted only to the periphery of American society as a sort of colonial people not fit for the total assimilation into American society that had been the plan of the Christian reformers in the 1880s and 1890s? This is the intriguing thesis of Frederick Hoxie.[18] (I prefer to see an evolution of the assimilationist doctrines rather than a sharp dichotomy between pre-1900 and post-1900 policies and practices.)

My own theory in regard to Indian policy is that we must look

16. See remarks in *Lake Mohonk Conference Proceedings,* 1902.
17. U.S. Office of Indian Affairs, "General Regulations for Religious Worship and Instruction of Pupils in Government Indian Schools," March 12, 1910.
18. Frederick E. Hoxie, "Beyond Savagery: The Campaign to Assimilate the American Indian, 1880–1920" (Ph.D. diss., Brandeis University, 1977).

beyond Indian affairs themselves; that we must pay attention to changes in the larger American society, for Indian policy reflected major characteristics of that society. For example, the Christian nation concept that dominated much of the nineteenth century began to erode in the early twentieth. The idea that the nation itself—not just the individuals composing it—was Christian has been well explained by recent writers in the history of religious thought in America. And they point to evidence that the idea was no longer viable by 1920.[19] Part of the decline was due to the fundamental division within the Protestant ranks. The individualistic, "private" brand of Protestantism, out of which the late nineteenth-century Indian programs came, was increasingly losing ground to a new social, "public" Protestantism, more concerned with regenerating society and social institutions than in reforming individuals.[20]

Another factor in the breakdown of evangelical Protestant domination was the advent of large numbers of Catholics. The effect of their political weight we have already touched upon. The Catholic input seriously weakened the drive for total assimilation and Americanization that had been part of the traditional American Christian reformers' dream. That dream called for absolute conversion—physical as well as spiritual—and demanded firm direction from the whites. Indian desires were simply brushed aside. But one of the recurrent Catholic demands after 1900 in their battles with the Protestants over Indian matters was that the Indians be allowed in some measure a voice in their own affairs.

The other side of the loss of religious force was the increasing secularization of American society, an inchoative spirit that burst out full-blown in the 1920s. I think there was evidence of this in the new importance attached to efficient administration on the part of Progressive government officials, which was a sort of secular force.

Rather than be moved along ineluctably by a theory or a set of beliefs (one historian has aptly described the Dawes Act as an "act of faith"), bureaucrats took a harder look at the practicalities of a situation. Commissioner Leupp is a fine example. He urged day schools rather than boarding schools for practical reasons; he was interested in Indians who could support themselves and their families no matter

19. See, for example, Martin E. Marty, *Righteous Empire: The Protestant Experience in America* (New York: Dial Press, 1970); Robert T. Handy, *A Christian America: Protestant Hopes and Historical Realities* (New York: Oxford University Press, 1971).

20. Marty, *Righteous Empire,* pp. 177–87.

how they dressed or wore their hair; he thought that Indian criminals should be treated as such and refused to be swayed by what he considered abstract theories of Indian rights. Leupp wrote just after he left office: "The Indian problem has now reached a stage where its solution is almost wholly a matter of administration. Mere sentiment has spent its day; the moral questions involved have pretty well settled themselves. What is most needed from this time forth is the guidance of affairs by an independent mind, active sympathies free from mawkishness, an elastic patience and a steady hand."[21]

The provisions of the Burke Act and the Lacey Act reflected a realistic evaluation of Indian possibilities, rather than the absolute principles of individualization that the Christian reformers had espoused. There was a willingness to move one step at a time, instead of overthrowing the past with a sudden reversal. Let me highlight the difference by two quotations. In 1885, Lyman Abbott, the liberal Protestant reformer, told his colleagues at Lake Mohonk:

> I declare my conviction then that the reservation system is hopelessly wrong; that it cannot be amended or modified; that it can only be uprooted, root, trunk, branch, and leaf, and a new system put in its place. We evangelical ministers believe in immediate repentance. I hold to immediate repentance as a national duty. Cease to do evil, cease instantly, abruptly, immediately. I hold that the reservation barriers should be cast down and the land given to the Indians in severalty; that every Indian should be protected in his right to his home, and in his right to free intercourse and free trade, whether the rest of the tribe wish him so protected or not; that these are his individual, personal rights, which no tribe has the right to take from him, and no nation the right to sanction the robbery of.[22]

But twenty years later, in 1906, Congressman Burke, explaining why he favored a very limited measure in place of the original proposal of Congressman Lacey to segregate and allot the Indian trust funds wholesale, said: "It is very much easier to legislate by degrees, than it is to undo what may be done by going too far in enacting new legislation, and the subject of the trust funds, belonging to the Indians of the United States, is of such importance that we should go very slow in enacting any legislation affecting the same."[23] A hard look at the

21. Leupp, *The Indian and His Problem*, p. vii.
22. *Lake Mohonk Conference Proceedings*, 1885, pp. 50–53.
23. Charles H. Burke to C. C. Binney, April 7, 1906, Indian Rights Association Papers (microfilm reel 18).

effects of allotment of lands, even in the early decades of the twentieth century, must have shown to all but those blinded by their dream that all was not working out as envisaged.

The torch of leadership in directing Indian affairs, for whatever deep and fundamental reasons, passed from the hands of the Christian reformers. One cannot, of course, put an exact date on the transfer. Like so many historical events and movements, it is only from a later perspective that one can see what had occurred. The social science approach to Indian affairs that came with John Collier was clearly at odds with the Christian motivation behind the reformers of the late nineteenth century. But the nation did not jump suddenly from one to the other. The beginnings of the change, however we identify or describe them, came in the Progressive Era. It was a transition age—the old evident still, the new not quite established—and perhaps we will never be able to characterize Indian affairs in that age to everyone's—or even to anyone's—satisfaction. But whatever the final formulation, it will, I think, have to include the decline of the old Christian reformers.

INDEX